1150

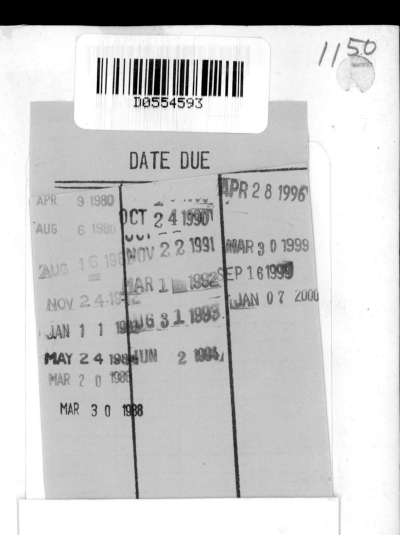

The Master Musicians Series

VIVALDI

Series edited by Stanley Sadie

THE MASTER MUSICIANS SERIES

Vivaldi

Michael Talbot

*With eight pages of plates and
music examples in text*

J.M. DENT & SONS LTD
LONDON, TORONTO AND MELBOURNE

First published 1978
© Text, Michael Talbot, 1978

Printed in Great Britain by
Biddles Ltd, Guildford, Surrey
and bound at the
Aldine Press, Letchworth, Herts
for
J. M. DENT & SONS LTD
Aldine House, Albemarle Street, London

This book is set in VIP 11 on 12 pt Garamond No. 3

Hardback ISBN 0 460 03164 3
Paperback ISBN 0 460 02204 0

British Library Cataloguing in Publication Data

Talbot, Michael
    Vivaldi. — (Master musicians series).
    1. Vivaldi, Antonio
    I. Series
    780'.92'4   ML 410.V82

ISBN 0-460 03164-3

79- 302925

To Shirley and Stephen

Preface

The admission of Vivaldi to the select company of the 'Master Musicians' is a sign of the growing esteem in which he has been held in recent decades. Fortunately, this surge of interest has stimulated research into Vivaldi's life and works, so that an author today can draw upon much information unavailable at the time of the pioneer studies. Gone are the days when he was regarded principally as a composer of concertos; we now have to see him as an important contributor to several *genres*: vocal as well as instrumental, sacred as well as secular.

I must gratefully acknowledge here the help of several musicians, scholars and librarians, among whom I should like to mention by name Eric Cross, Jean-Pierre Demoulin, Eleanor Selfridge-Field, Anthony Hicks, Wolfgang Reich and Reinhard Strohm. The University of Liverpool, and in particular the staff of the University Library, also aided me in many ways.

The musical illustrations Nos. 1–3, 8–11 and 18–32 are included by courtesy of the Biblioteca Nazionale di Torino; No. 13 by courtesy of the Sächsische Landesbibliothek; and Nos. 7 and 15 by courtesy of Manchester Public Libraries. Extracts from the correspondence of Charles Jennens and Edward Holdsworth are quoted by kind permission of the owner, Gerald Coke.

Liverpool 1977   Michael Talbot

Contents

Illustrations

1 The path to rediscovery

By the 'rediscovery' of a composer we seldom mean much more than his rescue from a presumably unmerited neglect, and sometimes as little as the dutiful revival of some of his major works on the anniversary of his birth or death. Vivaldi is one of the very few important composers to whom the notion of rediscovery applies in the most literal sense. He died almost two-and-a-half centuries ago, yet until fifty years ago the musical world was totally unaware of the existence of the great majority of the works, totalling over 760, that can today be ascribed to him. Until then not one opera, not one sacred vocal piece had, it seemed, survived for scholars to inspect and audiences to hear. Now scarcely a year passes without the announcement of some fresh discovery: one might mention a partly autograph set of twelve violin sonatas (seven hitherto entirely unknown and the rest known only in incomplete or variant form) as well as two violin concertos unearthed in Manchester in 1973, and a highly original sonata for violin, oboe and obbligato organ, also autograph, preserved in Dresden, which was brought to light as recently as 1976. As more and more private collections of old music are acquired by libraries accessible to the researcher and the bibliographer one should expect a narrowing of the avenues of discovery. That this has not happened in Vivaldi's case is a testimony to his enormous productivity and the unusually wide circulation of his music in his lifetime.

Naturally, rediscovery in the other, more figurative sense of revaluation has gone hand in hand from the earliest times with the growth of our knowledge of his life and works — a process sometimes slow, sometimes spectacularly rapid. After his death in 1741 his name continued to be mentioned by bibliographers, lexicographers and writers of memoirs, but his music plunged into oblivion almost immediately. Indeed, his reputation as a freakish violinist and eccentric cleric largely overshadowed his fame, even in retrospect, as a composer. To his sometime collaborator Goldoni, in the first, serialized version of the Venetian dramatist's memoirs, he was still a 'famous violin player . . . noted for his sonatas [sic], especially those called the *Four Seasons*',[1] but when Goldoni came to write the definitive account of his first meeting with Vivaldi a quarter of a century later he dismissed the musician as an 'excellent violin player and mediocre composer'.[2] E. L. Gerber's *Historisch-biographisches Lexicon der Tonkünstler*, a pioneer dictionary of musical biography written shortly afterwards, mentions Vivaldi as a composer merely in passing, turning Goldoni's vivid and amusing description of the Italian composer's exaggerated (and by implication feigned) piety into a claim that Vivaldi never let his rosary out of his hand except when he took up his pen to write an opera.[3] Even the comparatively generous amount of space allotted to Vivaldi in Count Grégoire Orloff's *Essai sur l'histoire de la musique en Italie*, representative of the contemporary French view, is largely filled with a romanticized account (which may nevertheless contain a grain of truth) of how Vivaldi once, while celebrating Mass, temporarily retired into the sacristy in order to write out a fugue subject which was obsessing him.[4]

Apocryphal anecdotes of this kind abound in historical writing of the late eighteenth and early nineteenth centuries; we

[1] *Commedie,* vol. xiii (Venice, 1761), p. 11.
[2] *Mémoires de M. Goldoni* (Paris, 1787), p. 287.
[3] Vol. ii (Leipzig, 1792), col. 736f.
[4] Vol. ii (Paris, 1822), p. 290.

find them also in biographies of Corelli, Benedetto Marcello and Pergolesi. The difference is that in the case of these composers and a few other Italians contemporary with Vivaldi at least some of the music retained a shadowy presence in the repertoire. Corelli's continually reprinted violin sonatas served a didactic purpose, while Marcello's *Psalms* and Pergolesi's *Stabat Mater* still found admirers among connoisseurs of church music. The complete void that was our knowledge of Vivaldi's music might have remained unfilled until the present century, had it not been for the almost fortuitous exhumation of a small part of it in the course of the Bach revival.

J. S. Bach's indebtedness to Vivaldi was first brought to public notice by his pioneer biographer J. N. Forkel much of whose information had been obtained at first hand from Bach's two eldest sons. The celebrated passage runs:

J. S. Bach's first attempts at composition were, like all such attempts, deficient. With no instruction to point a way forward and lead him on gradually, stage by stage, he had to begin like all those who set foot on such a path without guidance, and let things take their own course. To run or leap up and down the instrument, occupying the two hands as fully as their five fingers will allow, and to carry on in this undisciplined fashion until some point of repose is snatched quite by chance: these are the arts common to all beginners. Hence they can only be 'finger composers' (or 'hussars of the keyboard', as Bach called them in his later years): that is, they must allow their fingers to dictate what they write instead of telling their fingers what to play. But Bach did not remain for long on this path. He soon began to feel that all was not right with this ceaseless running and leaping, that order, coherence and inter-relatedness must be brought to the ideas, and that some form of instruction was needed for the attainment of this end. Vivaldi's violin concertos, which had just appeared, served this purpose for him. So often did he hear them praised as excellent pieces of music, that he hit upon the happy idea of arranging them all for his *clavier*. He studied the treatment of the ideas, their mutual relationship, the pattern of modulation and many other features. The adaptation of ideas and figurations intended for the violin but unsuited to the keyboard taught him in addition to think in musical terms, so that when he had finished he no longer needed to draw his ideas from his fingers, but instead preconceived them in his imagination.'[5]

Though Bach could hardly have arranged 'all' Vivaldi's violin concertos for keyboard, a good number of transcriptions were soon unearthed, totalling 17 concertos for solo harpsichord, four for solo organ and one for four harpsichords and string orchestra. A further organ transcription (BWV 596),[6] though in J. S. Bach's own hand, was believed until 1910 to be a composition by his eldest son on account of its ambiguous added inscription 'di W. F. Bach manu mei patris descriptum'. The original composer was scarcely ever mentioned (and then not always correctly) in the manuscripts, so scholars, acting on Forkel's lead, hunted through whatever original sources of Vivaldi's music were accessible, hoping to make a match. In 1850 C. L. Hilgenfeldt identified the concerto for four harpsichords as the tenth concerto of Vivaldi's op. 3. By the end of the century six harpsichord and two organ transcriptions had been established from concordant sources as Vivaldi works, to be joined soon by BWV 596. The identification of the authorship of the twelve remaining concertos, eight of which are known today to be by other composers, lagged behind, so that when the transcriptions came to be published by Peters in 1851 (16 works for harpsichord),[7] 1852 (four for organ) and 1865 (that for four harpsichords), and later in the 42nd (1894), 38th

[5] *Ueber Johann Sebastian Bachs Leben, Kunst und Kunstwerke* (Leipzig, 1802), p. 23f.

[6] *Bach Werke Verzeichnis* (BWV) numbers are taken from Wolfgang Schmieder, *Thematisch-systematisches Verzeichnis der musikalischen Werke von Johann Sebastian Bach* (Leipzig, 1950).

[7] One of the harpsichord transcriptions (BWV 592a), being concordant with the organ transcription BWV 592, remained unpublished.

(1891) and 43rd (1894) volumes of the Bach-Gesellschaft edition respectively, they were described collectively as concertos 'after Vivaldi' — an over-simplification whose unfortunate consequences have persisted.

The German scholars who first evaluated these Vivaldi concertos, comparing them with Bach's often very free arrangements, were ill-prepared to sit in judgment. Since they were infinitely more familiar with the music of Bach (and Handel) than that of the Italian masters of the late Baroque, they tended to see Vivaldi's music as deviant from the Bachian style (lines more scantily ornamented, inner parts simpler, fewer types of dissonance), whereas it would be more accurate historically and aesthetically to see Bach's music as deviant from the Vivaldian style (lines more richly ornamented, inner parts more complex, more types of dissonance). In the light of the performance practice then current, in which Bach, Mozart and Wagner would be played very similarly, they could scarcely imagine what crisp articulation and tasteful improvised embellishment could do to passages which on paper seemed jejune and repetitious. Undeniably, too, a general attitude towards Italian music which at best was patronizing and at worst distinctly hostile coloured their judgment. To have denied Vivaldi any merit whatever would have been to accuse Bach of a lack of discrimination. Some writers solved the dilemma by allowing Vivaldi the virtues of an artisan, while reserving for Bach those of an artist. The following passage from J. W. von Wasiliewski is not untypical:

'He [Vivaldi] belongs to those natures who, possessing considerable technique and exceptional skill at handling form, are always ready to compose, without thinking much about the significance and content of the result. Indeed, his compositions (we are thinking especially of those for violin) only very rarely contain stirrings of deeper feeling, notable power of thought and true dedication to art.' Or again: 'The less imagination and

5

depth Vivaldi evinces in his compositions, the more inventive he becomes in superficialities of all kinds.'[8]

Still, a trickle of Vivaldi's music began to be published in its original form, beginning with three concertos reproduced (one incompletely) as supplements to the transcriptions in the Bach–Gesellschaft volumes.

The great breakthrough came with the publication, in 1905, of Arnold Schering's classic monograph on the history of the concerto: *Geschichte des Instrumentalkonzerts*. The scope of Schering's study led him to view Vivaldi's music in its proper historical perspective; he had the added advantage of close acquaintance with the large collection of Vivaldi manuscripts preserved in the Saxon State Library, which revealed a composer of wider range, particularly in regard to instrumentation, than the works published in his lifetime suggested. He communicated his enthusiasm for the music vividly to the reader and ended with a bold declaration of Vivaldi's historical position: 'Vivaldi is as exemplary for the shaping of the violin concerto as Corelli was for that of the sonata.'[9]

Modern editions of Vivaldi's concertos, which still gave preference to works transcribed by Bach, slowly multiplied. The growing awareness of his stature is reflected in Fritz Kreisler's 'attribution' of one of his pastiche compositions to Vivaldi around 1905 — a charming deception which provoked a young French violinist and musicologist, Marc Pincherle, into initiating a lifetime's research into the music of the Venetian.

This phase of Vivaldi rediscovery closes with the publication, in 1922, of a thematic catalogue by Wilhelm Altmann containing virtually all the music seen in print during the composer's life, and few extra items.[10] Had no further works been dis-

---

[8] *Die Violine und ihre Meister,* 6th edn (Leipzig, 1927), p. 111f.
[9] *Geschichte des Instrumentalkonzerts* (Leipzig, 1905), p. 96.
[10] 'Thematischer Katalog der gedruckten Werke Antonio Vivaldis', *Archiv für Musikwissenschaft,* vol. iv (1922), pp. 262–79.

covered, Vivaldi's reputation might have remained to this very day on a par with, say, Corelli's: he would have occupied a niche in the concert repertoire, but a very small one.

The focus of our attention now shifts to Italy, which had been surprisingly slow in taking up Vivaldi's cause. One more pleasant consequence of the wave of patriotism after World War I was the direction of musicians' energies towards the rehabilitation of Italy's glorious pre-Classical past. In 1926 a collection of music belonging to the Salesian monks of the Collegio San Carlo in S. Martino (Monferrat) came up for sale. Despatched to investigate this collection with a view to its possible purchase by the Turin National Library, Alberto Gentili, a lecturer in musical history at Turin University, found that among its 97 volumes were 14 containing music by Vivaldi. These held manuscripts, mostly autograph scores, of 140 instrumental works, 29 cantatas, 12 operas (one in duplicate), three shorter dramatic works, one oratorio and numerous fragments. With the generous assistance of the banker Roberto Foà, after whose late son Mauro the collection was named, the library acquired all the volumes in 1927. Realizing from gaps in the original numbering of the Vivaldi volumes and the incompleteness of some compositions that the Foà collection was only one part of an originally larger library which had been divided, probably on inheritance, Gentili speculated whether a nephew of the Marquis Marcello Durazzo, who had bequeathed his collection to the Salesian monks, might possess the complementary volumes. This nephew, Giuseppe Maria Durazzo, was with great difficulty induced to show his collection of musical manuscripts to Gentili, confirming the hypothesis. By even more strenuous effots, Durazzo was persuaded to reunite the original collection by selling his manuscripts to the Turin National Library. A Turinese industrialist, Filippo Giordano, provided the funds, and the volumes passed to the library in 1930. By a strange coincidence, Giordano had also lost a young son, Renzo, after whom the new acquisition was named.[11]

Ownership of the Foà–Giordano collection (or 'Turin manuscripts', as they are commonly known) could be traced back to Count Giacomo Durazzo (1717–94), Genoese ambassador to Vienna from 1749 to 1752, director of theatrical performances at the Imperial Court from 1754 to 1764, and finally Imperial ambassador to Venice from 1764 to 1784. Durazzo's keen interest in music, particularly opera, and his patronage of Traetta and Gluck are well known to historians. How he came by the Vivaldi manuscripts awaits investigation. It is widely assumed that he acquired them, directly or indirectly, from the Ospedale della Pietà, the Venetian orphanage with which Vivaldi was associated for much of his life, but the character of the manuscripts belies this. That they belonged to the composer himself and constituted his 'working stock' of music is suggested by the following facts:

1. The wide coverage of *genres* and chronological spread. All *genres* in which the composer is known to have worked are represented (sonatas rather thinly, however). The operas stretch from *Ottone in Villa* (1713) to *Rosmira* (1738). No institution, religious or secular, would have a repertoire capable of accommodating such diversity.
2. Scores form an overwhelming proportion of the manuscripts. Any performing body like the Pietà's orchestra would need the music in parts.
3. Most of the manuscripts are autograph, and many of the remainder are partly autograph or contain autograph inscriptions. Composers normally retained their autograph manuscripts, having copies made as required.

[11] This highly condensed account is based on information in Gabriela Gentili Verona, 'Le collezioni Foà e Giordano della Biblioteca Nazionale di Torino', *Vivaldiana I* (Brussels, 1969), pp. 30–55.

4. Many of the scores are first drafts in a very rough state —
   suitable for copying but not for presentation. There are also
   several fragments in Vivaldi's hand which appear to be
   sketches or memory-aids.

Since all the works come in separate gatherings (or, for longer
compositions, series of gatherings) their binding into volumes
sometimes containing several dozen works must have taken
place, at the earliest, at the very end of Vivaldi's life. In general,
each volume contains works in a single broad category (secular
vocal music, sacred vocal music, concertos, operas), sometimes
subdivided into groups within the volume, but there are
anomalies arising from an exceptional format or leaf-size such as
the two lute trios at the beginning of Foà 40, a volume of sacred
music. The operas are preceded by uniform, non-autograph
title-leaves obviously inserted at the time of binding. These
cannot have been prepared under the composer's supervision or
by someone well acquainted with his operatic output, since the
date and place of performance, when supplied, are taken either
from the score itself or (for operas performed in Venice only)
from some contemporary reference work of the time.[12]

Only a close examination of the bindings of the Durazzo
collection as a whole will be able to reveal whether the Vivaldi
volumes were bound (probably, therefore, also acquired) in
Venice, Vienna or elsewhere. (As Vivaldi died in Vienna, he
could easily have taken his 'working stock' there.)

The discovery of the Turin manuscripts stimulated interest in
Vivaldi's biography. Very little was known beyond the few facts
already recorded by the earliest lexicographers, although in
1871 Federigo Stefani had published privately in Venice six
letters from Vivaldi to the Marquis Guido Bentivoglio
d'Aragona, initially more valued for their information about

[12] Possibly Antonio Groppo, *Catalogo di tutti i drami per musica recitati
ne' teatri di Venezia* (Venice, 1745).

9

operatic conditions generally than the wealth of data they contained on the composer's life.[13] In 1928 Arcangelo Salvatori published an article establishing, by reference to documents, some key facts about Vivaldi's training for the priesthood and subsequent employment at the Pietà.[14] Ten years later, Rodolfo Gallo was able to announce his discovery of the place and date (Vienna, 1741) of Vivaldi's death and identify some members of the composer's family (besides his already well-known father).[15]

The publication and wider diffusion of the Turin works was hampered during the 1930s by legal, economic, political and even personal factors, but the shape of things to come was revealed in 1939, when the Accademia Chigiana organized at Siena a Vivaldi 'week' (16th–21st September), during which a representative selection of his works, including sacred and secular vocal music, was heard. There were even two staged performances of *L'Olimpiade*.

The momentum, lost during the war years, quickly picked up again. In 1947 the publishers Ricordi began to bring out, on behalf of the newly-founded Istituto Italiano Antonio Vivaldi, the complete instrumental music. By 1972, the series was not far from its goal, 530 volumes having appeared. Although there are features of the editorial policy governing the series, as well as of the actual editing itself, which fall short of the scholarly standards expected of this kind of publishing venture, musicians everywhere have welcomed the opportunity to study and perform these works. More recently, Ricordi and Universal Edition have begun to issue systematically the sacred vocal music, and one can only hope that, this task complete, publishers will turn their attention towards the operas and cantatas,

---

[13] *Sei lettere di Antonio Vivaldi veneziano.*
[14] 'Antonio Vivaldi (il Prete Rosso)', *Rivista della città di Venezia*, vol. vi (1928), pp. 325–46.
[15] 'Antonio Vivaldi, il Prete Rosso: la famiglia, la morte', *Ateneo Veneto*, fasc. xii (December 1938).

The path to rediscovery

still very meagrely represented in print.[16] In the last few years, however, the world of recording has done a little to redress the imbalance favouring the instrumental music.

In the 1940s two large-scale studies of Vivaldi's life and music appeared: Mario Rinaldi's *Antonio Vivaldi* (Milan, 1943) and Marc Pincherle's *Antonio Vivaldi et la musique instrumentale* (Paris, 1948). The first was justly superseded by the second, a beautifully written work of massive erudition which had been in gestation (if one discounts a few articles which appeared on the way) for some 40 years. An abridged version of Pincherle's book soon appeared in an English translation.[17]

Several general introductions to Vivaldi's music, all heavily indebted to Pincherle, have since appeared in a variety of languages. Readers of English will be most familiar with *Antonio Vivaldi: His Life and Work* (London, 1970) by Walter Kolneder, a German scholar who has contributed several monographs on specialized aspects of Vivaldi's music.[18] One must also mention Remo Giazotto's *Vivaldi* (Milan, 1965) and *Antonio Vivaldi* (Turin, 1973), biographical studies containing some precious new material from Venetian archives.

The recent publication of a thematic catalogue of all Vivaldi's works by the Danish scholar Peter Ryom is an event of great importance.[19] Vivaldi has been cursed with more catalogues — which is to say unsatisfactory catalogues — than any other composer. Since no catalogue has yet succeeded in winning universal acceptance, no less than four (including Ryom's) are

---

[16] Of the operas only *La fida ninfa* has appeared in a modern edition (ed. R. Monterosso, Cremona, 1964).

[17] *Vivaldi* (Paris, 1955); *Vivaldi: Genius of the Baroque* (New York, 1957).

[18] This book is a translation, with additions, of the same author's *Antonio Vivaldi: Leben und Werk* (Wiesbaden, 1965).

[19] *Thematisches Verzeichnis der Werke Antonio Vivaldis: kleine Ausgabe* (Leipzig, 1974). A 'large' edition (*grosse Ausgabe*) is in preparation.

11

current today. The earliest (1945), by Rinaldi, is not merely inaccurate and incomplete, but groups Vivaldi's works into fictitious opus numbers reminiscent of the 'suites' into which Longo grouped Scarlatti's harpsichord sonatas.[20] Pincherle's *Inventaire-Thématique* (1948) would have been adequate, save that he was not consistent in distinguishing between two variants of the same work and two different works with common elements, and that his main series of numbers (1–443) comprises only concertos (sinfonias have a separate series (1–23). Sonatas, though listed by incipit, have no numbers at all, and vocal works are entirely absent).[21] Because of the unusually complex relationships between Vivaldi works in different *genres*, it is essential that all his works be brought within the scope of the same catalogue. Antonio Fanna's *Catalogo numerico-tematico delle opere strumentali* (Milan, 1968), being in essence a finding list for the Ricordi edition, which does not include incompletely preserved works or some important variants and tacitly or expressly 'modernizes' the instrumentation (Vivaldi's *flauto* is always given as 'flute' instead of 'recorder'), will clearly not do.

Ryom's catalogue passes the tests of comprehensiveness, accuracy and rationality of organization incomparably better than its predecessors. Instrumental works, *Ryom-Verzeichnis* (RV) 1–585 and late entries RV 751–768, are grouped first by the size of ensemble required (from one instrument and continuo up to several instruments, double orchestra and continuo), then by instrumentation. This arrangement corresponds closely to the generic distinction between sonata and concerto; sinfonias are perhaps treated inconsistently, however, some being listed among the concertos for strings (without soloist)

---

[20] *Catalogo numerico tematico delle composizioni di A. Vivaldi* (Rome, 1945).

[21] Vol. ii of *Antonio Vivaldi et la musique instrumentale*.

and continuo, while others share the number of the operatic or other work to which they are attached. Sacred (RV 586–648) and secular (RV 649–740) vocal works are grouped by genre (Mass movement, psalm, hymn, etc.). RV 741–50 are works which for one reason or another cannot be assigned to any group, and there is a long appendix (*Anhang*) listing 68 works of dubious or disproved authenticity.

As this book is being written, Ryom's numbers are rapidly passing into general circulation. It will nevertheless take some time for those accustomed to Pincherle numbers to abandon them. For this reason, the Pincherle numbers for concertos (those for sinfonias have never achieved wide currency) will be quoted in addition to Ryom numbers in the present work unless an original opus number renders them superfluous.[22]

It is salutary to consider, three hundred years after Vivaldi's birth, what is not known about him. First, there are tantalizing lacunae in his biography from one end of his life to the other. Research in archives, no doubt aided by serendipity, will surely yield discoveries in years to come. Second, we have hardly begun to establish the chronology of Vivaldi's music. For this, the most painstaking study of paper types and copyists' hands will be needed, and there is no guarantee of a high degree of success. The most sobering thought, however, is that we are still unfamiliar as listeners with well over half of Vivaldi's surviving music, as measured by the time taken to perform it. To remedy this ignorance must be our foremost task.

[22] A concordance table of Pincherle and Ryom numbers is included as Appendix F.

2 Venice

By the early eighteenth century, when Vivaldi was just beginning his career, Venice's once considerable economic power had ebbed to a point where culture rather than trade or manufacture was her most characteristic field of activity. Like a magnet she drew visitors in huge numbers from all over Europe, who observed her institutions, admired her buildings, wondered at her ceremonies, thronged to her theatres and gaming houses, and frequently departed with a memento, perhaps a painting or a musical score. The dependence of Venetian painting and music on foreign patronage, which we can date very roughly from the beginning, around 1660, of that custom known as the Grand Tour, obviously benefited the Republic's exchequer and for a long while stimulated creativity, although eventually it was bound to devitalize the arts by cutting them off from the roots of their inspiration. Just as the favourite genres of *settecento* Venetian painters — portraits and views of the city — seem 'made for export', so too composers came to put more and more of their effort into readily exportable types of music (for example, the opera and the concerto) at the expense of *genres* serving local needs. For this reason it is important to view Venetian music of Vivaldi's time not merely in the perspective of a long and noble indigenous tradition but also in that of its newly-acquired rôle as a setter of fashion for the whole of Europe.

In the later Middle Ages and Renaissance Venice had been anything but an international playground. Her wealth and power stemmed on the one hand from trade — for which her situation on the Mediterranean at the crossroads (politically if not quite geographically) of Europe and Asia ideally suited her — and on the other from manufacture, especially of textiles. Her military and naval power had held the Ottomans at bay in southern Europe for centuries.

The discovery of the New World and the Cape route to the Orient dealt a blow to Venice's position as a trading intermediary from which she never recovered. Even in the eastern Mediterranean English and French merchant vessels came in time to outnumber Venetian ones. As for manufacturing, Venice underwent the same decline as the rest of Italy after 1600. Once again, it was the northern Europeans who supplanted her, producing more cheaply and selling more vigorously, even to the Turks, Venice's traditional customers. Many of her monied citizens abandoned commerce and invested in agricultural estates on the mainland.

The effect of this economic shrinkage on Venetian political life in the eighteenth century was to reduce drastically the influence of the Republic on most affairs of European importance. Her independence was rarely threatened, however, for with her considerable territories on either side of the Adriatic she formed too large an entity to be absorbed into some other state without upsetting the balance of power. Besides, Venice's history of unbroken independence since her foundation in the seventh century as a refuge from the barbarians — an absence of foreign domination almost unique in Italy — would have made annexation difficult to justify, while her republican form of government rendered her immune to dynastic squabbles in which foreign powers could have had an interest. She became in effect a neutral buffer state.

Population statistics taken from official censuses bear out these changes in the character of Venice. The territorial limits of the capital (built, as everyone knows, on a partly man-made archipelago inside a lagoon) were fixed at the beginning of the seventeenth century. Already then the population had failed to make good the losses sustained in the plague of 1575–6; its slow climb was set back once more by the plague of 1630, and by 1696 the numbers had reached only 138,067 — over 30,000 short of the 1563 figure. But for immigration from the Italian mainland the stagnation would have been even greater, for the birth rate declined. In particular the *nobili veneti*, the Republic's governing class, shrank in proportion to the other estates — the *cittadini* ('citizens', comprising merchants and members of the professions) and *popolani* (populace) — so that some dilution of their ranks became unavoidable.

The *Terrafirma veneta*, or *Veneto*, as these mainland posssessions of the Republic were known, formed a large wedge of territory stretching westwards below the Alps just beyond Bergamo, and southwards to Chioggia. It included the famous university city of Padua, whose celebration on 13th June of the feast of the patron saint, St Anthony, was attended by many Venetians at the start of their customary *villeggiatura*, or stay in the country. This annual exodus from the capital helped to disseminate its culture in provincial centres such as Vicenza and Verona, where operas were often staged during the summer months by companies recruited in the main from Venice.

In cultural and economic terms Venice's eastern possessions were somewhat less significant, though hardly less extensive, for they comprised the provinces of Istria (separated from the *Veneto* by the Duchy of Carniola, an Imperial territory at whose narrow opening to the sea lay the port of Trieste) and Dalmatia, further down the coast of present-day Yugoslavia. Venice could claim in addition innumerable islands and trading posts in the eastern Mediterranean; from the Treaty of Karlowitz (1699) to that of Passarowitz (1718) she also governed the Peloponnese, or *Morea*, wrested a decade earlier from the Ottomans in what was to prove her last successful military adventure.

Rather remarkably for an age in which *la carrière ouverte aux talents* was steadily winning acceptance, the Venetian state still drew its senior administrators exclusively from the ranks of the nobility. The head of state was the Doge (Venetian dialect for *Duce*), who was elected for life. He presided over the College, a kind of cabinet. Supreme legislative power was vested in the Great Council (*Maggior Consiglio*), on which 600 nobles aged over 25 served; 120 of its members were chosen by ballot to serve on the Senate, the highest executive body. Of the numerous more specialized bodies, the Council of Ten (*Dieci Savii*), appointed annually by the Great Council, deserves mention. It was from these ten 'sages', that three Inquisitors of State were chosen every month to act as watchdogs against blasphemy, indecency and subversion. One of their more routine tasks was to license theatres at the start of each new season; the Inquisitors inspected the librettos of all operas, and if they were satisfied gave them their *faccio fede*, or affirmation of approval.

Next to the office of Doge, the highest honour coveted by the nobles was that of becoming one of the Procurators of St Mark's. Until the nineteenth century the Basilica of S. Marco was not Venice's cathedral church, but it became early on the focal point of her ceremonial sacred music through the combination of a favoured situation, adjoining the ducal palace and looking out on to the principal square, and the attendance at services of the doges. It was the procurators' task to appoint a *Primo Maestro*, or senior musical director, whenever the post fell vacant. The director's pay was excellent, rising during Monteverdi's tenure (1613–43) from 300 to 400 ducats annually, and it remained at that figure for over a century.[1] With this and other enticements the Basilica ought to have secured the services of Italy's foremost musicians, but like many a lay committee the procurators were cautious men who preferred to pick musicians they knew.

[1] A ducat of 'current' money (as distinct from the slightly more valuable ducat used in banking) was worth a little over half a crown in contemporary English currency.

Consequently, in the century following Monteverdi's death, all the *Primi Maestri* were men who had served in the *Cappella* previously, generally as the deputy director, or *Vice-Maestro*. Perhaps this helps to explain their lack of lustre, with the exceptions of Cavalli (1668–76), Legrenzi (1685–90) and arguably Lotti (1736–40). Of these three, however, it is notable that only the last made his principal contribution in sacred music, the others being better known as composers of opera.

The more talented musicians tended to use the *Cappella* as a stepping stone to higher things. The outstanding example is the Venetian Antonio Caldara (1670/1–1736), who joined it on an occasional basis as a cellist in 1688, served as a contralto from 1695 to 1699, and then became in fairly rapid succession *Maestro di Cappella* to the Duke of Mantua (1700), a musician in the service of the Archduke Charles, claimant to the Spanish throne (1708), *Maestro di Cappella* to Prince Ruspoli in Rome (1709) and finally Deputy *Kapellmeister* to the same Charles, now Emperor Charles VI (1716). Even Lotti spent a three-year period (1717–19) away from the *Cappella*, organizing church music and opera in distant Dresden. Many musicians of St Mark's held other posts concurrently. Giacomo Filippo Spada (*c* 1640–1704), second organist from 1678 and first organist from 1690, served the Ospedale della Pietà for many years as *Maestro di Coro*; the same post at the Ospedaletto was held by Benedetto Vinaccesi (?–1719), second organist from 1704; a *Vice-Maestro*, Carlo Francesco Pollarolo (1653–1723), directed music at the Incurabili, while the *Primo Maestro* himself, Antonio Biffi (*c* 1666–1732), occupied a like post at the Mendicanti, having as his *Maestro di Istromenti* the same Giorgio Gentili (*c* 1668–after 1731) who from 1693 played the violin solos in the St Mark's orchestra.

These four *ospedali*, literally 'hospitals', were charitable institutions for orphaned, abandoned, illegitimate or indigent girls. Since one of them, the Pietà, deserves our especial attention, being not only the most famous (and most thoroughly researched), but also the one with which our composer was closely associated during most of his life, it will be useful to describe it in some detail. Founded in 1346, it occupied in Vivaldi's time a building on the site of the present *Istituto provinciale degli espositi* in the Riva degli Schiavoni, which faces the island of S. Giorgio Maggiore across the Canale di S. Marco. Its adjoining chapel, greatly enlarged in 1745, is now the Church of La Pietà. The Pietà, like its sister institutions, was supported by the state and run by a board of governors appointed by the Senate. Its population was reported in 1663 to lie between 400 and 500; by 1738 it held 1,000.

The girls were divided into two categories: the *figlie di commun*, or commoners, who received a general education, and the *figlie di coro*, whose education was specifically musical. Not all in the latter group served regularly in the chapel choir and orchestra, as one might have thought from the description *di coro*; for one thing, there was too little room in the chapel, although the addition in 1724 of two *choretti* on either side of the main choirstalls relieved the congestion a little.[2] Exactly how large a minority the *figlie di coro* were is unknown, but whatever their proportion one is justified in calling the Pietà a conservatory, by analogy with the four conservatories of Naples (where, in contrast, only boys were admitted), on account of the primacy accorded to music. One almost suspects the good faith of the Pietà's governors when they speak, in a resolution concerning the *figlie di coro,* of the need to avoid harming the amenities

---

[2] Remo Giazotto, *Antonio Vivaldi* (Turin, 1973), pp. 374 and 375, gives brief details of two entries in the governors' minutes book (*Nottatorio*) dated 4th June 1723 and 27th January 1724, which refer to the decision to have these additional stalls built and to the execution of the work: Venice, *Archivio di Stato Veneto* (*ASV*), Pietà, Busta 691 (N.I), ff. 177 and 216.

of the *figlie di commun*,[3] for in the eyes of the general public the non-musicians might as well not have existed.

According to a set of regulations dating from 1745 or a little later the active members (*attive*) of the *coro* comprised 18 singers, eight string players, two organists, two soloists (presumably vocal) and a *maestra* (director) for each of the sections, vocal and instrumental. Fourteen 'initiates' (*iniziate*), some as young as nine years old, acted as their assistants and deputies.[4] The performers must often have been reinforced, especially by wind instruments, if Charles De Brosses's statement that they numbered around 40 is reliable.[5] A decision of 1st March 1705 permitted *figlie di coro* not belonging to the *coro* proper to take an occasional solo part if deemed worthy.[6] Another privilege, restricted to a dozen of the girls, was that of taking one female, fee-paying pupil from outside the Pietà. Originally, as laid down in the governors' resolution of 5th June 1707, these pupils could belong to either the noble or the citizen estate, but later— perhaps in response to the competition for places— girls from the citizenry were excluded.[7] The senior girls and in particular the various *maestre*, who were responsible within their designated spheres of competence (such as singing or playing stringed instruments) for maintaining discipline as well as teaching, organizing and directing performances, enjoyed other privileges. Some of them took part in musical activities outside

[3] *ASV*, Pietà, Busta 688, f. 181 (5th June 1707); transcribed in Giazotto, op. cit., p. 354f.

[4] *ASV*, Provveditori sopra Ospedali, Busta 48. Articles 45–99 ('Del Coro') are transcribed in Giazotto, op. cit., pp. 384ff.

[5] *Le président De Brosses en Italie: lettres familières écrites d'Italie en 1739 et 1740*, ed. R. Colomb, vol. i (Paris, 1858), p. 194 (letter to M. De Blancey of 29th August 1739).

[6] *ASV*, Pietà, Busta 688, f. 138v; transcribed in Giazotto, op. cit., p. 352f.

[7] *ASV*, Pietà, Busta 688, f. 181 (5th June 1707) and Busta 691 (N.I), f. 169 (30th April 1723).

the Pietà's walls and even outside Venice.

Tuition at the Pietà in singing, theory (*solfeggio*) and instrumental playing was organized on a pyramidical basis, the advanced girls teaching the less advanced, and the less advanced the beginners. Although the Pietà's inmates are always referred to in documents as *figlie* or *figliole* (both meaning 'girls'), the really proficient musicians among them who were loath to retire into the anonymity of marriage or the nunnery at the onset of adulthood had no option, given the exclusion of their sex (singers excepted) from the world of performing musicians, but to remain at the Pietà into middle age, to the delight of the audiences which flocked to its frequent services open to visitors and which contributed handsomely to its — and, incidentally, to the girls' — income. The 'stars' of the Pietà, and the other *ospedali* ranked with the foremost virtuosi of their time in the opinion of connoisseurs. De Brosses averred of the Pietà, whose orchestra he praised above those of the other *ospedali* and even that of the Paris opera for the perfection of its ensemble, that in a certain Chiaretta it would surely posssess the best violinist in all of Italy, if she were not surpassed by Anna Maria of the Ospedaletto.[8] Indeed, not a few of the girls must have outdone the average virtuoso in versatility. The celebrated Anna Maria of the Pietà (not her namesake just mentioned), who appears in that institution's records in 1712, 1720 (by which time she was already a *maestra*) and 1722, is claimed, in an anonymous MS. poem on the subject of the Pietà's girls, datable at shortly before 1740, to be proficient on the harpsichord, violin, cello, viola d'amore, lute, theorbo and mandolin.[9] Many girls were both expert singers and instrumentalists, a combination more common in the Baroque period (among composers, Henry Purcell,

[8] Loc. cit.
[9] Venice, Museo Correr, Ms. Cicogna, Cod. 1178, pp. 206–12. The poem, entitled *Sopra le putte della Pietà di coro*, is transcribed in Giazotto, op. cit., pp. 389ff.

21

Tomaso Albinoni and Domenico Alberti possessed this double aptitude) than it became later. The range of instruments played aroused comment. De Brosses wrote: '[They] play the violin, the recorder, the organ, the oboe, the cello, the bassoon; in short, there is no instrument large enough to frighten them.'[10] In fact, the Pietà made a speciality of unusual instruments, perhaps with the aim of attracting the curious to its services (in addition to keeping its girls from idleness). Besides those played by Anna Maria or mentioned by De Brosses one can cite the chalumeau, the *viola all'inglese* and the psaltery, all of which were employed during Vivaldi's period of service, which stretched, with some breaks, from 1703 to 1740. As for other, more familiar instruments, the clarinet was introduced by 1716, the transverse flute by 1728, the horn in 1747 and timpani in 1750.[11] Several works by Vivaldi suggest that the trumpet was also played, although it is possible that trumpets were brought in from outside. (If they were always available, it is difficult to see why so many of Vivaldi's compositions for the Pietà simulate the sound of trumpets on oboes, clarinets and even violins.) There are a number of reasons why brass instruments were at first little favoured at the Pietà. Until the establishment of the modern orchestra later in the eighteenth century their use, unlike that of oboes and bassoons, was restricted to solo parts. Because of their specialized technique it was unlikely that a teacher of woodwind instruments could

[10] Loc. cit.

[11] Denis Arnold, 'Instruments and Instrumental Teaching in the Early Italian Conservatories', *Galpin Society Journal*, vol. xviii (1965), p. 78f, records the repair of two clarinets in 1740 (they had been used as early as 1716 in Vivaldi's *Juditha Triumphans*, however) and the purchase of two horns in 1747 and two timpani in 1750. *ASV*, Ospedali, Busta 1009 (13th March 1740 and 7th December 1747) and Busta 693 (T.II), f. 42. In 1728 the Pietà reappointed Ignazio Siber as a flute (rather than oboe) master.

instruct the girls in them, hence the expense of a new teacher would be entailed. The governors may have considered them unladylike if not profane, for although the trumpet had long been used in sacred music as well as in pageantry, the horn was still associated with the worldly culture of courts and their favourite pastime of hunting.

The Pietà seems to have regarded its small staff of male teachers and instrument keepers as a necessary evil. They were required when new instruments were introduced and the girls had not yet acquired the necessary expertise, when a drop in performing standards had occurred, or when instruments had to be purchased or serviced. It has been shown by Denis Arnold how eager the governors were to terminate the contract of the timpani teacher once the girls were deemed able to manage on their own;[12] the same must have been true of the other teachers. Between 1703 and 1740 a violin or cello master and an oboe or flute master (who between them would have supervised tuition in all the stringed and woodwind instruments), a singing master, a teacher of *solfeggio*, and two men, one to maintain the organ and the other the harpsichords, were engaged with varying degrees of continuity. An appointment, even of the *Maestro di Coro*, was tenable for one year, at the end of which it was renewed only if the incumbent obtained two-thirds of the votes cast at a meeting of the governors. As a violin teacher Vivaldi was in a disadvantageous position, for the tradition of string playing was firmly established; as a *Maestro de' Concerti* (leader-cum-conductor of the orchestra) or as house composer he was less dispensible, indeed a bright feather in the Pietà's cap.

It has been suggested that the Pietà's male staff were drafted into the choir to sing tenor and bass. The idea is a little naïve, for the teachers would surely have wished to maintain a social distance from their pupils. Little can be said for the other common proposition, that singers from St Mark's or other

[12] Ibid., p. 79f. *ASV,* Ospedali, Busta 693 (T.II), f. 50.

23

churches were brought in, for they would have been expensive to hire and probably unavailable on the main feast-days, when their services would have been needed. The records so far made available indicate that the girls themselves supplied the tenor and bass voices. In contexts where a reference to instruments is excluded one sees girls listed as 'Paulina dal Tenor' or 'Anneta dal Basso' (since many of the girls must have lacked surnames, it was logical to identify them by a combination of christian name and voice or instrument). The roll of new entrants to the *coro* dated 4th December 1707, from which the above names are taken, contains two sopranos, four contraltos, three tenors and one bass.[13] The tenors will have sung their parts at notated pitch,[14] the basses probably in the higher octave like violins or violas reading from the bass clef. Since the instrumental bass could supply the eight-foot and sixteen-foot registers (unaccompanied choral writing is hardly found in Vivaldi's church music), the result would not have been unpleasing.

Women singing tenor and bass may have been a novelty, but men singing soprano and alto were commonplace in Vivaldi's Venice, not only in churches but also in the many opera houses. (The sopranos were invariably, the altos very often, *castrati*.) Since opera was in those days Venice's main tourist attraction, the city could sustain a level of operatic activity far beyond the capability of other major centres of opera in Italy such as Naples, Bologna, Rome and Milan. The number of theatres offering opera varied from season to season, as houses burned down or were rebuilt, closed or reopened, or switched between opera and comedy, but one may gain a good idea from the statement of

[13] *ASV*, Pietà, Busta 688, f. 195v; transcribed in Giazotto, op. cit., p. 357f.
[14] The poem cited above unflatteringly describes a certain Ambrosina as 'un tenor che contralteggia'. In fact, the aria 'Esurientes' designated for Ambrosina in one version (RV 611) of Vivaldi's *Magnificat* has her part written in the tenor clef.

Luigi Riccoboni, a contemporary observer of the European operatic scene, that 'at certain seasons they play every day, and in six theatres at the same time'.[15] The length of an operatic run depended on the work's popularity and the place it occupied within the season's repertory. Perhaps a record was established by G. A. Ristori's *Orlando furioso*, which ran for between 40 and 50 nights at the S. Angelo theatre during the Autumn of 1713 and had to be repeated the following Autumn.[16]

Venice had pioneered the opening of opera, hitherto the preserve of courts, to the general public. In 1637 the world's first public opera house, S. Cassiano, opened its doors, to be followed within a few years by those of SS. Giovanni e Paolo (1639), S. Moisè (1639), S. Angelo (1677) and S. Giovanni Grisostomo (1678), to name only those theatres which continued to accommodate operas in the next century. In most cases the name of the parish in which the theatre was situated served to identify it (the Venetians, oddly, canonized certain Old Testament prophets, hence S. Moisè, S. Samuele and S. Giobbe).

The proprietor of each theatre was a noble or group of nobles. Members of the Grimani family actually owned three theatres: SS. Giovanni e Paolo, S. Giovanni Grisostomo and S. Samuele. The proprietor normally appointed a director to take charge of the day-to-day running of the theatre, or sometimes leased it to an independent entrepreneur. The economics of opera were precarious at the best of times. An anonymous French pamphleteer wrote:

[15] Lewis (Luigi) Riccoboni, *An Historical and Critical Account of the Theatres in Europe* (London, 1741), p. 74; translated from *Réflexions historiques et critiques sur les différens théâtres de l'Europe* (Paris, 1738).
[16] The librettist, Grazio Braccioli, speaks in his next libretto, *Orlando finto pazzo* (set by Vivaldi), of nearly 50 performances, while Giovanni Carlo Bonlini, *Le glorie della poesia e della musica* (Venice, 1730), p. 169, reports that the opera ran for over 40 evenings.

The [Italian] entrepreneurs hardly ever manage to recoup their outlay. These entrepreneurs are usually people of rank — rich people who, banding together, bring honour on themselves by making sacrifices for their compatriots' entertainment. If they recover their expenses, it is most often because games of chance in which they keep the bank and which are at present tolerated, make good the deficits of the enterprise.[17]

Stage properties, scenery and the elaborate machinery were the least of the impresario's financial worries for, being interchangeable in large part between opera and opera, they could be regarded as fixed assets. The engaging for a season of the half-dozen or so principal singers required in every opera would prove the most expensive item in the budget, for the fees demanded by singers, particularly the pampered *castrati*, grew ever more exorbitant. If a chorus, a *corps de ballet* or extra singers for the intermezzos were required in addition, the burden would be increased in proportion. The income from ticket sales was often inadequate, since competition between the theatres kept down the price of tickets. When S. Cassiano opened in 1637, the price of a ticket of admission to an opera was four *lire*.[18] This price remained in force throughout the theatres until 1674, when Francesco Santurini, an impresario holding the lease of S. Moisè, lowered the price to a quarter ducat, little more than one and a half *lire*. Saturini soon ran into opposition and had to give up the lease, but in 1676 he erected an opera house of his own on a site owned by the Marcello and Cappello families (we will return later to the question of this site). When this theatre, S. Angelo, opened one year later, the same low price was introduced. Within a few years the other theatres, with the exception of S. Giovanni Grisostomo, the largest and most

[17] *Reflexions d'un patriote sur l'opera françois et sur l'opera italien* (Lausanne, 1754), p. 6f.

[18] The *ducato corrente* was equivalent to six *lire* and four *soldi* (20 *soldi* made up one *lira*).

magnificent of them, followed suit. By Riccoboni's time the price had climbed to only three *lire*. This sum covered admission only; an additional sum had to be paid for a seat in the pit or in a box. Many of the boxes were rented for the season, while others were virtually the property of a single family, passing from generation to generation.

The principal operatic season (in other cities generally the only season) was Carnival, which stretched from St Stephen's Day (26th December) to Shrove Tuesday. This festive season was marked by the wearing of masks by the whole of Venetian society, clergy included. A theatre would normally mount two, sometimes three, operas during Carnival. Since the season straddled two years, there was some confusion as to which year it belonged to. It was most common (and we shall follow this practice here) to take the date from the year in which the bulk of the season occurred. A work performed on 26th December 1709 would thus belong to the Carnival of 1710. Some preferred, however, to identify the season by the year in which it began; in Venice this practice was encouraged by the peculiarity of a local calendar used in legal and ecclesiastical documents, in which the start of the new year was delayed until 1st March, so that, *more veneto*, 1st January to 28th February 1709 was the same as 1st January to 28th February 1710 according to the normal calendar.

The Autumn season opened in the first week of October and continued until mid December. It was primarily a season for comedy, but from November onwards many theatres put on an opera as a foretaste of Carnival. Indeed, until the Council of Ten in 1699 decreed the closing of theatres over Christmas, the Autumn and Carnival seasons were virtually one. For purposes of identifying works by their order of performance within the season (when one sees in a score, for example, that an aria is taken from the 'third' work performed at S. Angelo in a given year) the Autumn opera is often to be regarded as the first work

27

of Carnival. Since the cast lists of operas performed in the Autumn and the following Carnival seasons at the same theatre so often have a majority of names in common, it seems that where possible singers were engaged for a 'combined' season.

By permission of the Council of Ten one or two theatres were allowed each year to present an opera during the 15 days of the Ascensiontide Fair, a practice begun in 1720.

Although public opera was performed within well defined seasons, dramatic works staged privately in the palaces and gardens of the nobility carried on all the year round. These works, generally of the small-scale type requiring a mere handful of singers and known as *serenata* on account of its performance in the evening (*sera*), commonly celebrated the success of, or extolled the virtues of, some high-born person in whose honour they were presented. Foreign ambassadors to Venice often commissioned *serenate* from local poets and composers to mark the birthday or name-day of their monarch or a member of his family.

Music of a more intimate kind was heard at 'academies' (*accademie*), which we should today term musical soirées or private concerts. De Brosses tells us not only that these musical occasions were frequent but also that they were eagerly overheard by the uninvited: 'There is hardly an evening when there is not an academy somewhere. The populace rushes out onto the canal to listen to it with as much keenness as if it were for the first time.'[19] Used in a rather different sense, the word 'academy' also meant a learned society like the Accademia degli Animosi founded by the Venetian dramatist and historian Apostolo Zeno in 1691, which in 1698 became affiliated to the famous Arcadian Academy of Rome. Such academies concerned themselves mainly with literary, aesthetic and philosophical matters but did not neglect music entirely. Two of Venice's musically most gifted dilettanti (in eighteenth-century usage

[19] Op. cit., vol. i, p. 193.

28

the term was one of commendation rather than disparagement), the Marcello brothers Alessandro (1669–1747) and Benedetto (1686–1739), belonged to the Arcadian Academy, as did many of Italy's best known opera librettists.

Our far from exhaustive review of Venice's musical life must end with an examination of how, and in what form, music was circulated. At least until the middle of the eighteenth century a musician was much more likely to perform from a manuscript than a printed copy. In Italy (perhaps less in northern Europe) music printing was a luxury industry whose products were more expensive, note for note, than the same music written out by a professional copyist. Further, the medium of print presupposed, by the very act of replicating one score or one set of parts, a uniformity of performing resources that simply did not yet exist in many areas of music. This explains in part why the *genres* in which the performing resources were most standardized — notably the violin sonata and concerto — were the ones favoured by music publishers. An opera house or a *cappella*, however, needed a version of a work tailored exactly to its immediate resources. The copyists employed by establishments of this kind (the Pietà retained two girls for this purpose) performed a valuable service by adapting their exemplars as their instructions or experience dictated. A copyist would often be called upon to piece together an ostensibly new work (a *pasticcio*) from fragments of earlier works, not necessarily by the same composer.

Composers often employed copyists on their own behalf. One thinks of the father and son, both named John Christopher Smith, in Handel's service. It is clear that Vivaldi worked in close association with several copyists (among them perhaps two nephews of his who belonged to the profession), for partly autograph manuscripts containing other hands besides his and non-autograph manuscripts with additions and corrections by the composer are very common.

29

Copyists also worked on a freelance basis, supplying their customers (who in Venice were often visiting foreigners) with the latest music. The libraries of Europe and America are full of collections of operatic arias acquired in this way; they are often in short score, shorn of their instrumental accompaniment. Undoubtedly, most of the buyers acquiesced in these mutilations, though a real connoisseur like Charles Jennens was moved to protest when his friend Edward Holdsworth brought him some 'songs' in this form from Italy.

Insist on the whole scores being copied', he wrote, 'that if they deserve it we may have them performed on the English stage. I must therefore have the overture, songs, symphonies and recitatives entire in all their parts. I mention this so particularly, because some songs of Porpora which you brought over with you the last time you was [sic] abroad were of no use to me, the symphonies being omitted, and nothing copied but the voice part and the bass . . .'[20]

The two firms which dominated Venetian music printing in Vivaldi's lifetime were those of Giuseppe Sala and Antonio Bortoli. Sala's period of activity runs from 1676 to 1715, that of the much less productive Bortoli from 1705 to 1764.[21] With rare exceptions, the Italian music-publishing industry was technically and commercially backward. Sala, Bortoli and their colleagues in other cities still employed the technique of movable type introduced by Attaingnant in the early sixteenth century and, moreover, kept a fount which had remained basically unchanged ever since. In this cumbersome method each section of stave line, each note head, each stem and each tail occupied a separate piece of type, which gave the music a broken, untidy appearance. When groups of shorter note values

[19] Op. cit., vol. i, p. 193.
[20] Letter of 10th July 1741. By 'symphonies' Jennens meant all the purely instrumental movements or sections.
[21] Dates from Claudio Sartori, *Dizionario degli editori musicali italiani (tipografi, incisori, librai-editori)* (Florence, 1958), pp. 137 and 32.

(increasingly common in the eighteenth century) were employed, clarity was difficult to achieve, as each note had a separate tail. The accurate placing of ties and slurs was another problem.

There is no evidence that Italian publishers sought sales outlets north of the Alps, and few of them, in their rôle as retailers, seem to have stocked music in any quantity published by their confrères elsewhere in Italy. This lethargy cannot have depressed their sales appreciably so long as northern Europeans (and Italians from other cities) were willing to travel to the point of production, but the rise at the end of the seventeenth century of a vigorous music-publishing industry in the north-west of the continent transformed the situation.

The doyen of north-European music publishing, Estienne Roger, who opened his firm in Amsterdam around 1697, made a practice from the very start of 'pirating' works published in Italy, sometimes within a year of their appearance.[22] Neither the composer, who had often paid for the first edition out of his own pocket (and, with luck, recouped his expenses from the dedicatee), nor the original publisher was protected by copyright legislation (save, in certain circumstances, in France and England), so there was no impediment to piracy if the publisher thought it worth while. Since the new publisher bore all the production costs, however, it was essential to achieve large sales. To this end Roger established a network of agents in the principal commercial centres of northern Europe: London, Paris, Rotterdam, Liége, Brussels, Hamburg, Cologne and Berlin. It became possible for customers to order his publications by post, identifying a work by its number quoted in his regularly up-dated catalogue and stamped on the plate of the respective title-page.

[22] François Lesure, *Bibliographie des éditions musicales publiées par Estienne Roger et Michel-Charles Le Cène* (Paris, 1969), is the standard work on the Amsterdam publishing house.

After Roger died in 1722, his son-in-law, Michel Charles Le Cène, carried on the business until 1743. Meanwhile, several competitors sprang up in neighbouring countries and even in Amsterdam itself, sometimes pirating works from Roger in their turn. Chief among these was John Walsh of London, who, working with a succession of associates, cornered the largest share of the British market between 1695 and 1760; but one should also mention Pierre Mortier of Amsterdam, who conducted a furious sales war with Roger between 1708 and 1711, Gerhard Fredrik Witvogel, active in Amsterdam after 1731, the younger Le Clerc in Paris and Leopold in Augsburg.

All these men used the new technique (not literally new, but applied to music for the first time on a mass scale) of engraving. This process reproduced the features of contemporary copyists' hands (see Plate 6), including the use of beams for groups of quavers or shorter values. Neat, round note-heads replaced the ungainly lozenges. In the years following 1700 engraving was made quicker and cheaper by the substitution of pewter (a softer metal) for copper and the use, where possible, of a punch in place of a graver. One great economic advantage of having music engraved was that new issues could be drawn at will from the original set of plates without extra cost. In contrast, a printer using movable type would distribute his type after running off the first edition; the type would have to be reset for any subsequent edition of a popular work (as occurred, for example, when Albinoni's *Sinfonie e concerti a cinque*, op. 2, first brought out by Sala in 1700, were republished in 1702 and 1707).

In the opening two decades of the eighteenth century Italian music publishers suffered a double blow from which they never recovered. First, the availability of the latest Italian music in northern European editions made it possible for the transalpine purchaser to satisfy his needs without setting foot in the 'land of music'. Second, Italian composers began after about 1710 to send their music directly to Amsterdam (after about 1730 to Paris), by-passing their native publishers. Hence Albinoni's op. 5 (1707) was entrusted to Sala, but his op. 6 (before 1712) to Roger. On his way back to England from Italy in 1733 Edward Holdsworth acquired for Charles Jennens in Le Cène's shop the newest collection (op. 2) of Tartini — a work probably unobtainable in the composer's own town of Padua.

The musical consequences of this shift to Amsterdam are interesting. Since those Italian composers who published abroad (primarily composers of instrumental music) had the transalpine market in mind from the beginning, a streak of cosmopolitanism — elements, for example, of the French style — crept into their music, contributing to the breakdown of barriers between the French and Italian idioms and preparing the way for the emergence of the international early classical style. But composers working in branches of music such as opera, on which publishing impinged only marginally, felt no need to broaden their style. Here, perhaps, one glimpses the beginning of the rift between Italian instrumental and vocal music, which was to lead to the attenuation of one and the provincialism of the other in the next century.

3 The red-haired priest

The surname Vivaldi is known from the twelfth century. In 1165 one Guglielmo Vivaldi from Taggia near San Remo was Governor of Sicily. In 1291 the Genoese brothers Guido and Ugolino Vivaldi were members of the ill-fated expedition led by Tedisio Doria, which, in search of a sea route to the Indies, disappeared mysteriously somewhere off Morocco. From the fifteenth century members of the Vivaldi family were prominent in Genoa, giving the Republic senators, ambassadors, a general and even a doge (Gerolamo Vivaldi, 1559–61). At the beginning of the sixteenth century Bernardo Vivaldi, an exile from Genoa, took refuge in Savona, founding a branch which is said to have multiplied rapidly and spread throughout Italy. Today the name Vivaldi is concentrated in no particular locality, though, perversely enough, it seems to be absent from Venice.

Agostino Vivaldi, the composer's grandfather, was a bakery worker living in Brescia, a city of the Veneto famous for its violin makers.[1] Either immediately before or after his death in 1666 (the case is unclear) his wife Margarita, whom he had married in 1642, came to Venice with their young son Giovanni

[1] The information concerning Agostino Vivaldi and the early years of Giovanni Battista Vivaldi comes from a paper read by Eric Paul to the First International Vivaldi Colloquium, held in Brussels on 16th December 1963, the contents of which were summarized in *Vivaldiana I* (Brussels, 1969), p. 159. No full transcript of the paper survives; Dr Paul died shortly afterwards.

Battista (or Giambattista). Although Giovanni Battista is generally supposed to have been born in Brescia in about 1655, his age is given as 70 in a membership list of the Venetian *Arte di sonadori* (an instrumentalists' guild) dated 20th June 1727.[2] If, as seems likely, this figure is to be interpreted literally, Giovanni Battista will have been born between 21st June 1656 and 20th June 1657.

In his marriage banns, dated 6th June 1676, Giovanni Battista's address is described as 'nelli forni in contrà S. Martin' (at the bakery, parish of S. Martino).[3] By implication he still had some connection with his father's trade, although he is known to have been a barber. His bride, Camilla Calicchio, was a tailor's daughter. Their wedding took place later that month.[4]

In the following year Giovanni Battista's profession is stated as 'sonador' (instrumentalist) in the record of Antonio's baptism. He must have been a good player, for on 23rd April 1685 (the day of Legrenzi's appointment as *Primo Maestro*) he joined the orchestra of St Mark's as a violinist.[5] His annual salary, originally 15 ducats, was raised to 25 ducats on 21st August 1689 in consideration of 'a major increase of new functions

[2] *ASV*, Milizia da Mar, Busta 553, fasc. 'Sonadori'; see Eleanor Selfridge-Field, 'Annotated Membership Lists of the Venetian Instrumentalists' Guild 1672–1727', *RMA Research Chronicle*, No. 9 (1971), p. 48.

[3] Venice, Church of S. Giovanni in Bràgora, Registro di stato libero; reproduced and transcribed in Giazotto, op. cit., pp. 14 and 132. The parish of S. Martino lies between the Arsenal and the Riva degli Schiavoni.

[4] Walter Kolneder, *Antonio Vivaldi: his Life and Work*, p. 7, gives the date of marriage as 6th August 1677 (if this were true, Antonio would have been conceived out of wedlock). Since no documentation is adduced, the earlier date (*Vivaldiana I*, p. 116) seems more likely.

[5] *ASV*, Basilica di S. Marco, Reg. 148; transcribed in Giazotto, op. cit., p. 96.

involving the use of orchestral instruments and organs'.[6] As two colleagues, the violinist Lorenzo Novelloni and the 'cellist Bernardo Cortella, received the same increases, Giovanni Battista's new duties probably included playing in a trio or (in its orchestral context) a *concertino*.

Very significantly, he was first engaged under the name of 'Gio: Baptista Rossi'. We know from many sources including Goldoni, who writes that the Abbé Vivaldi (Antonio) was called the 'red-haired priest' (*il Prete Rosso*) and even simply 'Rossi' by those unaquainted with his proper surname, of the unusual hair-colouring of the composer.[7] Evidently, the trait was inherited. In the light of this well-established sobriquet one may well wonder whether the Giambattista Rossi who composed the music to *La fedeltà sfortunata*, an opera performed in 1688 at an unknown theatre, possibly in Venice, was the elder Vivaldi.[8] As we shall see, he participated in opera as a performer, at the very least.

He was a founder-member, in 1685, of the *Società S. Cecilia*, a self-governing association of musicians whose moving spirit was his fellow-parishioner Giandomenico Partenio, Vice-Maestro of St Mark's, and to which Legrenzi also belonged. Growing age seems to have impaired his abilities as a violinist little, for in the 1713 edition of Vincenzo Coronelli's *Guida de' forestieri*, a kind of visitor's handbook to Venice, he is listed alongside his by now more famous son as one of the city's foremost virtuosi on that instrument. On 30th September 1729, now in his seventies, he petitioned the procurators of St Mark's to be released from his duties in the Ducal Chapel for one year in order to accompany a

---

[6] Ibid., Reg. 147, f. 288v; quoted in Eleanor Selfridge-Field, *Venetian Instrumental Music from Gabrieli to Vivaldi* (Oxford, 1975), p. 219.

[7] *Commedie*, vol. xiii, p. 11.

[8] See Livio Niso Galvani, *I teatri musicali di Venezia nel secolo xvii, 1637–1700* (Milan, 1879; facs. reprint, Florence, 1969), p. 166.

son of his (Antonio, certainly) to Germany.[9] As the man designated as his deputy, Francesco Negri, kept the position for over 20 years, while Giovanni Battista disappears thereafter from the *Cappella*'s records, one must presume that he died on this tour, from which his son may have returned to Venice as late as 1732.

The marriage of Giovanni Battista and Camilla Vivaldi produced six children of whom we have certain knowledge: Antonio Lucio (4th March 1678); Margarita Gabriela (7th December 1680); Cecilia Maria (25th January 1682); Bonaventura Tomaso (18th March 1685); Zanetta (Giannetta) Anna (17th February 1687); Francesco Gaetano (14th January 1689).[10] Only Antonio seems to have taken up music as a profession (and then, one must remember, after training for the priesthood), but Cecilia and Francesco were each the parent of a music copyist, respectively Piero Mauro and Carlo Vivaldi. Bonaventura married in 1718 and went to live outside Venice.[11] Francesco became a barber and wigmaker like his father. What is probably the earliest notice we have of him is a report in the Commemorali Gradenigo, a memoir preserved in the Museo Correr, that 'Francesco Vivaldi, a young wigmaker, brother of the famous Don Antonio, violin player', used insulting behaviour towards the nobleman Antonio Soranzo, for which he was banished from Venice.[12] He had evidently returned to Venice by 1727, when his name appears on a document giving a consortium engaged in re-paving the *piazza* of St Mark's permission to unload on the Riva degli Schiavoni.[13] Later, he

---

[9] *ASV*, Basilica di S. Marco, Reg. 153, f. 117. Though the tour was centred on Bohemia, Giovanni Battista's citation of 'Germany' was not inaccurate, given the political and linguistic subjection to Austria of the Czech lands.

[10] Details from 'Pedigree of A. L. Vivaldi' (genealogical table after Eric Paul), *Vivaldiana I*, p. 116.

[11] Giazotto, op. cit., p. 236.

[12] *Commemorali Gradenigo*, iv, p. 77.

[13] Giazotto, op. cit., p. 234.

turned his hand to publishing; his application to the *Riformatori* dated 18th December 1730 was granted on 15th January 1731.[14] In an official register of barbers living in the Cannaregio *sestiere* (one of six districts into which Venice was divided) dated 18th July 1732, Francesco is listed as a 'master barber'.[15]

Although Eric Paul, to whom we are indebted for the most recent discoveries concerning the Vivaldi family, concluded that one Iseppo (Giuseppe) Vivaldi, sentenced on 18th May 1729 to be banished for five years from Venice for wounding Giacomo Crespan, a grocer's errand-boy, had no direct connexion with the other Vivaldis, the circumstances in which three witnesses linked him with that family are extraordinary enough to justify continued speculation.[16] One witness, Giovanni Antonio Zanchi, did not know Iseppo's surname but recognized him as a 'brother of the red-haired priest who plays the violin' (fratello del prete rosso che sona il violin). Another, Zuane (Giovanni) Pignol, thought him to be a brother of the barber who, so he believed, resided at the top of the Calle dell'oca (Street of the Goose) in the parish of SS. Apostoli. (Since this parish lies within the Cannaregio *sestiere*, the barber in question must have been Francesco.) The third, Bastian Maggi, confirmed Zanchi's identification and, when questioned about the so-called 'Rossi' family, said that he thought there were four brothers (Antonio, Bonaventura, Francesco — and Iseppo?), of whom he knew one from hearsay to be outside Venice, supposedly banished. Whether Pignol was mistaken in believing Francesco to be still at his shop in Venice, or Maggi confused Bonaventura and Francesco, the fact that four brothers are mentioned cannot be ignored.

Until Paul's discovery in 1962 of a baptismal register con-

---

[14] Loc. cit.

[15] *ASV*, Milizia da Mar, Busta 58.

[16] *ASV*, Avogaria di comun, Penale, Busta 110, fasc. 11, and Reg. iii, raspe, 11th May 1729.

taining Antonio's date of birth scholars had to rely on Pincherle's inspired conjecture, which placed it 15 years before the date of his tonsure (1693), or else take refuge in approximations, of which 1675 was the most common. The entry in the baptismal register reads:

6th May 1678. Antonio Lucio, son of Signor Giovanni Battista Vivaldi, son of the late Agustin, instrumentalist, and his wife Camilla Calicchio, daughter of the late Camillo, born on 4th March last, who was baptised at home, being in danger of death, by the midwife Madama Margarita Veronese, was today taken to the church and received the exorcisms and holy oils from me, Giacomo Fornacieri, parish priest, at which he was held by Signor Antonio Veccelio, son of the late Gerolemo, apothecary, at the sign of the dose in the same parish.[17]

What was this *pericolo di morte*? One immediately recalls the chest ailment which troubled Vivaldi all his life. In a letter of 16th November 1737 to his Ferrarese patron Count Guido Bentivoglio d'Aragona he wrote: 'I have not said Mass for 25 years, nor will I ever again, not because of a ban or an order — may it please His Excellency [Cardinal Ruffo, Legate of Ferrara] to learn — but from choice, because of an ailment from which I have suffered from birth and by which I am afflicted.' And later on: 'For this reason I almost always live at home and go out only in a gondola or carriage, since my chest ailment, or constriction

---

[17] Venice, Church of S. Giovanni in Bràgora, Libro de' battesimi; reproduced in Giazotto, op. cit., p. 33 and *Vivaldiana I*, p. 116: 'Adi 6 Maggio 1678. Antonio Lucio figliolo del Sig.re Gio: Batta q. Agustin Viualdi Sonador et della Sig.ra Camilla figliola del q Camillo Calicchio sus Cons.te nato li 4 marzo ult.o caduto, qual hebbe L'acqua in casa p pericolo di morte dalla Comare allev.ce mad.ma Margarita Veronese, hoggi fù portato alla chiesa riceuè gl'essorcismi, et ogli ss.ti da me Giacomo Fornacieri Piouano à quali lo tene il Sig.re Antonio q Gerolemo Veccelio specier all'insegna del Dose in Contrà.'

of the chest, prevents me from walking.'[18] This *strettezza di petto* is usually identified as asthma. Remo Giazotto, however, suggests another possible cause of anxiety: an earth tremor which shook Venice on the day of Antonio's birth.[19]

The young Antonio learned the violin from his father and — if the report of the nineteenth-century Venetian historian Francesco Caffi, culled from unknown sources, is trustworthy — played on occasion in the orchestra of St Mark's as a supernumerary violinist or as Giovanni Battista's deputy.[20] Little credence should be placed in an oft-repeated statement that he took composition lessons from Legrenzi. Too often the mere presence in the same city of an old and a young talent has led to the presumption of a master-pupil relationship, as if genius observed some kind of apostolic succession. Although Legrenzi has also been claimed as the teacher of Albinoni, Bassani, Biffi, C. F. Pollarolo, F. Gasparini, Lotti, Varischino and M. A. Gasparini, confirmation exists only in the last three cases.[21] Vivaldi had less chance than most, as Legrenzi died when he was twelve.

It is probable that Antonio also received some instruction in the harpsichord, for in a report to the Inquisitors of a banquet given by the Spanish ambassador to Venice in celebration of the marriage of the Infant Philip to Princess Marie-Louise-Elizabeth of France on 26th August 1739 a certain Giovanni Gilli recounted that the abbé Vivaldi was seated at the harp-

---

[18] Transcribed in Stefani, op. cit., p. 21f. The present location of this letter is unknown.

[19] Op. cit., pp. 4ff.

[20] *Storia della musica teatrale in Venezia* (MS notes, *c* 1850). Venice, Biblioteca Nazionale Marciana, Cod. It. IV–747 (= 10465), 310r. The section dealing with Vivaldi (ff. 310r–315r) is in the hand of Caffi's daughter Amalia.

[21] See Ursula Kirkendale, *Antonio Caldara: sein Leben und seine venezianisch-römischen Oratorien* (Graz–Cologne, 1966), p. 23.

sichord, where he directed the instruments accompanying the singer Anna Girò (of whom much more will be said later).[22]

That he, the eldest son, was directed towards the priesthood, a career that offered some hope of social mobility, was in keeping with his humble origins (in wealthier families one would more commonly find a younger son taking holy orders). From available records it appears that he did not attend a seminary, perhaps on account of his infirmity, but received instruction from the clergy of two local churches, S. Giovanni in Oleo and S. Geminiano. His progress up to full ordination can be charted as follows:[23]

Tonsure	18th September 1693
Minor Orders	
Porter (*Ostiario*)	19th September 1693
Lector	21st September 1694
Exorcist	25th December 1695
Acolyte	21st September 1696
Holy Orders	
Sub-Deacon	4th April 1699
Deacon	18th September 1700
Priest	23rd March 1703

If one takes at face value Vivaldi's claim, in the letter to Bentivoglio quoted above, not to have said Mass for 25 years, 1712 becomes the year in which he performed this rite for the last time. A much earlier date is suggested, however, by the sentence which comes between the two already cited: 'Barely ordained a priest, I said Mass for a year or a little longer, and

[22] *ASV*, Inquisitori, Busta 604; quoted in Giazotto, op. cit., p. 309f.
[23] Venice, Archivio Patriarcale, Registro sacre ordinazioni, anni 1688–1706, ff. 129f, 131, 163f, 205ff, 314, 380f, 463f; extracts reproduced in Giazotto, op. cit., opp. pp. 48, 49, and transcribed p. 397f.

then I abandoned it, having had to leave the altar three times because of the same complaint.' Herein we see, perhaps, the source of Orloff's anecdote: Vivaldi was observed to terminate Mass prematurely, for which a member of the congregation supplied his own over-fanciful explanation. A few lines further down Vivaldi continues his justifications: 'Immediately after eating, I can usually move about [*andare*], but never on foot; this is the reason why I do not celebrate Mass.' Convenient pretext (to allow more time for the practice — and business — of music) or genuine excuse? Very likely something of both.

His association with the Pietà can be traced back to a resolution debated by its governors on 12th August 1703. Reading between the lines, one gathers that Francesco Gasparini, barely two years in office as *Maestro di Coro*, wished to improve the standard of string playing and consolidate, or perhaps even inaugurate, the teaching of wind instruments.

New Music Teachers

To increase ever further the perfection of the orchestra [Coro] and to introduce more polish into its performances, in accordance with the wishes of Signor Gasparini, it is moved that teachers of the *viola*, the violin and the oboe be appointed by the Officers in charge of Music [*Deputati sopra il Coro*] at a salary that shall be deemed proper, and no great expense to this venerable institution, and that their services be retained for as long as believed necessary, their duties being laid down by this Congregation [Board of Governors].

For the resolution	8	
Against	2	carried[24]
Abstentions	1	

[24] *ASV*, Pietà, Busta 688, f. 102v; transcribed in Giazotto, op. cit., p. 352. In Vivaldi's day *viola*, when not a generic term for instruments of the violin family, usually denoted the cello; the modern viola was known either as the *violetta* or (by reason of its rôle within the ensemble) as the *alto viola* or *tenore viola*.

That Vivaldi was engaged soon after emerges from a series of payments, the first dated 17th March 1704, recorded in one of the Pietà's account books.[25] An itemized list of payments made to 'D. [Don] Antonio Vivaldi Maestro di Choro' (his full title would be *Maestro di Violino di C(h)oro*) shows that the 30 ducats received by him on that date represented his salary for the six months ending in February 1704. Subsequent payments on 3rd May (20 ducats), 27th June (30 ducats), 4th August (20 ducats), 3rd October (20 ducats), 13th December (20 ducats) and 13th February 1705 (20 ducats) are puzzling in one important respect: although the scale of payment (where made explicit) remains with one exception five ducats per month,[26] the gross payment over the period of 130 ducats would represent 26 months' work, an impossibility even if he were paid in advance.

Discounting the possible existence of double entries or errors of transcription by Pincherle, from whom our information is derived,[27] there remains the possibility that at least some of the money resulted from an increment to Vivaldi's salary awarded by the governors on 17th August 1704:

Since the sustained efforts of Don Antonio Vivaldi, the girls' violin teacher, have borne fruit, and since he has also rendered diligent assistance in the tuition of the *viola inglese*, which is considered by Their Excellencies [the governors] part of his duties, it is moved that 40 ducats be added to his normal salary on account of his teaching of the *viole all'inglese*, making a total of 100 ducats per annum, so that he may be encouraged in his tasks, and for the greater profit of those girls.

For .... 9 ⎫
 carried[28]
Against .... 1 ⎭

[25] Ibid., Reg. 999, *passim*.
[26] The 20 ducats paid on 4th August represented three months' work.
[27] *Antonio Vivaldi et la musique instrumentale*, vol. i, p. 292f.
[28] *ASV*, Pietà, Busta 688, f. 128v; transcribed in Giazotto, op. cit.,

Vivaldi

Quarterly payments of 25 ducats to Vivaldi during 1706–7 show that this new salary, and the duties encompassed by it, remained in force.[29] In his main employment he was now earning only half the amount paid to the Pietà's musical director, but already his salary was four times greater than his father's.

His ancillary duties included the acquisition of instruments for the chapel: a violin in 1704; another violin and four *viole* (? of different sizes) in 1705; a violin bow for a certain Madalena Rassa in 1706; a violin and a cello in 1708; strings for a viola d'amore in 1708 and 1709 (January).[30] In all probability he was also unofficial *Maestro de' Concerti*, directing (and playing in) orchestral performances, and composing instrumental music for both private and public consumption.

His first publication, a set of trio sonatas, appeared from Sala in or before 1705. Until quite recently only the 'pirated' edition by Roger (1715) was known, but a solitary first violin part of the Italian edition survives in the library of the Venice Conservatoire. The trio sonata was still the most popular instrumental genre in Italy, though beginning to lose ground to the solo sonata and the concerto, and was commonly regarded as the touchstone of a composer's ability; Corelli's four great collections provided both a model and a yardstick of excellence. Small wonder, then, that emerging composers of Vivaldi's generation, men such as Gentili, Albinoni and Caldara, nearly always made their début in print with a set of trio sonatas.

---

p. 352. The family of instruments known generically as *viole (all')* *inglese* is discussed on p. 159f below.

[29] See Pincherle, *Antonio Vivaldi et la musique instrumentale*, vol. i, p. 293.

[30] Pincherle, loc. cit.; Denis Arnold, 'Instruments and Instrumental Teaching in the Early Italian Conservatoires', *Galpin Society Journal*, vol. xviii (1965), p. 76f.

Opus 1 was dedicated to Count Annibale Gambara, a Venetian of Brescian extraction. Vivaldi's little-known dedication is worth quoting in full:

My devotion, ambitious to make itself known to Your Excellency, has suffered enough from the torments of desire. I confess that many times I restrained my ardour, mindful of your merit and mistrustful of my talent, but, no longer able to contain my ambition, I thought it proper to free it from its longing, since what was earlier a mere propensity had become a necessity. When considering whether to dedicate to Your Excellency the first fruits of my feeble efforts in the form of these sonatas, I realized that it was no longer in my power not to do so. Your lofty prerogatives took my judgement captive and rewarded my decision with the bounty of a Maecenas. I will not lose myself in the vast expanse of the glories of your most noble and excellent family, for I would not find my way out again, since they are so immense in greatness and number. Knowing that I possess no other adornments than those of my feebleness, I have sought the patronage of a great man, who can not only protect me from the tongues of Aristarchuses [pedants — named after a grammarian of the second century B.C.], and in whose shade my labours — perhaps when maligned by critics, who in these times like to flaunt their impertinences — can enjoy a safe refuge, but can also perform these flaccid harmonies, which with so much humility I dedicate to Your Excellency. May your exalted generosity then deign to accept in respectful tribute these first, most humble products of my labours, and meanwhile grant me the honour of declaring myself:
the most humble, devoted and obliged servant of Your Excellency,
D. Antonio Vivaldi

One need only compare this dedication with the generality of dedications written by his contemporaries to realize how entirely conventional its tone and imagery are.[31] The composer's apology for his inadequacies; his eulogy of the dedicatee;

[31] See the examples quoted in Claudio Sartori, *Bibliografia della musica strumentale italiana stampata in Italia fino al 1700* (Florence, 1952).

his invocation of the Classical age: all these occur over and over again, down to the very phraseology. Even the plea to the dedicatee to shield the composer from malevolent critics is a commonplace, especially in first publications (like those of Corelli and Caldara), although Vivaldi's tone is more bitter than usual, perhaps indicating that the sensitivity to criticism which he showed in later life was already one of his characteristics.

Two curious features of the surviving Sala edition suggest that it is a reprint of a work brought out earlier, perhaps in mid 1703. The title-page bears the printer's own typographical emblem (a seated King David playing the harp), normal in Sala's reprints, instead of the dedicatee's coat of arms, normal in first editions.[32] Further, although Vivaldi is identified as a cleric ('Don'), he is styled merely 'Musico di violino professore veneto' (professional violinist from Venice) with no mention of his post at the Pietà. Highly conscious of rank, even for his times, Vivaldi would hardly have omitted this detail from a title-page drawn up in 1705. Against this one can argue that the retention of the dedication is rare in a Sala reprint, but not entirely unknown, for the 1707 edition of Gentili's *Capricci da camera*, op. 3, possesses one, although it must be a reprint, since a pirated edition by Roger was advertised in April 1706.[33]

The dedication of Vivaldi's next opus, twelve sonatas for violin and harpsichord, is a perfect example of the opportunism an eighteenth-century composer had to practise in order to prosper, or merely to survive. A catalogue of the publisher Antonio Bortoli attached to the libretto of Caldara's opera *Sofonisba*, first performed in November 1708, lists second from the end Vivaldi's op. 2. Very likely, the composer's manuscript was already in Bortoli's hands. Then on 29th December Venice received a visit arranged at very short notice by Frederick IV of

---

[32] Compare, for instance, the 1700 edition of Albinoni's op. 2 with the 1702 and 1707 reprints.

[33] Lesure, op. cit., p. 44.

Denmark and Norway, who was by his own request to remain incognito (a state facilitated by the wearing of a Carnival mask). On the very day after his arrival Frederick attended a Sunday service at the Pietà. In the words of a contemporary account:

'His Majesty appeared at the Pietà at 11 o'clock after receiving ambassadors from Savoy, to hear the girls singing and playing instruments under the direction of the master who was occupying the rostrum in the absence of Gasparini. Great was the applause for the *Credo* and *Agnus Dei* which were performed with instruments, and afterwards there was a concert very much after his taste, as befitted him.[34]

One can well imagine that this deputy was Vivaldi, who managed to present the sonatas, duly dedicated, to the king before he departed on 6th March 1709.

What of concertos? That Vivaldi did not publish any until 1711 may indicate simply that he could not afford the cost earlier. We have the rather pathetic testimony of the Roman composer Giuseppe Valentini from the foreword to his *Idee per camera a violino e violone o cembalo*, op. 4 (1706 or 1707), on this subject:

. . . I have made so bold as to publish, further, the present work, which contains my first collection of sonatas, for one violin, reserving my second for sonatas with two and three stringed instruments; these I cannot consign to print at the moment, however, on account of the great expense involved: nevertheless, I will not take long, if you show me favour, to publish these too, likewise my theatrical concertos [*concerti teatrali*] and other things which I am now preparing.[35]

---

[34] Giazotto, op. cit., p. 105.
[35] Sartori, *Bibliografia*, p. 591. The identification of the composer and work is the author's. The trio-sonatas of which Valentini writes were published in 1707, the concertos only in 1710.

Strangely enough, the earliest datable manuscript copies of concertos by Vivaldi to have survived are not of works for principal (i.e. solo) violin, strings and continuo, a type he can hardly have neglected to write in abundance, however) but of concertos with an obbligato cello part. Among the eight cello concertos attributed to Vivaldi preserved in the library of the counts of Schönborn (Wiesentheid/Unterfranken, W. Germany) are three (RV 402, 416, 420) in the hand of Franz Horneck, a young musician in the service of Johann Philipp Franz von Schönborn who stayed in Venice from November 1708 till March 1709.[36] The works were destined for Count Rudolf Franz Erwein von Schönborn, an enthusiastic cellist who also acquired some cello sonatas by Vivaldi. Between 1708 and 1713 the Schönborn brothers purchased a great deal of music from Venice, including unidentified instrumental works by Vivaldi, via the merchant Regaznig, who acted as 'resident' (consul) for the Elector of Mainz, their uncle.

Vivaldi's appointment at the Pietà was renewed in 1706 and in the following two years, though in 1707 he scraped a bare two-thirds majority (six votes to three), perhaps on account of the appointment of a new teacher, the oboist Lodovico Erdmann. He was less fortunate in a ballot held on 24th February 1709, when seven votes were cast in favour of his retention and six against. In a fresh vote one of his supporters changed sides: he was out of office. It is often surmised that his independent personality and outside interests and ambitions harmed his relationship with the Pietà's governors, but real evidence is lacking. Meanwhile, we should not overlook the Pietà's readiness to reappointment him when the moment arrived, nor the even greater liability to dismissal of some of his colleagues.

Reappointment, evidently as violin teacher without special

---

[36] Karl Heller, *Die deutsche Überlieferung der Instrumentalwerke Vivaldis* (Leipzig, 1971), pp. 178ff.

responsibilities for the *viole all'inglese*, came on 27th September 1711:

Realising the necessity of securing ever better instrumental tuition for the girls studying music in order to increase the reputation of this pious establishment, the post of violin master being vacant, we move that Don Antonio Vivaldi be appointed violin master at an annual salary of 60 ducats, this governing body being certain that he will exercise his talent to the utmost in the good service of this pious establishment, and for the greater profit of those girls.

Abstentions	0	
Against	0	carried[37]
In favour	11	

The renewal of his post went through without serious opposition in 1712 and 1713. Then, on 23rd April 1713 there occurred an event of great importance for Vivaldi's career and orientation as a composer. Francesco Gasparini was granted sick leave, nominally of six months, and permission to go outside Venice. This may well have been a strategem on Gasparini's part, for he never returned, passing via Florence to Rome, where in 1716 he became musical director to Prince Ruspoli, in 1717 *Maestro di Cappella* at S. Lorenzo in Lucina, and in 1725, two years before his death, *maestro* of St John Lateran.

Gasparini's departure left a void which the Pietà had difficulty in filling for many years, as the record of the four succeeding *maestri di coro* reveals:

Pietro Dall'Olio	appointed on interim basis 11th June 1713	? dismissed before 4th March 1714

---

[37] *ASV,* Pietà, Busta 689, f. 182r; transcribed in Giazotto, op. cit., p. 365.

Carlo Pietro Grua	appointed 26th February 1719	died 29th March 1726
Giovanni Porta	appointed 24th May 1726	left soon after 28th September 1737
Alessandro Gennaro	appointed 21st August 1739	dismissed 21st April 1741

The regular composition of new works was an important part of the *maestro*'s duties. In a memorandum of 6th July 1710 the requirements are specified: a minimum of two new Mass and Vespers settings annually (one for Easter and the other for the feast of the Visitation of the Blessed Virgin, to whom the Pietà was dedicated); at least two motets every month; occasional compositions as required for funerals, the offices of Holy Week, etc. The scores had to be delivered to the *maestra di coro*, who would have them copied into parts and draw up a list of new compositions every six months for the inspection of the governors.[38]

For whatever reason, Dall'Olio was evidently unable to take over this side of Gasparini's activities, and the opportunity passed to Vivaldi. We learn this from a motion debated by the Governors on 2nd June 1715:

This pious congregation [the governors] having noted from the petition of the Reverend Don Antonio Vivaldi, violin master in this pious establishment, and the deposition of the Officers in charge of Music just read out, the acknowledged services and well-rewarded labours performed by him, not only in the successful and universally approved teaching of musical instruments to the girls, but also the excellent musical compositions supplied after the departure of the above-mentioned *maestro* Gasparini — a complete Mass, a Vespers, an

---

[38] Ibid., f. 136r; transcribed in Giazotto, op. cit., p. 363f.

oratorio, over 30 motets and other works — and seeing fit in its generosity to give him a token of its gratitude and recompense him in part for these services outside his normal duties, resolves that a single payment of 50 ducats be made to him from our exchequer in apprecia-tion of his efforts and special contributions. And may this reward also stimulate him to make further contributions and to perfect still more the performing abilities of the girls of this our orchestra, so necessary to the musical standards and the good reputation of this our chapel.

Abstentions	0	
Against	2	carried[39]
In favour	10	

Vivaldi no doubt continued to provide the Pietà's chapel with vocal works until Grua's appointment in 1719 and thereafter intermittently, particularly during the two interregna (March–May 1726 and September 1737–August 1739).

One can only hazard a guess at the main line of his activity during his own period of absence from the Pietà (1709–11). Giazotto refers to a document of 1710 connecting G. B. Vivaldi (as a debtor) with the S. Angelo theatre, whose lessee and impressario was still Francesco Santurini mentioned earlier. It was perhaps around then that Antonio established his first close links with the operatic world. The S. Angelo theatre enjoyed little support from the local nobility and for its survival had to cultivate a popular, ear-catching style. It rarely engaged singers of the highest class, and the composers most in the public eye (Albinoni, Gasparini, Lotti and Pollarolo) had their hands full elsewhere. For its librettos it relied on refurbishments of old texts and, for a brief period, on the prolific output of Grazio Braccioli, a Ferrarese poet living in Venice, nine of whose librettos were set to music for S. Angelo between 1711 and 1715. Despite his membership of the Arcadian Academy, Brac-

---

[39] Ibid., f. 172v; transcribed in Giazotto, op. cit., p. 368.

cioli showed little finesse either of language or of plot construction, but his subjects were colourful and his style vigorous.

If S. Angelo librettos tended to be old or (in Braccioli's case) old-fashioned, its composers were young, rising talents. The experience of one composer, Johann David Heinichen, forms an enlightening prelude to Vivaldi's association with S. Angelo. Paying the almost mandatory visit of a promising German composer to Venice, Heinichen was engaged by its impresario (? still Santurini) to write a pair of operas (*Calfurnia* and *Le passioni per troppo amore*) for the 1713 Carnival season. In his highly anecdotal account J. A. Hiller relates how the impresario tried to take one of Heinichen's operas off after only two performances, intending to substitute a work by a local composer, but was forced by the public outcry to restore it to the stage. When he then attempted to withhold the agreed payment of 200 ducats (a typical amount for an operatic score) from Heinichen, the composer initiated a lawsuit against him; this proving successful, the impresario became liable for 1,600 ducats, including damages and costs.[40]

If a bankruptcy resulted, as one might well imagine, from this affair, it may not be unconnected with Vivaldi's appearance at S. Angelo as an entrepreneur and resident composer in the two years following. In the meantime he had blooded himself in the comparative obscurity of the provinces. By a unanimous vote the Pietà's governors granted him, on 30th April 1713, one month's leave of absence outside Venice 'for the exercise of his skill' (*all'impiego delle sue virtuose applicazioni*).[41] The place was Vicenza; the purpose, the performance of his first opera, *Ottone in Villa*, whose librettist was Sebastiano Biancardi alias

---

[40] *Lebensbeschreibungen berühmter Musikgelehrten und Tonkünstler neuerer Zeit,* vol. i (Leipzig, 1784), pp. 133f, 136.

[41] *ASV*, Pietà, Busta 689, f. 88v; transcribed in Giazotto, op. cit., p. 367.

Domenico Lalli, later to become manager of the S. Giovanni Grisostomo and S. Samuele theatres.[42]

Although S. Angelo was to remain the Venetian theatre with which Vivaldi was most frequently associated as a composer — no less than 18 of his scores, from *Orlando finto pazzo* (1714) to *Feraspe* (1739), were first performed there, not to speak of numerous revivals — his involvement in its management seems to have begun in 1713–14 (i.e. Autumn 1713 and Carnival 1714, regarded as a single season) and to have ended the following year. On 20th January 1714 he wrote the dedication of the libretto (by Braccioli) of Marcantonio Gasparini's *Rodomonte sdegnato*.[43] His *Orlando finto pazzo* opened the Autumn of 1714, to be followed by a revival of Ristori's *Orlando furioso* (the huge success of the previous year), to which he contributed several new numbers.[44] Carnival was launched with a revival of L. A. Predieri's *Lucio Papirio*, whose libretto was once again dedicated by Vivaldi. In February there followed *Nerone fatto cesare*, on an old libretto by Matteo Noris first set by Perti in 1693 for S. Salvatore. Vivaldi arranged the work as a *pasticcio*, contributing twelve arias (and, very likely, also the recitatives) himself, but borrowing the remainder from other sources.[45] A conventional explanation for such hotch-potches is the haste

---

[42] A mistaken belief that Vivaldi's *Tieteberga* (Venice, S. Moisè, Autumn 1717) was originally performed there ten years earlier arose from a typographical error (a missing Roman numeral 'X') on the title-page of a revised libretto issued later that same year.

[43] This is probably the reprinted, slightly altered libretto mentioned by Bonlini; presumably Braccioli wrote the original dedication.

[44] The first two acts of this score are preserved in Turin, Biblioteca Nazionale, Giordano 37, ff. 161–250.

[45] Two arias are attributed in the libretto (the score is lost) to Orlandini and to Perti, one to F. Gasparini, A. Carli and D. Pistocchi, and twelve to unknown composers identified either as 'N.N.' or 'P.P.'. It is probable that *Nerone fatto cesare* was preceded by a first version

with which operas often had to be written, copied into parts and rehearsed, but in this case it is equally likely that the borrowed arias were popular favourites which the singers or the public wished to have included. From a *faccio fede* discovered by Giazotto it appears that Vivaldi's *Arsilda, regina di Ponto*, performed at S. Angelo during the Autumn of 1716, was originally destined for the Ascension of 1715; Lalli's libretto was not approved, however, by the censors.[46]

While Venice was becoming acquainted with a new personality in the realm of opera, all Europe was revelling in the sounds of his first published set of concertos, *L'estro armonico*, op. 3 — perhaps the most influential collection of instrumental works to appear during the whole of the eighteenth century. 'Estro' means oestrus, or heat (though a translator will do well to avoid a too narrowly biological term), but it was less the undoubted passion and energy of the concertos that startled Vivaldi's contemporaries than the novelty of their design.

The set was dedicated to Grand Prince Ferdinand of Tuscany (1663–1713), son of Grand Duke Cosimo III (1642–1723). Ferdinand was a skilled and enthusiastic amateur musician, who bestowed his patronage upon Alessandro and Domenico Scarlatti, Albinoni, Pasquini and Handel, as well as Bartolomeo Cristofori, reputed inventor of the pianoforte. Vivaldi may well have met the prince on one of his frequent visits to Venice for the opera. Although Ferdinand failed to outlive his father and

---

called *Agrippina*, since the *faccio fede*, dated 12th February 1715, identifies the cast as 'the same that sang in *Agrippina* with [the addition of?] Marietta della Pietà'. Uffenbach, whose report we shall come to shortly, records having heard '*Agrippina*' on 19th February but '*Nerone fatto cesare* or *Agrippina*' on 28th February. See Giazotto, op. cit., p. 114, and Eberhard Preussner, *Die musikalischen Reisen des Herrn von Uffenbach* (Kassel and Basel, 1949), pp. 67f, 70.
[46] Op. cit., p. 141.

become a reigning grand duke, he was universally known in flattering affection as Ferdinand III; the dedication of their third *opera* to him by Albinoni, Gentili and Vivaldi is probably a sly allusion to this fact.

If Vivaldi's dedication contains nothing of note other than a renewed disparagement of his critics, his preface addressed to performers ('Alli dilettanti di musica') is very informative:

The kind indulgence you have so far accorded to my feeble efforts has persuaded me to seek to gratify you with a work containing instrumental concertos. I must acknowledge that if in the past my compositions have suffered from printing errors [*il discapito della stampa*] in addition to their own defects, their greatest distinction will now be that of having been engraved by the famous hand of Monsieur Estienne Roger. This is one reason why I have tried to please you by having the concertos published, and I shall venture before long to present you with another set, comprising *concerti a quattro*. . . .

No doubt Vivaldi spoke for many of his compatriots in lauding the handiwork of the Dutch publisher. What he omitted to mention was the straightforward commercial advantage of having his music published north of the Alps, where its impact would be greatest. In Italy, where the concerto had been in existence for several years, composers such as Torelli and Albinoni had already moved some distance along the path taken by Vivaldi; consequently, his ideas were absorbed by slow diffusion among composers of his own generation, reluctant to abandon well-tried practices overnight. The first native composer to betray his influence strongly was the young Bolognese Giuseppe Matteo Alberti (1685–1751) in his *Concerti per chiesa e per camera*, op. 1 (1713), but it was not until the generation of Locatelli (1695–1764) and Tartini (1692–1770) that Italian concertists as a whole embraced the Vivaldian method. In northern Europe, where concertos had not yet achieved a wide dissemination (Roger had published a mere handful by 1711, when *L'estro armonico* appeared)[47], Vivaldi's concertos, spearheaded by op. 3, quickly established themselves as the norm. In Germany, particularly, they were received with enthusiasm. Johann Joachim Quantz, later famous as flautist and theorist, described his first acquaintance with them at Pirna (1714): 'As a then entirely novel type of musical composition, they impressed me considerably. I made sure to collect a good number of them. Henceforth, the magnificent ritornellos of Vivaldi served me as excellent models.'[48] Bach obviously knew *L'estro armonico*, for he transcribed five of its works for keyboard while at Weimar and another (BWV 1065, for four harpsichords and strings) at Leipzig.

Amateurs responded equally warmly, as Johann Friedrich Armand von Uffenbach, a member of a distinguished Frankfurt family of merchants and civic dignitaries, found when he introduced Vivaldi's op. 3 in 1713 to a Strasbourg music society.[49] Uffenbach's travel diary is of especial interest, for in it he recorded a visit to Venice in 1715, during which he visited S. Angelo four times and met Vivaldi.

He paid his first visit to the opera house on 4th February:

I remained here [at the casino] until it was time to go to the opera, and then went with some acquaintances to the S. Angelo house, which is smaller and also not as expensive as the one described above [SS. Giovanni e Paolo]; its *entrepreneur* was the celebrated Vivaldi, who also composed the opera, which was really nice, and very attractive to the eye; the machines were not as expensive as in the other theatre and the orchestra not so large, but none the less it was well worth hearing. . . . Towards the end Vivaldi played a solo accompaniment —

[47] The *Post Man* of 16th October 1711 carried an advertisement for the works.
[48] 'Herrn Johann Joachim Quantzens Lebenslauf, von ihm selbst entworfen' in Friedrich Wilhelm Marpurg, *Historisch-Kritische Beyträge zur Aufnahme der Musik,* vol. i. (Berlin, 1755), p. 205.
[49] Heller, op. cit., p. 6.

splendid — to which he appended a cadenza [*phantasie*] which really frightened me, for such playing has never been nor can be: he brought his fingers up to only a straw's distance from the bridge, leaving no room for the bow — and that on all four strings with imitations [Fugen] and incredible speed. With this he astounded everyone, but I cannot say that it pleased me, for it was not so pleasant to listen to as it was skilfully executed.[50]

The opera was probably Predieri's *Lucio Papirio* in the altered version for whose libretto Vivaldi wrote the dedication. Uffenbach's belief that he also composed the music may not have been without foundation if he contributed some new numbers, as in *Orlando furioso*. The mention of an elaborate cadenza brings to mind Quantz's statement that the most recent form of cadenza, in which the soloist played without accompaniment, arose 'roughly between 1710 and 1716'.[51]

On his next visit (19th February) Uffenbach heard a new opera, *Agrippina*. Neither the subject nor the ill-assorted costumes pleased him, and he regretted that Vivaldi this time played only a short solo 'air' (?obbligato accompaniment) on his violin. He thought better of *Nerone fatto cesare* (which, as we have seen, was probably only a revised version of *Agrippina*) and went to hear it twice, on 28th February and 4th March.[52]

On 6th March Uffenbach's attempt to meet Vivaldi was successful. With great satisfaction he noted in his diary:

After supper I received a visit from Vivaldi, the famous composer and violinist, having several times sent an invitation to his house when discusssing some *concerti grossi* which I wished to order from him, and also having a few bottles of wine fetched for him, knowing that he

---

[50] Preussner, op. cit., p. 67.

[51] *Versuch einer Anweisung, die Flöte traversiere zu spielen,* third complete German edn. (Breslau, 1789; facs. Reprint, Kassel and Basel, 1953), p. 152.

[52] See p. 53 f.

57

was a cleric.[53] He let me listen to his very difficult and quite inimitable fantasias on the violin, so that, being close at hand, I could not but marvel even more at his skill. It was clear to me that although he played exceptionally difficult and animated pieces he lacked a pleasant and cantabile style.[54]

And three days later:

This afternoon Vivaldi came to me and brought me, as requested, ten *concerti grossi*, which he claimed to have composed especially for me. I bought some of them, and in order that I might have a better idea of them, he wanted to teach me to play them on the spot, and to visit me every so often, so that this occasion would be [just] a start.[55]

Uffenbach's reservations about Vivaldi's manner of playing suggest that like many Germans he was more at home with the French style than the less discreet Italian style, of which the Venetians, known for their extravagance in all things, were the boldest exponents. The composer's aggressive sales technique, in which the supply of music becomes a pretext for an offer of tuition, reveals something about his character; more generally, the whole transaction demonstrates how music could, in the Venetian environment, become a simple commodity turned out to order for the casual visitor.

The *concerti a quattro* (concertos for four-part strings and continuo with solo violin) promised in the foreword to op. 3 duly appeared from Roger in about 1714. They were collectively entitled *La stravaganza* and dedicated to Vettor Dolfin (the surname is given in its Tuscan form Delfino), a young Venetian noble to whom Vivaldi had taught the violin. In 1716–17 Roger brought out three further Vivaldi collections — one of sonatas and two of concertos — under the imprint of his daughter Jeanne. Although all these have regular opus num-

---

[53] The remark 'Da er unter die Cantores gehört' implies that the Venetian clergy were notoriously partial to drink.
[54] Preussner, op. cit., p. 71.
[55] Loc. cit.

bers, the lack of a dedication, the numerous textual errors and some problematic features in their make-up (to be discussed later) indicate that Roger published them on his own initiative, possibly even bypassing the composer altogether. Such action was still quite uncommon, the rather special case of anthologies excepted, and reflects the quite extraordinary demand for Vivaldi's instrumental music in the wake of opp. 3 and 4.

By 1716 Vivaldi's merits as an operatic composer must have become widely recognized, for he was commissioned to write the Carnival opera, *La costanza trionfante degl'amori e degl'odii,* for S. Moisè. At the Pietà, however, his position as *Maestro di Violino* was growing vulnerable, either because economies were necessary or because the governors looked askance on his extra-mural activities. In a ballot held on 29th March 1716 the governors were initially seven to five (less than the required two-thirds) in his favour; a fresh count merely lost him one vote.[56] But his partisans must have been tenacious, for he was reinstated, now as *Maestro de' Concerti* (the change of nomenclature is probably not significant), on 24th May, by a near-unanimous vote.[57]

His restoration to favour may not be unconnected with his composition of the music to *Juditha triumphans*, a 'topical' oratorio to words by the local poet Giacomo Cassetti performed at the Pietà in November 1716. Designated a 'sacred military oratorio', the work was conceived as an allegory on Venice's struggle against Ottoman belligerence, and in particular on the Venetian fleet's efforts to relieve beleaguered Corfu. The war — Venice's sixth against the Turks — had begun in 1714. Badly led and prone to mutiny, the Republic's forces in the Peloponnese and the Aegean had suffered severe reverses in 1715. In July 1716 the Turks began their siege of the strategic island of Corfu. Since *Juditha triumphans* was approved by the inquisitors

[56] *ASV,* Pietà, Busta 690, f. 18v.
[57] Ibid., f. 26v.

on 7th August, Cassetti probably composed his libretto in the shadow of this threat. Although direct reference to the affairs of 1716 is confined to a sort of epilogue in which Ozias, High Priest of Bethulia (really an amalgam of the biblical Ozias, Governor of Bethulia, and Joakim, High Priest of Jerusalem), prophesies Venetian victory, a *Carmen allegoricum* published at the end of the libretto provides a key for the allegorical interpretation of the entire oratorio: Judith represents the Adriatic (Venice) and Holophernes the Sultan; her handmaiden Abra (an invented character) and his servant Vagaus (Bagoas) respectively stand for Faith and the Turkish commander (perhaps to be identified with Ali Pasha, who had earned a reputation for brutality in the campaigns of 1715). Ozias personifies the union of Christians and the honour of virgins.

It was this union of Christians— more concretely, an alliance with Austria concluded on 25th May — which enabled Ozias's prophecy, in the short term, to be fulfilled. The Turks were defeated, and Ali Pasha killed, at Petrovaradin on 5th August. In consequence, they abandoned the siege of Corfu on 22nd August. So it was that *Juditha triumphans*, written in fearful hope, was performed in an atmosphere of relieved jubilation.

Vivaldi's operas returned to S. Angelo on the following year. *Arsilda, regina di Ponto* was performed, belatedly as we saw, in Autumn 1716, the following Carnival closing with *L'incoronazione di Dario*.[58] It was next the turn of S. Moisè: *Tieteberga* occupied Autumn 1717, while the second and third Carnival works were *Artabano, rè de' Parti*, a modified version of *La costanza trionfante*, and *Armida al campo d'Egitto*.

Revivals, presumably in Venice, of *Orlando finto pazzo* (Autumn 1716) and *L'incoronazione di Dario* (Carnival 1718) received the inquisitors'. assent, but no record of their performance has survived.[59] One is tempted to imagine that application

[58] The date of 1716 in the libretto is to be interpreted *more veneto*.
[59] Giazotto, op. cit., pp. 138, 144.

to perform these operas was made as an insurance against possible hitches with new works.

During the 1710s several of the young German composers fortunate enough to obtain leave from their employers to study in Venice made Vivaldi's acquaintance. First there was Heinichen, joined at the end of 1713 by Gottfried Heinrich Stölzel. Daniel Gottlob Treu, sometimes known by his italianized name Daniele Teofilo Fedele, became Vivaldi's pupil in 1716. The most important figure, however, was Johann Georg Pisendel (1687–1755), a violin virtuoso in the service of the Dresden court, who, having previously studied with Torelli at Ansbach, was already well versed in the Italian style.

Pisendel arrived in Venice in April 1716 as a member of an élite group of four musicians, the *Kammermusik*, sent from Dresden to join the visiting prince-elector of Saxony (from 1733 Frederick Augustus II of Saxony and Augustus III of Poland). Since the *Kammermusik* remained in Venice until the end of the year it became well integrated into Venetian musical life; Pisendel, moreover, revisited Venice in 1717. He became a friend as well as a pupil of Vivaldi. Their association is recorded in two delightful, if uncorroborated, anecdotes from Hiller. The first recounts how Vivaldi, walking with Pisendel in St Mark's Square, suddenly broke off the conversation and urged the visitor to return home with him immediately. Privacy regained, Vivaldi explained that he had observed four constables shadowing Pisendel and asked him whether he had done or said anything forbidden by the authorities. Since Pisendel could think of nothing, Vivaldi sought the advice of one of the inquisitors, from whom he learned that they were looking not for Pisendel but for a man resembling him.[60] The second anecdote concerns a concerto identifiable as RV 571 (P.268) which Pisendel was asked to play, at the prince-elector's behest,

---

[60] Op. cit., p. 189f.

Vivaldi

as an operatic *entr'acte*. During an extended solo passage in the upper register his accompanists tried to discomfit him by rushing ahead, but he kept his composure and forced them to slow down by marking the beat vigorously with his foot, much to Frederick Augustus's amusement.[61]

Pisendel used his stay in Venice to amass a large quantity of musical manuscripts containing the latest works by her most eminent composers — principally, of course, Vivaldi. Some of these were presented to him by the composer, for instance the autograph manuscripts of five sonatas and six concertos by Vivaldi, all purporting to have been written for 'Monsieur Pisendel' (although the dedication seems in nearly all cases to have been an afterthought), and those of three sonatas by Albinoni, one with a formal dedication. The bulk of the music, however, was copied out by Pisendel himself. We possess his scores of 22 concertos and seven violin sonatas by Vivaldi, as well as complete sets of parts of 15 further concertos. His copies of concertos by Albinoni and B. Marcello are also preserved.[62] Whether by annotating manuscripts that came into his hands or by editing music in the act of making his own copy, Pisendel was in the habit of subjecting the originals to considerable revision. The purpose of these alterations was doubtless manifold: to exercise his talents as a composer; to afford his virtuosity on the violin greater scope (more necessary in the case of Albinoni, the less adventurous composer, than in that of Vivaldi); to bring the scoring into line with the practice of the

[61] *Wöchentliche Nachrichten und Anmerkungen die Musik betreffend* (Leipzig, 10th March 1767). The opera might well have been either *Arsilda, regina di Ponto* or *L'incoronazione di Dario*, as scores of the overture to both works copied in Pisendel's hand are preserved in Dresden, Sächsische Landesbibliothek, Mus.2389/N/2(4).

[62] All these MSS. except, curiously, that of one violin sonata (RV 19) dedicated to Pisendel by Vivaldi, which is found in the collection of the Paris Conservatoire (Rés. ms. 2225), are today in the possession of the Sächsische Landesbibliothek.

Dresden court orchestra, where wind instruments were prominent in both solo and *ripieno* functions; to eliminate infelicities of phrase balance or part-writing. At its most overt this re-shaping could result in added or substituted solo passages, cadenzas or even entire movements; at its most covert, in written-out embellishments, added *ripieno* parts for recorders, oboes and bassoons or simple marks of expression.

Pisendel returned to Dresden in 1717 to become acting (later, official) leader of the court orchestra. As a result of his influence Vivaldi's concertos and sinfonias came to occupy a place of honour in its repertoire, making Dresden the centre of the Vivaldian cult in Germany. One may add that Vivaldi's church music was also cultivated there, as shown by the inclusion of his *Magnificat* in an inventory drawn up by Jan Dismas Zelenka, one of Pisendel's colleagues in the *Kammermusik* and subsequently official composer of church music to the court.

No musicians' names appear in the list of staff members appointed at the Pietà on 9th May 1717, and Vivaldi was not one of the musicians seeking re-appointment on 24th April 1718. The second absence is easily explained, however: he had just left Venice for Mantua.

4 Years of travel

The duchy of Mantua, bordering the *Veneto*, was a flourishing centre of the arts during the seventeenth century. Indirectly, lavish spending on court entertainment led to the downfall of the Gonzaga dynasty, for the last Duke, Ferdinando Carlo, being greatly in debt, was bribed into an alliance with the French during the War of the Spanish Succession. As Mantua was a fief of the Austrian Empire, this constituted treason; accordingly, the victorious Austrians made Mantua an hereditary Imperial possession, appointing as governor the younger brother of the Landgrave of Hesse-Darmstadt, Prince Philip. Fortunately, Mantua's cultural life continued much as before under Philip's governorship (1714–35).

The movement of musicians between Venice and Mantua was a two-way traffic of long standing. If Vicenzo di Gonzaga had lost Monteverdi to Venice in 1613, Ferdinando Carlo's recruitment of Caldara in 1700 showed that the pull could as well come from the other direction. A period of service at even a small court like Mantua's offered a musician from republican Venice a type of experience and a species of patronage for which his city provided no equivalent.

It has long been known that Vivaldi spent three consecutive years at Mantua in the service of Prince Philip, since he wrote in his letter to Bentivoglio of 16th November 1737: 'In Mantova sono stato tre anni al servigio dell piissimo principe Darmstadt'. Pincherle proposed the years 1720 to 1723 and Kolneder 1719 to 1722, but more recent research based on the dates of newly-discovered librettos leaves little room for doubt that the period spanned 1718 to 1720.

Vivaldi's position, as we learn from title-pages, was that of *Maestro di Cappella da Camera*. What this curious, possibly unique formula seems to indicate is that he enjoyed the status of a *Maestro di Cappella* but concerned himself only with secular music. There are some parallels between Vivaldi's activity at Mantua and Bach's at Cöthen (1717–23). Both men had to write occasional works for local festivities, such as Vivaldi's cantatas *O mie porpore più belle* celebrating the installation of Monsignore da Bagni as bishop of Mantua or *Qual in pioggia dorata* in praise of Prince Philip. The last-named cantata and the operatic scores Vivaldi provided for Mantua's Teatro Arciducale point to another similarity: the frequency and prominence of horn parts.

Opera was indeed Vivaldi's main concern. Scarcely off the stage of S. Moisè, his *Armida al campo d'Egitto* was presented during April and May 1718. The following Carnival season witnessed the *premières* of *Teuzzone* and *Tito Manlio,* on old librettos by Apostolo Zeno and Matteo Noris. Vivaldi's autograph score of *Tito Manlio* in Turin is inscribed 'Musica del Vivaldi fatta in 5 giorni' (music by Vivaldi written in five days);[1] even Handel never achieved such speed. The last opera he produced for Mantua while resident there was *La Candace* (otherwise, *Li veri amici*), heard during Carnival 1720. His departure did not mean, however, the severance of links with the Teatro Arciducale, for *Artabano, rè de' Parti* was given in 1725, and the already much-travelled *Farnace* in 1732. A *Semiramide* performed in 1732 may have been specially commissioned, for no earlier setting of Francesco Silvani's libretto is attributable to Vivaldi; the composer may even have revisited Mantua for the occasion on his homeward journey from

[1] Giordano 39, ff. 172–365. A partly autograph score of the same opera survives in Foà 37, ff. 119–306.

65

Bohemia. As he retained his Mantuan title without, apparently, incurring the displeasure of the court, he probably retained vestigial duties *in absentia* after his initial sojourn was over.[2]

Many, perhaps the bulk, of Vivaldi's solo cantatas must have been written for Mantua. Most of the non-autograph cantata scores in Turin are in the hands known from the manuscripts of Vivaldi operas copied in Mantua (e.g. *Teuzzone*). The solo cantata was the courtly genre *par excellence*, for the virtuoso singers to whom nobles lent their patronage had few other outlets during the operatic off-season, when they returned to their employers. He must also have composed instrumental music there, but until more solid evidence is found, one can do no more than surmise that those instruments having important solo parts in the Mantuan operas (horns and recorders) also had concertos written for them.

Perhaps Vivaldi made the acquaintance of the contralto Anna Girò (Giraud) at Mantua, for in her earliest appearances on the Venetian stage, beginning with the rôle of Clistene in Albinoni's *Laodice* (S. Moisè, Autumn 1724), she is described as 'mantovana'. This fact has been taken by Pincherle to indicate that, contrary to Goldoni's statement that she was born in Venice to a wig-maker of French origin, she came from Mantua.[3] We must remember, however, that sobriquets formed from place-names denoted not only places of birth but also places from which a celebrity had recently arrived — hence the nickname '(il) bolognese' acquired in Rome by Corelli, a native of Fusignano who had made his reputation in Bologna. Girò became Vivaldi's pupil; the inseparability of composer and

---

[2] *Questa Eurilla gentil,* a serenata written for Philip's birthday in 1726, supports this hypothesis.

[3] Pincherle, *Antonio Vivaldi et la musique instrumentale,* vol. i, p. 29n. Anna Girò is termed 'viniziana' in F. S. Quadrio's *Della storia e della ragione d'ogni poesia,* vol. iii/2 (Milan, 1742), p. 539. If Goldoni's description of her parentage is correct, G. B. Vivaldi will surely have known her father.

singer led her to be dubbed, a little maliciously, 'L'Annina del Prete Rosso'. She also appears as 'Annina della Pietà', but as it is hard to identify her with any similarly named *figliola* of that institution except, perhaps, a girl who sang the part of a messenger in *Moyses deus Pharaonis* of 1714), her connexion with the Pietà may have been merely through her teacher. A sister, Paolina, also attended Vivaldi, probably as a nurse.

Not surprisingly, intimacy in matters other than musical was suspected; had not many of the most eminent Venetian composers — including Albinoni, Caldara, Lotti and Marcello — chosen singers as their companions (albeit clerically sanctioned) for life? Gilli's report to the inquisitors identifies Anna by the fact of her living in Vivaldi's house.[4] Aware of these allegations, which had evidently been revived at a most inopportune moment for him, the composer bitterly denied them in his letter to Bentivoglio of 16th November 1737: for 14 years he had travelled with the Girò sisters all over Europe and their virtue had never been impugned, nor their piety; he admitted to a friendship with Anna, but claimed (in a following letter dated 23rd November) that the Girò sisters lived in a house far from his own. Despite, or perhaps because of, the wealth of 'evidence' Vivaldi musters in his defence, his case carries little conviction. It is so noticeable how he tries to divert the issue of *his* relationship with *one* of the sisters (Anna) into a discussion of the morals of *both* women, as appraised by their spiritual mentor. Besides, it takes little cynicism to concur with the suggestion that Vivaldi would hardly have courted scandal for so long without enjoying some of its fruits.

We are well informed by Goldoni of Anna's qualities as an operatic singer. In 1761 he remembered her as 'bella e graziosa', while in his later account, which is both fuller and less charitable in tone, he denied that she was actually pretty, though complimented her on her grace, good figure, attractive eyes and

[4] See page 41.

hair and charming mouth. He found her voice weak but praised her acting ability, a rare quality in singers. Indeed, the mission on which Goldoni had been sent to Vivaldi's house primarily concerned the rewriting of part of the text of Zeno's *Griselda* so that *La Girò,* in the title-rôle, could be shown off to best advantage; her teacher had decided, no doubt wisely, that *arie d'azione*, emphasizing her talent for movement, suited her better than *arie cantabili*.

Nevertheless, her first few operatic seasons (S. Moisè 1724–5, S. Angelo 1726–8) were triumphantly successful, earning her many admirers. The Abbé Conti wrote that she performed marvels,[5] while Zuane Zuccato, newly appointed Venetian resident at Naples, found her incomparable and mentioned the furore she was then (1726) causing.[6] The fact that she was engaged for rôles in operas by composers other than Vivaldi (among them, Galuppi and Hasse) during his lifetime and even afterwards[7] proves that she was not simply his creature. If anything, it was he who was more dependent on her, declaring in the first letter to Bentivoglio just quoted: 'To put on the opera without *La Girò* is not possible, for a comparable prima donna is not to be found.' It is remarkable how well her absences from the Venetian stage correspond to premières of Vivaldi operas outside Venice, in which— so one gathers from his next letter — he liked to lead the orchestra on the opening night. Herself performing or not, she must have been a faithful member of his entourage. Giazotto believes, perhaps on insufficient evidence, that she acted as his secretary.[8]

[5] *Lettres de M. L'Abbé Conti, noble vénitien, à Mme. de Caylus,* Venice, Biblioteca Marciana, Ms. fr. append. 58 (= 10102); quoted in Giazotto, op. cit., p. 214.

[6] *ASV,* Serenissima Signoria, Terra, 1726; quoted in Giazotto, op. cit., p. 215.

[7] Her last known appearance was in G. B. Runcher's *Achille* at S. Samuele in Ascension 1747.

[8] Op. cit., p. 217f.

Vivaldi's return from Mantua was signalled by the performance of *La verità in cimento* at S. Angelo in Autumn 1720. At
the height of his fame, he must have been disconcerted by the
appearance in December of an anonymous satirical volume,
whose author was soon revealed as Benedetto Marcello, entitled
Il teatro alla moda (The Theatre in Fashion). It was advertised as a
compendium of hints for librettists, composers, singers of both
sexes, players, engineers, scene painters, performers of comic
parts (in *intermezzi*), costumiers, pages, supers, prompters,
copyists, protectors (of singers), mothers of lady singers and
others connected with the theatre. The imprint identifies
through anagram, pun or other allusion some of the persons at
whom Marcello's barbs are aimed (all were prominent in the
world of Venetian opera during 1720): the composers Vivaldi
('Aldiviva'), Porta and Orlandini; the librettist (of *La verità in
cimento*) Giovanni Palazzi; the impresarios Modotto (S. Angelo)
and Orsatti (S. Moisè); the singers Caterina Borghi, Cecilia
Belisani, Antonia Laurenti and Anna Maria Strada. In an amusing engraving above the imprint a suitably ursine Orsatti is
shown together with Modotto in a rowing boat (an allusion to
the latter's previous involvement in the boat trade); a fiddling
angel in a priest's hat, representing Vivaldi and his S. Angelo
connexions, has one foot on the rudder and the other in the air
marking the beat to symbolize his commanding position both as
musician and entrepreneur. Throughout the book Vivaldi is
obviously a prime target. Marcello pretends to endorse—that is
to say, he attacks as slipshod or meretricious — some of Vivaldi's favourite practices, such as *all'unisono* accompaniments,
the elimination of lower strings in accompanimental passages,
lengthy cadenzas, special effects (e.g. muting) and the introduction of rare instruments. Giazotto suggests, no doubt correctly up to a point, that Marcello bore Vivaldi a special grudge
arising from legal wrangles over the S. Angelo theatre, built, as

we saw earlier,[9] on a site partly owned by his family. Three years earlier Vivaldi and Santurini had been cited as debtors and mismanagers in respect of that theatre.[10] Be that as it may, Vivaldi could hardly have escaped Marcello's censure, since he was responsible, in one capacity or another, for so much of what then went on in the opera houses.

Judging from contemporary references, some in later satires, *Il teatro alla moda* quickly won the approval of discerning opera-goers. Perhaps it put Vivaldi for a time under a cloud, for after the opening Carnival work of 1721 at S. Angelo, *Filippo, rè di Macedonia* (of which he wrote only the last act, the previous two being by Giuseppe Boniventi), his operas disappeared from the Venetian stage until 1725–6.

Despite his vacillating fortunes at home, the major Italian opera houses were one by one opening their doors to him. Discounting revivals of older operas and the appearance of individual arias in pasticcios, we have five scores from the period 1715–25: *Scanderbeg* (Florence, Summer 1718); *La Silvia* (Milan, Autumn 1721); *Ercole sul Termodonte* (Rome, Carnival 1723); *Giustino* and *La virtù trionfante dell'amore e dell'odio ovvero il Tigrane* (Rome, Carnival 1724).[11]

In his letter to Bentivoglio of 16th November 1737 Vivaldi claimed to have spent three Carnival seasons at Rome in connexion with opera. Two are evident from the above list, but the third has not yet been ascertained. It is not even clear whether Vivaldi meant *consecutive* seasons. In the same letter and its sequel (23rd November) he boasted that the Pope had asked him

---

[9] See p. 26.

[10] Giazotto, op. cit., p. 185.

[11] *Il Tigrane* was a joint composition of B. Micheli (Act I), Vivaldi (Act II) and N. Romaldi (Act III). A version of *Tito Manlio* with acts composed by G. Boni, G. Giorgio and Vivaldi respectively (the last's contribution drawing in part on the Mantuan score) opened the 1720 Carnival season at the Teatro della Pace, Rome.

to play the violin, courteously receiving him on two occasions in a private apartment. Circumstantial evidence indicates that he also enjoyed the patronage of Cardinal Pietro Ottoboni (1667–1740), Corelli's last and most generous Maecenas. The famous sketch of Vivaldi drawn in 1723 by Pier Leone Ghezzi is one of several he made of persons in the Cardinal's circle, while remnants of Ottoboni's large music collection preserved in the Central Library, Manchester, include copies of Vivaldi concertos that are of unmistakable Roman provenance. Coming from a noble Venetian family, but prevented by a decree of 1712 from returning to his native city because he was deemed to have compromised the Republic's neutrality by becoming Protector of France at the Vatican, Ottoboni would have had every reason to welcome Venice's foremost musician.

Contacts with the Pietà were re-established (perhaps they had never been broken) in 1723. Since 1720 the Pietà had employed a cello master, first the famous Antonio Vandini and subsequently Bernardo Aliprandi, but neither man had the facility in composition (not to speak of the reputation) of Vivaldi.[12] On 2nd July the governors passed a motion that Vivaldi, who had just supplied two concertos for the celebration of the Visitation of the Blessed Virgin Mary, be asked to provide two more every month at one sequin each; this arrangement could hold even during his absence from Venice, provided that their postage was not charged to the Pietà. While in Venice, he would be required to direct personally three or four rehearsals of each piece. The intimate but at the same time patronizing manner in which the governors' minutes normally refer to members of staff is drop-

---

[12] Giazotto's suggestion (op. cit., p. 165f) that Vandini was the same man as Vivaldi must be rejected; however, it is a strange coincidence that Vivaldi chose to anagrammatize his name as Lotavio Vandini in the libretto of the comic opera *Aristide*. A cello sonata in the Bibliothèque Nationale, Paris, shows Vandini to have been a competent but unexciting composer.

71

ped: Vivaldi is an outsider with whom a bargain is to be struck.[13]

On 14th December 1725 the *Gazette d'Amsterdam* advertised his op. 8, twelve concertos collectively entitled *Il cimento dell' armonia e dell'inventione*, the contest between harmony (representing the rational side of composition) and invention (imagination). Some of the concertos had been circulating in manuscript for several years; in his dedication, to the Bohemian count Wenzel von Morzin (1676–1737), a cousin of Haydn's patron at Lukavec, Vivaldi acknowledges this in the case of the opening four works, *Le quattro stagioni* (The Four Seasons). The novelty in Le Cène's edition of these works is the appearance before each of an explanatory sonnet (*sonetto dimostrativo*) containing the complete 'programme'. Cue-letters and portions of the sonnet texts engraved over the notes locate precisely the depicted events. Vivaldi speaks of having served Morzin (whose name he gives as Marzin) for several years as his 'Maestro di musica in Italia'. This probably means simply that he provided the count with music when requested; one bassoon concerto (RV 496/P.381) in the Turin collection is headed with the name of Morzin.

No doubt because of the programmatic nature of half the works in it, op. 8 was received with especial enthusiasm in France.[14] From 1728 *The Four Seasons* were often heard at the Concert Spirituel; the *Mercure de France* reported that on 25th November 1730 the king commanded an impromptu performance of *La primavera*, for which a scratch orchestra containing several nobles was assembled.[15] Such was the vogue for this particular concerto that it was subjected to many arrangements,

---

[13] *ASV*, Pietà, Busta 691, f. 179; reproduced in Giazotto, op. cit., p. 256.

[14] In addition to *Le quattro stagioni*, op. 8 contains works entitled *La tempesta di mare* (The storm at sea) and *La caccia* (The hunt).

[15] December 1730, i, p. 2758.

of which the most extraordinary were a motet, *Laudate Dominum de coelis*, by Michel Corrette (1765) and a version for unaccompanied flute by Jean-Jacques Rousseau (1775).

Three serenatas were written by Vivaldi during the 1720s in honour of the French royal house. A work of which the title-page (and perforce the title) is lost, but which is generally known by the names of its two allegorical characters, Gloria and Imeneo (Hymen), commemorates Louis XV's wedding on 5th September 1725 to the Polish princess Maria Leczinska. *L'unione della pace e di marte*, of which only the libretto survives, celebrates the birth of royal twins, 'Mesdames de France', on 14th August 1727; it may have formed part of the festivities on 19th September at the residence of Count Languet de Gergy, Ambassador to Venice, about which the *Mercure de France* reported that towards eight o'clock in the evening there was 'a very beautiful concert of instrumental music lasting nearly two hours, whose music, as well as that of the *Te Deum*, was by the famous Vivaldi'.[16] The event for which the grandest of the serenatas, *La Sena festeggiante* (The Seine rejoicing), was composed has not yet been established. Lalli's libretto pays homage in a very general way to the young monarch Louis XV. At all events, the work can date from no earlier than 1724, for its final chorus is a slightly lengthened arrangement, to new words, of the final chorus in *Giustino*. A suggestion by Roland De Candé that the serenata commemorates the birth of the Dauphin on 4th September 1729 must be ruled out:[17] firstly, because the libretto refers to the king's *sons* (in the hypothetical context of the future), when a single living son would surely have been alluded to more concretely; secondly, because Albinoni provided a serenata (*Il concilio de'pianeti*) for that occasion, which, after its *première* at the ambassador's residence, was repeated with success at the French court. There are hints in Vivaldi's

[16] October 1727, p. 2327.
[17] *Vivaldi* (Paris, 1967), p. 75n.

score that *La Sena festeggiante* was intended for a performance which he knew he would not be able to supervise — possibly, therefore, one in Versailles. The rubric '2 hautbois (flauti) o più se piace' at the head of the first chorus implies that he anticipated the doubling of wind parts (a French rather than Venetian practice), while the choral chaconne borrowed from *Giustino* has its tenor part marked as optional, indicating that Vivaldi was uncertain of the vocal forces available.[18] Although he often adopted elements of the French style for the sake of variety, their quite exceptional prominence in *La Sena festeggiante* (which even boasts a French overture to its second part) strongly suggests that, unlike the other serenatas, it was aimed at a French audience.

During the Carnival seasons (with preceding Autumn) of 1726, 1727 and 1728 Vivaldi once more stood at the helm of the S. Angelo theatre. *L'inganno trionfante in amore*, on a libretto adapted from Matteo Noris's original by G. M. Ruggieri, a Venetian musical and literary dilettante whom we shall encounter again when examining Vivaldi's church music, occupied Autumn 1725. Two of the Carnival works were also Vivaldi's: *Cunegonda* and *La fede tradita e vendicata*. In 1726–7 *Dorilla in Tempe* (Autumn) and *Farnace* (Carnival) were staged.[19] Vivaldi even found time to write *Ipermestra* for Florence. The Abbé Conti reported to Mme de Caylus on 23rd February 1727: 'Vivaldi has composed three operas in less than three months, two for Venice and the third for Florence; the last of these has restored the reputation of the theatre of that city and earned him

---

[18] Peter Ryom, *Les manuscrits de Vivaldi* (Copenhagen, 1977), points out that, to judge from its almost identical text in the libretto, the lost final number of *La verità in cimento* may well have been the first incarnation of this movement. If so, 1720 and not 1724 is the *terminus post quem* of *La Sena festeggiante*.

[19] The date of 1726 on the title-page of the libretto to *Farnace* is *more veneto*.

ATTORI.

Farnace Re di Ponto.
  La Sig. Maria Maddalena Pieri. Virtuo-
  sa del Seren. Duca di Modona.
Berenice Regina di Cappadocia Madre
  di Tamiri.
  La Sig. Angela Capuano Romana detta la
  Capuanina.
Tamiri, Regina Sposa di Farnace.
  La Sig. Anna Girò.
Selinda Sorella di Farnace.
  La Sig. Lucrezia Baldini.
Pompeo Pro-Console Romano nell'Asia.
  Il Sig. Lorenzo Moretti.
Gilade Principe del Sangue Reale , e
  Capitano di Berenice.
  Il Sig. Filippo Finazzi.
Aquilio Prefetto delle Legioni Romane.
  Il Sig. Domenico Gioseppe Galletti.
Un Fanciullo Figlio di Farnace, e Ta-
  miri.

Il Luogo dell'Azione in Eraclea.
Cori di Soldati Romani, e Asiatici.

La Musica è del celebre Sig. D. Antonio
  Vivaldi Maestro di Cappella di S. A. S.
  il Signor Principe Filippo Langravio d'
  Hassia D'armstath.
Li Balli sono invenzioni del Sig. Giovan-
  ni Galletto.

                    A 3   MU-

Cast-list of the libretto of *Farnace* (Carnival, 1727)

a lot of money.'[20] Vivaldi's position at S. Angelo is made clear in a contract, dated 13th October 1726, drawn up privately between himself and the singer Lucrezia Baldini, in which he is named as 'direttore delle opere'.[21] The contract contains some interesting details: the singer was to appear in the third and last opera (*Farnace*) of the season and was to be paid 200 ducats in three instalments — the first just before the opera opened, the second half way through its run, and the third on the last Thursday before Lent. For the following season Vivaldi provided *Orlando furioso* (Autumn),[22] using a slightly altered version of Braccioli's libretto for Ristori, and *Rosilena ed Oronta* (Carnival). With these two works his second period of intense activity at S. Angelo abruptly closes.

Vivaldi's standing as an operatic composer had reached, and would soon pass, its high point. At the time when he started to compose works for the Venetian stage the dominant figures were all natives or at the very least residents of that city — men like Albinoni, Gasparini, Lotti, Caldara and the two Pollarolos. While it would be an exaggeration to speak of a Venetian 'school', one can with justice point to a regional style. Now a degree of cosmopolitanism had arrived, and a younger generation of composers, mostly Neapolitan (Leo, Vinci, Porpora) or Naples-influenced (Hasse), was coming to the fore, borne aloft by the new lyricism of Metastasian verse. Among younger Venetian composers only Baldassare Galuppi (1706–85) could still count as a front-runner. True, Venice did not wholly desert her favourite sons, Albinoni and Vivaldi, and a trickle of operas, new or refurbished, by both men continued to reach the stage in the smaller theatres for several years, but both found difficulties

---

[20] Op. cit.; quoted in Pincherle, *Antonio Vivaldi et la musique instrumentale,* vol. i, p. 22f.
[21] Reproduced from the original in *ASV* in Giazotto, op. cit., p. 193.
[22] The title is shortened to *Orlando* in the libretto, but not in the autograph score.

in updating their style to conform with current fashion. In general, their greatest successes after 1728 were to be enjoyed in northern Europe or the Italian provinces, where audiences were more conservative or simply less fashion conscious. From now on, Vivaldi was to pay increasing attention to the promotion of his operas outside Venice. In Sping 1728 *Siroe, rè di Persia*, his first setting of a Metastasio libretto, was staged in Reggio Emilia; *Atenaide* received its *première* in Florence during Carnival 1729, while *Ottone in Villa* was performed in Treviso (Autumn 1728) and *Farnace* in Livorno (Summer, 1729).

In the late 1720s Vivaldi came into close contact with the Austrian emperor Charles VI and at some point visted Vienna, if his affirmation to Bentivoglio: 'Sono stato chiamato a Vienna' (letter of 16th November 1737) is to be believed. The first sign appears in the dedication to Charles (curiously, without a letter of dedication) of his op. 9, twelve concertos entitled *La Cetra* (The Lyre). The set was advertised in the *Gazette d'Amsterdam* of 31st January 1727 as soon to appear, and its publication was announced in the issue of 28th November. The dedication was evidently well received, for on the occasion of Charles's visit to Carniola, during which he inspected the port of Trieste, Vivaldi was received by the Emperor and treated very handsomely. In the words of the Abbé Conti (letter of 19th September 1728): 'The Emperor has given Vivaldi much money, together with a golden chain and medal; and tell him [the son of Mme. de Caylus] that he has made him a knight.' And again (letter of 23rd September): 'The Emperor conversed with Vivaldi for a long time about music, and people say that he spoke more to him in private in a fortnight than he speaks to his ministers in two years.'[23] It may have been this meeting which prompted Vivaldi to dedicate and present to the Emperor a second, this time manuscript, set of violin concertos entitled *La Cetra* and dated 1728 in the autograph parts (lacking only the solo part)

[23] Op. cit.; quoted in Giazotto, op. cit., p. 233.

preserved in the Österreichische Nationalbibliothek.[24] Until recently scholars generally presumed the manuscript *La Cetra* to be the same as the published set of that name, but in reality only one work (RV 391/P. 154) is common to them. Nothing more is known for certain about Vivaldi's links with the Viennese court, except that a serenata, *Le gare della Giustitia e della Pace*, was performed for Charles's name-day in Venice; the year is not recorded.

La Cetra was quickly followed by a set of six concertos, op. 10 (*c* 1728), for flute and strings, the first for that combination ever to be published. (They were not quite the first published concertos to include flute, however, as Boismortier's *Six concerts pour cinque flûtes traversières sans basse*, op. 15, had appeared in Paris in 1727.) Twelve violin concertos, opp. 11 and 12 (really two volumes of a single opus), came out in 1729. Like op. 6 and 7, these three new collections included no dedication, and like opp. 8 and 9, they were said in the imprint to be published at Le Cène's expense.

His visit to Bohemia, already mentioned in connexion with G. B. Vivaldi's application for leave, probably began shortly after Anna Girò's appearance in Hasse's *Dalisa* (Ascension 1730). Between 1724 and 1734 a Venetian troupe led by Antonio Denzio mounted a total of 57 operas (discounting intermezzi) at the theatre of Count Franz Anton von Sporck in Prague.[25] Already, Denzio had used arias by Vivaldi (including several from *La costanza trionfante*) in *La tirannia gastigata* (Carnival 1726), for which Antonio Guerra wrote the recitatives.

Vivaldi probably reached Prague in time for the revival of his popular *Farnace* (Spring 1730). Having familiarized himself with conditions in Prague, he proceeded to compose a new

[24] Cod. 15996.
[25] The best account of the activity and repertoire of Denzio's company is in Pravoslav Kneidl, 'Libreta italské opery v Praze v 18. století', Strahovská knihovna (Prague, 1966), pp. 97–131.

opera, *Argippo* (Autumn 1730), and write arias for *Alvida, regina de' Goti* (Spring 1731). It is less likely that he was present for the revivals of *La costanza trionfante* (as *Doriclea,* Carnival 1732) and *Dorilla in Tempe* (Spring 1732).

The evidence for Vivaldi's residence in Bohemia is circumstantial. The fact that *La costanza trionfante*, retitled *L'odio vinto dalla costanza*, was staged at S. Angelo during Carnival 1731 with its music arranged by A. Galeozzi bespeaks Vivaldi's absence from Venice, for we know from his later Ferrara projects that he was extremely jealous of the privilege of arranging his music. A stronger hint is provided by the autograph scores of two trios for lute, violin and bass and one concerto for lute, two violins and bass, all from the Turin collection.[26] They are written on an unusual paper of non-Venetian provenance, and each has on its opening page the following superscription: 'Per Sua Eccellenza Signor Conte Wrttbij' (abbreviations spelt out). This nobleman can be identified (not with certainty, as his family had several branches) with Count Johann Joseph von Wrtby (1669–1734), who held some of the highest offices in Bohemia, including those of royal governor, president of the Court of Appeal and hereditary treasurer. Wrtby was a regular visitor to the Prague opera, and his collection of librettos, which passed first to the Křimice branch of his own family, then to the Lobkowitzes, and latterly to the National Museum in Prague, includes several in which the Count recorded how well the opera had been received. *Farnace*, for instance, earned 'great approbation', and *Argippo* 'very great approbation'.[27] A meeting with Wrtby in Prague could explain both the commission (perhaps for six trios, as the surviving pair are numbered 2 and 5) and the unusual paper of the scores.

[26] RV 82 (Foà 40, ff. 6–9), RV 85 (Foà 40, ff. 2–5) and RV 93/P.209 (Giordano 35, ff. 297–301).
[27] Kneidl, op. cit., p. 114f.

79

Vivaldi

By Carnival 1732 Vivaldi was probably back in Italy. He was asked, in place of Orlandini, the original choice, to compose the music for Scipione Maffei's *La fida ninfa*, an opera written by this celebrated savant to inaugurate Verona's Teatro Filarmonico (6th January 1732). His *Semiramide* was given during the same season at nearby Mantua.

He was certainly in Venice on 13th February 1733, when Edward Holdsworth met him. One gathers that Charles Jennens, for whom Holdsworth was ceaselessly carrying out 'commissions' during his visits to Italy, had asked his literary friend to seek out Vivaldi and explore the possibility of buying works from him. It is obvious that Jennens greatly admired Vivaldi's music, for in the sale catalogue of Puttick and Simpson for 25th August 1873, when part of the musical library of the Earl of Aylesford (to whose family Jennens had bequeathed his collection) was put on auction, we find all the published sets except op. 5. Holdsworth writes:

I had this day some discourse with your friend Vivaldi who told me that he had resolved not to publish any more concertos, because he says it prevents his selling his compositions in MSS which he thinks will turn more to account; as certainly it would if he finds a good market for he expects a guinea for every piece. Perhaps you might deal with him if you were here to choose what you like, but I am sure I shall not venture to choose for you at that price. I had before been informed by others that this was Vivaldi's resolution. I suppose you already know that he had published 17 concertos.

Jennens took the reference to '17 concertos' to mean that number of *sets* of concertos or sonatas, and in his reply, alas lost, seems to have disputed the figure. Hence another interesting passage in a letter Holdsworth sent him on 16th July 1733 from Antwerp:

Monsieur La [sic] Cene who has published Vivaldi's and Albinoni's works assured me that if you have 12 of Vivaldi's op. [sic] and 9 of Albinoni, you have all. Let Vivaldi, he says, reckon as he pleases. He has published no more than 12, and must count several of them double to make up the number 17, which piece of vanity suits very well with his character. . . .

Vivaldi was undoubtedly vain, but on this occasion there was a grain of sense in his calculation, if he meant to count double those five sets of concertos divided into two *libri*.

In 1733–4 he returned to S. Angelo. *Motezuma* (Autumn) was followed by *L'Olimpiade* and a revived *Dorilla in Tempe*. The following year it was the turn of Verona with *L'Adelaide* and *Bajazet* (or *Tamerlano*), a *pasticcio* including arias by G. Giacomelli and Hasse. Later in 1735 Vivaldi came back to the Venetian stage. Let Goldoni take up the story:[28]

His Excellency Grimani was accustomed to have an *opera seria* performed at the same theatre [S. Samuele] during the Ascensiontide fair. Normally, old librettos were used, and these always needed to be altered in part, either because the composer required it or to suit the whims of the singers. So for this purpose, as well as that of directing and coaching the actors [i.e. singers], it was necessary to have a poet capable of writing new aria texts and possessing some knowledge of the theatre. [There follows a description of how Domenico Lalli, Grimani's manager, used to delegate this work to Goldoni, and some introductory remarks (to which reference has been made earlier) concerning Vivaldi and Anna Girò.] Vivaldi badly needed a poet to adapt, or rather to hash up, the drama to his taste, so that he could include for better or for worse the arias which his pupil had sung on other occasions, and I, charged with this task, presented myself to the composer on the instructions of my noble patron. He received me rather coldly. He took me for a novice, quite correctly, and finding me ill versed in the science of mutilating dramas, made obvious his great desire to send me away. He knew of the applause which had greeted my *Bellisario* and the success of my intermezzos, but he deemed the task of hashing up a drama a difficult one, which required a special talent. Then I remembered those *rules* which had driven me mad at Milan, when I read my *Amalasunta*, and I too wanted to depart, but

[28] *Commedie*, vol. xiii, pp. 10ff.

81

my position, my reluctance to disappoint His Excellency Grimani, and my hope of assuming the directorship of the magnificent theatre of S. Giovanni Grisostomo [also owned by Grimani] made me conceal my feelings and almost beg the *Prete Rosso* to try me out. He looked at me with a compassionate smile and picked up a libretto. 'Here you are', he said; 'this is the drama to be adapted: Apostolo Zeno's *Griselda*. The opera (he went on) is very fine; the part of the leading lady could not be better; but certain changes are needed . . . If you, Sir, knew the rules . . . Enough — how could you know them? You see here, for instance, after this tender scene, there is a *cantabile* aria; but as Miss Annina does not . . . does not . . . does not like this kind of aria (that is, she could not sing it) we need here an aria of action . . . to express passion without being pathetic or *cantabile*.'

'I see', I replied, 'I see. I will attempt to satisfy you: please give me the libretto.'

'But I need it', Vivaldi resumed; 'I have not finished the recitatives; when will you return it?'

'Straight away', I say; 'please give me a piece of paper and an ink-well. . .'

'What? You think, Sir, that an aria in an opera is like one in an intermezzo!'

I became a little angry, and cheekily replied: 'Let me have the ink-well'; and I took a letter from my pocket, from which I tore a piece of white paper.

'Do not take offence', he said gently; please— sit down here at this desk: here is the paper, the ink-well and the libretto; take your time;' and he returns to his study and begins to recite from his breviary. Then I read the scene carefully; I size up the feeling of the *cantabile* aria, and write one expressing action, passion and movement. I bring it and show it to him; he holds the breviary in his right hand, my sheet in his left hand, and he reads softly; having finished reading, he throws the breviary in a corner, gets up, embraces me, rushes to the door, and calls Miss Annina. Miss Annina comes with her sister Paolina; he reads them the area, shouting loudly: 'He did it *here*, he did it *here, here* he did it!' Again he embraces me and congratulates me, and I became his dear friend, his poet and his confidant; and from then on he never forsook me. I went on to murder Zeno's drama as much as, and in whatever way, he wanted. The opera was performed and met with success.

The pen-portrait emerging from this account is not a wholly unsympathetic one. Note how meagrely Vivaldi's breviary figures in it, compared with Goldoni's later and better-known account of the meeting. At any rate, the two men liked one another enough to collaborate (as Lotavio Vandini and Grolo Candido) on the 'heroic-comic' opera *Aristide*, performed at S. Samuele in the following Autumn.

We must now return to the Pietà, where on 5th August 1735 Vivaldi was once again engaged as *Maestro de' Concerti*, his salary 100 ducats as before.[29] Composing, teaching and rehearsal were to be his duties. Pincherle found a reference in the minutes book (whether for that same date or a later date is unclear) enjoining him to 'give up any idea of going away, as he had done in former years'.[30] One might as well ask a bird to remain in its nest.

The years 1737–9 are dominated by Vivaldi's three attempts, all unsuccessful in different ways, to mount a season of opera at Ferrara. Our information comes from his surviving correspondence with the Marquis Guido Bentivoglio d'Aragona, which comprises 19 letters, thirteen from Vivaldi and copies of six from the Marquis, to which one may add some letters to Bentivoglio from other persons concerned in the operatic projects. Eleven of the letters are preserved in the Ferrara State Archives, the others being in private ownership. To quote at length from this voluminous correspondence would be impossible here, so the content of each letter will be summarized.[31]

---

[29] *ASV*, Pietà, Busta 692, f. 113r; transcribed in Giazotto, op. cit., p. 378.

[30] *Antonio Vivaldi et la musique instrumentale*, vol. i, p. 24: '. . . senza idea di più partire come aveva praticato negli anni passati.'

[31] See Giazotto, op. cit., *passim*, for a complete series of transcriptions and information on sources.

Vivaldi

28th October 1736. Bentivoglio, replying to Vivaldi's proposal, in a letter (lost) of 20th October, to organize an operatic season at Ferrara in the coming Winter, informs the composer that the Abbé Bollani, impresario of the Ferrara opera, has come to Venice to discuss the project with him.

3rd November 1736. Thanking Bentivoglio for keeping a promise made (when?) in Rome to act as his patron, Vivaldi reports a successful meeting with Bollani. He has assembled a strong team of singers. Although he has just turned down an invitation to write the third opera of the season at S. Cassiano for 90 sequins, demanding his normal fee of 100 sequins, he will be able to let Ferrara have two operas specially arranged by him for six sequins — what it costs to have them copied — apiece. His responsibilities at S. Cassiano prevent him from coming in person to Ferrara, except, possibly, at the very end of the season. Anna Girò, who will be singing at Ferrara, offers her respects.

24th November 1736. After mentioning a point at issue in the contract of one singer (La Mancini), Vivaldi reports that he has had to rewrite the recitatives of *Demetrio* (identifiable as Hasse's opera performed at S. Giovanni Grisostomo in 1732) and provide some arias of his own. The first act is already in rehearsal at Venice.

26th December 1736. Vivaldi expresses hope that *Demetrio* has opened successfully. He is sending on the first act of another opera, ready for copying into parts. He proposes to alter a few lines of the libretto, which he is submitting for the Marquis's approval, rather than trouble the impresario (Bollani), who might take exception. Vivaldi disparages the incumbent impresarios of S. Cassiano, S. Angelo, Brescia and Ferrara, describing them as 'di poco prattica' (is their common fault to have obstructed his plans?). He finally asks Bentivoglio (obviously angling for a commission) whether he still enjoys playing the mandolin.

29th December 1736. Vivaldi brings to the Marquis's attention a matter which he had earlier wished to conceal. He reveals that it was originally agreed with Bollani that the two operas should be *Ginevra* and *L'Olimpiade* (his own operas of 1736 for Florence and 1734 for Venice). Having revised *Ginevra,* Vivaldi was suddenly informed by Bollani that the patrons of the Ferrara opera wished instead to have *Demetrio*. He obtained the score from the impresario Grimani, and, seeing that five out of six vocal parts needed reshaping, composed new recitatives. Grimani made him pay for the copying of parts, which resulted in an unforeseen expense of 20 *lire*. As Bollani was pressing him to have *L'Olimpiade* ready, Vivaldi, having greatly altered the original (as one can today verify from the autograph score in Turin), took it upon himself to start having parts copied. Then Bollani informed him that in place of *L'Olimpiade, Alessandro nell'Indie* (probably also Hasse's setting) was now wanted, and had the temerity to suggest that Grimani send the score in his possession to Ferrara — something no impresario would agree to. So Vivaldi has had to assume the cost of copying, another six sequins. Bollani therefore owes him six sequins and 20 *lire*. Vivaldi ends by bemoaning the impresario's incompetence. (One cannot altogether discount his pique at having his own scores rejected in favour of Hasse's.)

30th December 1736. Bentivoglio, who has not yet received Vivaldi's letter of the day before, approves the alterations to *Alessandro*, and agrees that Bollani is inexpert. He confesses, pointedly, that he takes his mandolin out only once a year, or even less often.

2nd January 1737. Vivaldi reports sending off the final act of *Alessandro*. He asks Bentivoglio to help him obtain the outstanding sum from Bollani. He has heard that *Demetrio* is thought overlong, and agrees that an opera lasting four hours is unsuitable for Ferrara. It was his intention to cut the recitatives, but Lanzetti (Bollani's underling) stopped him. He reports that S. Cassiano is being managed very badly, tickets being over-priced, for which reason he has turned down a commission worth 100 sequins for a new opera.[32] (Lanzetti, who on 9th January had written to Bentivoglio confirming Vivaldi's extra expenses, retracted his account in a further letter of 12th January, complaining that Vivaldi, who had exaggerated these expenses, had forced him by threats to write the first letter.)

17th March 1737. In a cool letter, which almost seems to suggest that Bentivoglio suffers Vivaldi for the sake of his female companions, the Marquis expresses his desire to show his appreciation of the Girò sisters. Vivaldi will be welcome in Ferrara, but should not put himself out . . .

3rd May 1737. Vivaldi writes excitedly from Verona, where his new opera (*Catone in Utica*) is enjoying great success, having covered its costs after only six performances.[33] A similar opera, with ballets in place of intermezzos, would suit Ferrara excellently — not during Carnival, when the ballets alone would cost 700 *louis*, but in the Summer, when they can be had for a knockdown price. He boasts of being an independent *entrepreneur*, capable of meeting costs from his own pocket without taking loans, and invites Bentivoglio to ask him to Ferrara that Autumn.

[32] No opera by Vivaldi, discounting his posthumous contribution to the *pasticcio Ernelinda* (1750), is known to have been composed for S. Cassiano.

[33] It was this opera which so delighted Charles Albert, Elector of Bavaria, and his wife on 26th March 1737. See Pincherle, *Antonio Vivaldi et la musique instrumentale*, vol. i, p. 24.

5th May 1737. Bentivoglio expresses pleasure at Vivaldi's success, but advises him against taking the opera to Ferrara in the Autumn, when he will be away.

6th November 1737. In the meantime, Bentivoglio has given Vivaldi his blessing for an opera in the following Carnival. Vivaldi is having trouble with Coluzzi, a dancer under contract with him, who has eloped with another dancer, Angelo Pompeati, 'a very bad man by nature and capable of any error or extravagance'.[34] Now there is talk of her dancing that Autumn in Venice, which will allow her less than the 16 or 18 days needed to rehearse a ballet. He begs Bentivoglio to write to the wife of the procurator Foscarini in order to compel Coluzzi to be in Ferrara by 2nd December. He will travel up towards the 15th (of November).

13th November 1737. Vivaldi thanks Bentivoglio for his intercession and continuing help in the Coluzzi affair. Whenever Coluzzi shows up, the opera will open on time, on 26th December. God willing, he is leaving for Ferrara on Monday.

16th November 1737. God, or rather one of his earthly representatives, is not willing! A distraught Vivaldi reports that the papal nuncio (in Venice) has just informed him that Tomaso Ruffo, Cardinal of Ferrara, will not allow him to enter Ferrara, citing his refusal to say Mass and his friendship with Anna Girò.[35] Contracts worth 6,000 ducats, of which more than a third has been paid out, are jeopardized. It is unthinkable to put on the opera without Girò, whose talents are unique, or

[34] Pompeati later became a dancing master and teacher of Italian, instructing the young Dittersdorf in both arts. Vivaldi evidently forgave him by 1739, when he choreographed the ballets in *Feraspe*.
[35] Ruffo (1664–1753) had a reputation for strictness, and in 1738 actually issued an edict forbidding the clergy under his jurisdiction to take part in the Carnival festivities. See Giazotto, op. cit., p. 286.

without him, since he cannot entrust so large a sum to other hands. Besides, the allegations are unfounded.

Then follows the *apologia per vita sua,* to which reference has been made earlier. Where Vivaldi is not wallowing in self-pity, he tries to pull rank with statements like: 'I have the honour to correspond with nine high princes, and my letters travel all over Europe'. He ends by asking Bentivoglio to use his good offices with Ruffo. If Ruffo still will not let him in, at least the opera should be prohibited, so as to release him from his contracts!

20th November 1737. Bentivoglio replies that Ruffo is immovable in his resolution to forbid Vivaldi's presence as impresario. Nor can he prohibit the opera, for no good reason can be cited, especially as comedies will also be playing during Carnival. The Marquis advises Vivaldi to put the opera in the hands of Picchi, a local impresario. He politely reproves Vivaldi for having sent Bollani to plead with Ruffo, for priests are the last people His Eminence likes to see mixed up with opera.

23rd November 1737. Vivaldi resigns himself to handing over the opera to Picchi. Continuing his self-defence, he pleads that he never demeans himself by standing at the door of the opera-house (?to sell tickets) like a common impresario, nor does he play in the orchestra like a common violinist, except on the first night. Defending himself against the charge of cohabiting with Anna Girò, he cannot forbear to mention that his house costs 200 ducats to rent.

30th November 1737. Picchi is evidently driving a hard bargain. Conscious of the weakness of his position, Vivaldi begs Bentivoglio to back him up.

Our sympathy for Vivaldi lessens a little when we learn that he had by no means put all his eggs in one basket. He travelled to Amsterdam for the centenary celebrations of the Schouwburg theatre, leading the orchestra and contributing a richly-scored concerto (RV 562a/P. 444). Moreover, he evidently took up the reins of S. Angelo once more, providing for Carnival one new opera, *L'oracolo in Messenia,* one revised opera, *Armida al campo d'Egitto*, and the pasticcio *Rosmira*. But let us pick up the threads of the Bentivoglio correspondence again:

2nd January 1739. Vivaldi is writing in great distress, having heard about the reception of his *Siroe* in Ferrara, which has been so bad that the management are refusing to follow it with his specially-revised *Farnace*, in defiance of contract. His recitatives have been declared miserable — an accusation that he, with 94 operas to his credit, will not stand for. The real villain is the first harpsichordist Pietro Antonio Berretta (*Maestro di Cappella* at Ferrara cathedral), who, finding the recitatives difficult, has tampered with them. Add to that his bad playing, and the result is bound to be dreadful. These are the same recitatives performed with great success at Ancona (Summer 1738), and which went well in rehearsal at Venice. In the original score no notes or figures have been struck out or erased: Berretta's alterations will therefore be identifiable. Imploring Bentivoglio to protect his reputation, Vivaldi blames his misfortune on his absence from Ferrara and his trust in an impresario.

7th January 1739. Bentivoglio commiserates, but writes that he is unwilling to become embroiled.

Ferrara had had enough of Vivaldi's operas, but Venice remained indulgent. *Feraspe* was heard at S. Angelo in Carnival 1739. A *faccio fede* for *Tito Manlio* dated 27th January 1739 (?*more veneto*) reported by Giazotto must refer to a projected but unrealized performance.[36]

[36] Op. cit., p. 310.

89

The Pietà, too, still kept him in the public eye. When Ferdinand of Bavaria, Charles Albert's brother, visited Venice around Carnival 1739, he heard there a performance of Vivaldi's 'piscatorial eclogue' *Il Mopso* (probably a kind of serenata), which he greatly admired. When Frederick Christian, Prince-Elector of Saxony, paid a state visit to Venice in 1740, three of the conservatories fêted him with music. The Pietà led off, on 21st March 1740, with a serenata, *Il coro delle muse,* for which Vivaldi wrote a sinfonia (RV 149) and three concertos, all exploiting unusual combinations of instruments (RV 540/P.266, RV 552/P. 222 and RV 558/P. 16). (A division of labour where one composer wrote the vocal music and another the instrumental music (overture, entr'actes, etc.) to the same work was very common at the time, corresponding to the respective composers' terms of employment; even ostensibly independent works like Corelli's *Concerti grossi* often originated as parts of a greater whole.)

There is no doubt, however, that Vivaldi's opportunities in Venice were drying up. The point is made in de Brosses's much-quoted letter of 29th August 1739, where one reads:[37]

Vivaldi has made himself one of my intimate friends in order to sell me some concertos at a very high price. In this he partly succeeded, as did I in my intention, which was to hear him play and have good musical recreation frequently. He is an old man with a mania for composing. I have heard him boast of composing a concerto in all its parts more quickly than a copyist could write them down. To my great astonishment, I have found that he is not as well regarded as he deserves in these parts, where everything has to be fashionable, where his works have been heard for too long, and where last year's music no longer brings in revenue.

The reason why Vivaldi, now aged 62, ventured on a final journey in 1740 remains mysterious. Since Vienna was his destination, one might guess that he had been invited by

[37] Op. cit., vol. i, p. 193.

Charles VI, who died in October 1740. Alternatively, his original destination might have been different, and his decision to make for Vienna a result of the accession of Empress Maria Theresa's consort Francis Stephen, Duke of Lorraine (and latterly Grand Duke of Tuscany), since in opera librettos from 1735 onwards Vivaldi had styled himself *Maestro di Cappella* of the Duke, proof of some form of association. We first get wind of his imminent departure in a resolution debated by the Pietà's governors on 29th April 1740:[38]

It has been brought to our attention that our orchestra needs concertos for organ and other instruments to maintain its present reputation. Having heard also that Reverend Vivaldi is about to leave this capital city and has a certain quantity of concertos ready for sale, we shall be obliged to buy them outright.

It is moved that the Officers in charge of the Chapel and of Music be empowered to buy these from our funds as they see fit at the rate of one sequin each, the action being justified.

abstentions . . . . 3 ⎫
against . . . . 3 ⎬ lost
for . . . . 4 ⎭

Although the motion, when put to the vote again, was lost by a greater margin, the governors must have relented, for on 12th May Vivaldi was paid 70 ducats and 23 *lire* for 20 concertos.[39] We then lose track of him for over a year. His presence in Vienna on 28th June 1741 is attested by an autograph receipt for the sale of an unspecified number of compositions to Antonio

[38] *ASV*, Pietà, Busta 692, f. 78; reproduced in Giazotto, op. cit., p. 257. The date of 29th August given in Salvatori, op. cit., p. 341, and accepted by many later writers including Pincherle, is thus incorrect.

[39] *ASV*, Pietà, Reg. 1009, f. 541. Another record of what must be the same payment (Ibid., Busta 704, III, f. 41) cites the mathematically more explicable figure of 440 *lire* (22 sequins).

Vinciguerra, Count of Collalto, a nobleman of Venetian origin whose main residence was at Brtnice in south-west Moravia.[40] Death overtook the composer a month later. When he breathed his last, on Friday 28th July 1741, he was living in the house of the widow of a saddler named Waller (or Wahler), hence its description in the necrology as 'saddler's house' (*Satlerisches Haus*).[41] This house, demolished to make way for the new Ringstrasse in 1858, stood at the end of the Kärntner Strasse nearest the Kärntner Tor (Gate of Carinthia). The cause of death was stated to be an internal inflammation (*innerlicher Brand*). Later that day Vivaldi was unceremoniously buried in the Hospital Cemetery (*Spitaler Gottesacker*), which also no longer exists. His funeral was accompanied by a *Kleingeläut* (small peal of bells), and the expenses, which totalled 19 florins and 45 kreutzers, were kept to the minimum. If Mozart's burial 50 years later was that of a pauper, Vivaldi's deserves that sad epithet equally. His straitened circumstances are confirmed by a brief report in the Commemorali Gradenigo that 'the Abbé Don Antonio Vivaldi, known as the *Prete Rosso*, an excellent performer on the violin and a much-admired composer of concertos, once earned over 50,000 ducats (? annually), but through excessive prodigality died a pauper in Vienna'.[42]

There are two, possibly three, portraits of Vivaldi still surviving, one of which was much copied during the eighteenth century and exists in several variants. This 'Effigies Antonii Vivaldi' was an engraving made by François Morellon La Cave (a Frenchman resident in Amsterdam) in 1725. The composer is shown full-face, holding up a sheet of music over a table on

---

[40] The compositions may be among the 16 recorded in an inventory of the Collalto collection preserved in Brno, Moravské Muzeum.

[41] Vienna, Parish of St Stephen, necrology, vol. xxiii, f. 63. See Gallo, op. cit., and Hedy Pabisch, 'Neue Dokumente zu Vivaldis Sterbetag', *Österreichische Musikzeitschrift*, vol. xxvii (1972), pp. 82–3.

[42] Venice, Museo Correr; reproduced in Giazotto, op. cit., p. 289.

which an ink-well stands. His expression is a little sanctimonious and, as Pincherle says, ovine (though the shape and texture of his wig contribute to this impression). Ghezzi's ink sketch (Rome, 1723) shows the head and shoulders in profile, lightly accentuating the nostrility of his nose and the pugnacious thrust of his chin. Lastly, there is an anonymous portrait in oils of an unnamed violinist in the Liceo Musicale of Bologna, which was identified as that of Vivaldi by Francesco Vatielli on account of its similarity to other portraits and the hint of red hair showing at the edge of the blond wig. Indeed, it has so many features in common with La Cave's engraving (Vivaldi's gown, his chemise, the ink-well and paper, the proportions of his face) that it might well have served as its model. If La Cave's engraving stresses self-satisfaction, and Ghezzi's caricature avidity, the oil portrait gives Vivaldi's face a sweet, almost angelic cast.

The character revealed by what details we possess of the composer's life is complex, and — like those of Lully and Wagner, two other composers famous for their entrepreneurial zest — not always sympathetic. Vivaldi's ailment, which restricted his movements, must be held to account for many traits. Was it not to compensate for physical immobility that he played at such breakneck speed, wrote down his music in a tearing hurry (in many original drafts he begins by writing neatly, but in his impulsiveness allows his hand to degenerate into a scrawl), and allowed himself to be transported in a carriage back and forth across Europe? Did he not compensate for his physical dependence on others by stubbornly refusing to delegate matters concerning his career to collaborators, even at the cost of overstretching his capacity to keep a grip on events? Was not the inferiority complex to which invalids are susceptible inverted to become a superiority complex — a megalomania, even — making the composer intolerant of all criticism and full of his musical accomplishments and social connexions?

This contrast between Vivaldi's knowledge of himself and the face which he wished to present to the world comes out in his music, where frenetic gaiety is found side by side with dreamy withdrawal or brooding introspection. The melancholy repetitiveness of a movement such as the Largo of op. 4 no. 9 (RV 284), suggestive of great loneliness, is paralleled in its period only in the music of Zelenka, whose service at Dresden was marked by deep frustration.

One cannot so easily explain Vivaldi's obsession with money and, more generally, with quantification of all kinds. Even when inflating his statistics, he never uses round figures.

Vivaldi's religiosity seems, superficially at least, to be confirmed by the famous motto standing at the head of many of his longer scores: L. D. B. M. D. A. As this motto is usually presented as a monogram, the letters superimposed on one another, its elucidation has escaped many commentators, who preferred to see in it the initials of Vivaldi's name; but since the letters are spelt out consecutively in the scores of *Bajazet, L'Olimpiade* and *Teuzzone,* their identity cannot be questioned. Reinhard Strohm has suggested the expansion of the initials to 'Laus Deo Beataeque Mariae Deiparae Amen', which seems entirely convincing.[43] One might liken this motto to the formula 'Adsit scribenti Virgo Beata mihi' found in autograph scores of Benedetto Marcello, himself something of a religious recluse in later life.

Fortunately, Vivaldi did not lack a somewhat rough sense of humour. One remembers the inscription 'per li coglioni', rather too delicately rendered as 'for blockheads', in the finale of the autograph score of the concerto RV 340/P.228 dedicated to Pisendel, where Vivaldi had included, no doubt for a copyist's benefit, some bass figures, which, if left in, could be interpreted as a slight on Pisendel's musicality. One also smiles at the

[43] 'Eine neuentdeckte Mantuaner Opernpartitur Vivaldis', *Vivaldi Informations,* vol. ii (1973), p. 105.

exasperated comment written over the score of an aria in *Orlando finto pazzo* intended to replace the one originally composed, probably at the singer's behest: 'Se questa non piace, non voglio più scrivere di musica' (If you don't like this, I'll stop writing music). Some of the descriptive titles of concertos are attractively whimsical — *La disunione, Grosso Mogul, Il Proteo* — and the intriguingly enigmatic dedication of the concerto RV 574/P.319 to 'S.A.S.I.S.P.G.M.D.G.S.M.B.' must be in jest, satirizing the eighteenth century's fondness for abbreviation.

There was kindliness, too, in the man. Once his initial suspicions had been overcome, he treated Goldoni with real warmth. Also, one doubts whether the devotion of the Girò sisters was inspired merely by self-interest. Let us not judge Vivaldi's character on the strength of the surviving documentation alone, since this is inevitably weighted towards his business activities, which brought out his less attractive side, but let us rather infer from his music what nobler qualities lay, perhaps latently, in his personality.

5 Vivaldi's musical style

Many listeners must have discovered how much easier it is to mistake one Vivaldi composition for another than to identify its composer wrongly. To say this is neither to endorse Stravinsky's supercilious observation, inherited from Dallapiccola, that Vivaldi could 'compose the same form so many times over',[1] nor to make an obvious deduction from the fact that he borrowed copiously from his own works but sparingly from those of other composers. Even by the standards of his age, when plagiarism from other composers was frequently castigated by critics but self-borrowing raised hardly a murmur, his style remained remarkably constant. It was almost fully formed in op. 1 (1705) and complete in its essentials in op. 2 (1709); thereafter it underwent little change except in its more superficial melodic characteristics, which evolved continuously to keep abreast of current fashion. Had his style been half as malleable as that of his contemporary Telemann (1681–1767), who began as a neo-Corellian and ended as an immediate precursor of the Classical style, he would hardly have countenanced including his contributions to the 1714 revival of Ristori's *Orlando furioso* in his own *Orlando* of 1727, or using movements from the original version of *Farnace* (1727) in the ill-fated score for Ferrara of 1738.

Nor does his style vary much from one *genre* or medium to another, when the potentialities and limitations of different

[1] Igor Stravinsky and Robert Craft, *Conversations with Igor Stravinsky* (London, 1959), p. 76.

instrumenents and the human voice have been taken into account. He was not one of those composers like Caldara and Lotti who could write in a 'strict' style for the church and a 'free' style for the theatre. Try as he might on occasion to compose in the learned style, the French style or even the *bel canto* style, Vivaldi proved (perhaps fortunately) a bad imitator incapable of suppressing his individuality.

Because his style was so distinctive in a consistent manner, it is useful to precede a discussion of Vivaldi's music with a look at some of the most original features of his style in general. The norm against which we shall be measuring him will be the mainstream of the Italian tradition, though inevitably major figures of the late Baroque from outside Italy will be drawn in.

In Vivaldi's melody one notes first a broad sweep and a great fondness for unusually wide intervals. Italian composers for the violin had long been accustomed to the practice of skipping back and forth between adjacent and even non-adjacent strings and were now beginning to move with greater freedom up and down the fingerboard; indeed, Venetian composers such as Legrenzi and (somewhat less) Albinoni often revelled in angularity for its own sake. The growing popularity around 1690 of unison writing for the string ensemble caused some types of melodic progression hitherto the prerogative of bass parts (especially the rising fourth or descending fifth at cadences) to be adopted by upper parts, which might retain them even when independent of the bass. What distinguishes Vivaldi is the expressive value he attaches to the octave and compound intervals — a value totally different from that of the corresponding simple intervals. Without historical awareness we might easily consider the opening of the *Gloria* RV 589 banal, even naïve:

Ex. 1

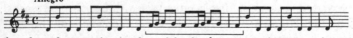

(bracketed notes in tenths with the bass, rest in octaves)

Vivaldi

To Vivaldi's contemporaries those pounding octaves were novel, exciting and worthy of imitation.

Where he uses large intervals we often find either that two-part writing is being simulated in a single line (the lower 'part' may be a pedal-note) or that an expected simple interval has been displaced upwards or downwards by one or two octaves, as at the beginning of the *Concerto funebre* RV 579/P.385:

Ex. 2

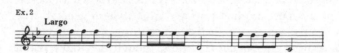

He shows no general preference for diatonicism or chromaticism in his melodies, tending to either as the occasion warrants, but it is remarkable how often melodic chromaticism is introduced without prompting from the harmonic progressions. A flattened ('Neapolitan') supertonic is common in minor tonalities, and a sharpened ('Lydian') subdominant in both major and minor tonalities. In minor keys the raised fourth degree is often preceded by a raised third degree — a curious reproduction of the structure at the upper end of the melodic minor scale (see the B natural and C sharp in the example below). He inflects (or fails to inflect) the sixth and seventh degrees of the minor scale in ways that still strike us as extraordinary: the 'descending' (i.e. lowered) forms can be used for an *ascending* line, and the 'ascending' (i.e. raised) forms for a *descending* line (outside the confines of dominant harmony, where they are conventional). Moreover, he exploits the augmented second of the 'harmonic' minor scale for frankly melodic purposes — this at a time when even in inner parts augmented seconds were carefully avoided, often being converted by octave displacement into diminished sevenths. The two augmented seconds in close succession in the next example, from an aria (sung originally by Anna Girò) for the

enchantress Alcina near the end of the second act of *Orlando*, lend
the vocal line an anguished intensity rare for its period.

Ex.3

tor - men — — — ti mi - nac — - - cia il dio d'a - mor

Sometimes, an unusual chromatic inflection suggests the influ-
ence of folk music, Italian or Slav. Given the location of the
Pietà on the Riva degli Schiavoni (Waterfront of the Slavs),
Vivaldi could hardly have escaped hearing daily the songs of
Dalmatian sailors.

The first fact to note about Vivaldi's rhythm is his liking,
particularly at the opening of phrases, for anapaestic patterns
such as ♫ ♩ or ♫♫, where two notes on the strong division
of a bar (or beat) are followed by one on a weak division. He also
evinces a fondness for the 'syncope' pattern ♪ ♩ ♪ and its
extensions, both in melodic and accompanying parts. These two
rhythmic traits are prominent in Slav (especially Czech) folk
music, by which they may have been inspired. Quantz claimed
that Vivaldi was one of the originators of 'Lombardic' rhythm
(the inverted dotted group ♫ or its variant ♫). In his
Lebenslauf he linked its introduction with the performance of
Vivaldi's operas in Rome shortly before his arrival there in
1724;[2] in his *Versuch* he stated that the formula emerged in
about 1722:[3] Vivaldi's scores seem to bear out his belief. As
Quantz himself admitted, however, Lombardic rhythm had
long been a characteristic of the Scottish style ('Scotch snap'), so
Vivaldi's popularization of it was innovatory only for the operatic idiom in which he worked. The *saccadé* rhythmic formula —
repetitive use of the normal dotted group — is adopted by

[2] Op. cit., p. 223.
[3] Op cit., p. 309f.

Vivaldi in certain stereotyped situations: the imposing tutti peroration; the illustrative accompaniment (in the central movement of *La primavera* to represent the rustling of leaves — in the 'Eja Mater' of the *Stabat Mater*, the lashing of whips); imitation of the French style (as in the aria 'Tornar voglio al primo ardore', headed *alla francese,* from the last act of *Arsilda*).

Vivaldi pushes to the very limit the characteristic Italian fondness, absent from French music of the same time, for sharply differentiated rhythms, often expressed by contrasted note-values, in the various components (melody, counter-melody, accompanying parts, bass) of a texture. Each component carries its own rhythmic stamp, often maintained in ostinato fashion for several bars (see Ex. 25, p. 174). Then the rhythms are redistributed or abandoned in favour of new patterns, and the process is repeated. Sometimes triple and duple (or quadruple) division of the same note-value appears simultaneously in different parts, in a context where 'assimilation' of one notated rhythm to the other (e.g. the performance of a dotted quaver and semiquaver in 2/4 as a crotchet and quaver in 6/8) is improbable. In the finale of the oboe concerto RV 453/P.187, notated *alla giga* in 12/8, the dotted crotchet is often divided into *four* quavers in the solo part, an effect used later by Mozart in the finale of his Oboe Quartet K.370.

Vivaldi's phrase structure is outstandingly fresh and original. Throughout most of musical history it has been normal to group cells, phrases and larger units in pairs, where the second unit (consequent) balances the first (antecedent). Sometimes — particularly at the lower levels of organization — antecedent and consequent are exactly matched in length, but their relationship can also be asymmetrical. In the late baroque period repetition and sequence are often used to spin out the consequent beyond the expected length. What Vivaldi did that was new was sometimes to group units of equal length in *threes* so that an antecedent in effect had two consequents, or vice-versa. Ternary

Portrait of Vivaldi from Sir John Hawkins's *A General History of the Science and Practice of Music*

Opening page of the autograph score of *Arsilda, regina di Ponto* showing Vivaldi's monogram formed from the letters LDBMDA

Autograph page from the quartet sonata by Vivaldi discovered in
Dresden in 1976

Farinelli's company. One of them is Marigha who was lately on ye English stage. The Compositions either here or at Milan are not esteem'd, and therefore I shall not have any more of them copied than some of the best Airs.

I am sorry that the loose airs wch I sent you from Rome were not to your mind; but this comes of employing a blockhead who knows no more of an air than he does of the language of China. I hope you have by this time found out Mr Bertie's tuner to put yr Harpsichord in order. I have wrote to Florence to acquaint the maker wth the ill state you found it in on it's arrival and to complain of his sending it out of his hands in so bad a condition. I suppose he will deny it, and indeed I was very much surpris'd to hear your account of it, because Mr Megnell had it tried by a good master few days before 'twas sent of, and the maker pack'd it up himself.

I had this day some discourse with your friend Vivaldi who told me yt He had resolv'd not to publish any more Concerto's, because He saith it prevents his selling his Compositions in Mss wch He thinks will turn more to account; as certainly it won'd if He finds a good market for he expects a Guinea for each piece. Perhaps you might deal with him if you were here to choose what you like, but I am sure I shall not venture to choose for you at that price. I had before been informed by others that this was Vivaldi's resolution. I suppose you already know yt He has publish'd 12 Concertos.

Whilst I was at Milan I rec.d yrs of a very old date April the 10th last, wch had been forwarded to Naples, & lay there till just before we left Milan. for that Letter you put me in mind of a very agreeable voyage I once made to Holland. but give me good reasons not to hope to have the pleasure of seeing you there again. We shall not leave this place till towards the latter end of the next month or yt beginning April. And from hence we shall go for Vienna. If you have any commands for me at either place let me know them, and in giving me an opportunity of serving you, you will very much oblige

Dear Sir
Your most affectionate
and obedt. humble serv.t

E Holdsworth

Mr Herbert desires his service
if you write immediately upon
the receipt of this, yr Letter may
reach me here.

Page from Le Cène's edition of Vivaldi's op. 8

Page (with some corrections in Vivaldi's hand) from the volume of violin sonatas discovered in Manchester in 1973

Sketch of Vivaldi (left) by Pier Leone Ghezzi

grouping of cells half a bar in length (in common time) lies behind most of the 'irregular' phrases including an odd half bar which occur so widely in his music. Another of his favourite devices, later to be used in a more polished form by Haydn and Mendelssohn, was to make the same structural unit serve as the consequent of the one preceding it and the antecedent of the one following it — a kind of elision. In the next example, from the finale of the violin concerto RV 356 (op. 3 no. 6), the irruption of the soloist turns the bracketed motive, which one would have taken to be the flourish immediately before a cadence, into the opening of a new musical paragraph.

Ex. 4

(Presto)

When Vivaldi recapitulates material, he likes to prune it drastically, eliminating the repetition of phrases or simply excising whole groups of bars. The consequences for the phrase-structure are often startling: what was previously symmetrical may now be asymmetrical, or vice-versa. He seems to regard a melody less as an organic entity than as a provisional arrangement of small units capable of recombination.

Much has been made by previous writers of Vivaldi's over-dependence on sequence as a means of continuation. This is in fact a weakness (as we now see it) that he shares with most of his Italian contemporaries. Bach uses sequence hardly any less, but he so often enriches (or disguises) it through melodic and harmonic paraphrase, and has besides a better sense of when to call a halt. When they are enlivened by counterpoint (as in the imitative play of the violins in Ex. 6, p. 103) or are chromatically inflected to produce modulation, Vivaldi's sequential

101

phrases bear repetition more easily than when such interest is absent. Some modern performers spare no effort to bring variety to Vivaldi's sequential writing, introducing long crescendos or decrescendos, or ornamenting each phrase differently, but these attempts often merely draw attention to the problem.

He likes to articulate his phrases by interpolating rests (sometimes amplified by a fermata) in all the parts. Interestingly, the breaks occur not only after imperfect cadences (e.g. I–V), where the incompleteness of the harmonic progression guarantees preservation of the momentum, but also after perfect cadences. In these cases the cadence will have occurred earlier than the listener anticipated, so that he is prepared for a continuation of the paragraph after the general pause.

Very occasionally, he anticipates the masculine-feminine antithesis beloved of the classical period, as shown in the next example (note the asymmetrical relationship of the two phrases), taken from the finale of the concerto RV 300 (op. 9 no. 10). Strange to say, Vivaldi does not use the graceful 'feminine' answer again after its double appearance in the opening ritornello. Although Quantz recommended that the 'best ideas' of the ritornello be extracted and interspersed among the solo passages,[4] Vivaldi often shows a disinclination to exploit the more memorable parts of his ritornello, preferring to repeat the more conventional material.

Ex. 5

---

[4] *Versuch*, p. 295.

His harmony is equally forward looking. No previous composer had used the seventh in a chord with greater licence. To be sure, he normally introduces the seventh in one of three ways current at the time: from the same note in the previous chord; from a note a step away; from another note of the same chord. Sometimes, however, the seventh is introduced by a leap from another chord, as the next example, from the finale of RV 279 (op. 4 no. 2), demonstrates (sevenths ringed):

Ex. 6

(Allegro)

Chords of the ninth (as distinct from suspended ninths resolving to the octave) are less common, but are treated in equally emancipated fashion when they do occur. 'Higher' discords (the eleventh and thirteenth) also appear, usually as a result of repeating a phrase a third higher over a dominant pedal.

Not all Vivaldi's discords resolve in the orthodox manner, particularly when concealed in the middle of the texture. The resolution is often transferred to another part, sometimes to a different octave. It is interesting that when Vivaldi indulges his fondness for arpeggiating a chord in two or three parts simultaneously, a dissonance such as the fourth (a suspension which must eventually resolve to the third) can be treated as a normal member of the chord and pass from one instrument to another, generating great tension. This is not an example that his imitators were quick to follow.

Another peculiarity of his harmony, and the cause of some pungent effects, is the inexact synchronization of a harmonic progression in the different parts: one part (or more) moves to the new chord before the beat; the others arrive on the beat. This can be observed in the next example, from the first movement of the violin sonata RV 755, where the ringed violin notes are the advance guard of the new chord, dissonating rather oddly against the notes of the established chord.

Ex.7

(Bass notes sound an octave lower.)

Then, there are cases of dissonance in Vivaldi's more florid writing which cannot be justified by any harmonic principle but seem to arise from the technique of the instrument itself — one might say, from the action of the fingers.

The harmonic rhythm of his music — the rate at which chords change — fluctuates more widely and more abruptly than in the music of any contemporary. An eight-fold or sixteen-fold reduction or acceleration, which may (or may not) be disguised by the maintenance of the same note-values or even the same figuration, is not uncommon. He seems to delight in teasing the listener, unexpectedly freezing the movement and then, once the ear has adjusted to the slower pace, suddenly unleashing a quickfire series of chords. We are miles away from the relatively steady tread of Bachian and Handelian harmony. One is tempted to cite this as an example of Vivaldi's 'dramatic' leanings, though it must be understood that the irregularities of harmonic rhythm are not prompted by extra-musical factors (they are no more marked in his operas) but are part of his natural musical thought.

Contemporary critics, anticipating some more recent voices, found his sometimes rather static basses, which for long stretches may consist of just a rhythmicized monotone, over-primitive. Quantz, obviously with Vivaldi especially in mind, inveighs against the non-melodic character of basses in Italian compositions and the 'drum bass' (*Trommelbass*) in particular.[5] It is true that Vivaldi's basses are often insubstantial, but their very simplicity may afford him an opportunity to produce dazzling flights of fancy in one or more melodic parts, unhampered by considerations of part-writing or balance.

Until the discovery of the Turin manuscripts it seemed not unreasonable to identify Vivaldi as a, if not the, prime mover in the retreat from counterpoint which was to lead first to the attenuation of baroque style and then to the emergence of the classical style. Critics of his own time who knew only the published instrumental music found the absence of traditional contrapuntal procedures disconcerting. In a section of his *Essay on Musical Expression* headed 'On the too close attachment to air and neglect of harmony' Charles Avison observed the following:[6]

It may be proper now to mention by way of example on this head the most noted composers who have erred in the extreme of an unnatural modulation, leaving those of still inferior genius to that oblivion to which they are deservedly destined. Of the first and lowest class are Vivaldi, Tessarini, Alberti and Loccatelli [sic], whose compositions being equally defective in various harmony and true invention, are only a fit amusement for children; nor indeed for these, if ever they are intended to be led to a just taste in music.

Interestingly, a rejoinder to Avison's strictures published anonymously in the following year cited in defence of Vivaldi

[5] Ibid., p. 313. C. P. E. Bach shared Quantz's dislike of the *Trommelbass*.
[6] *An Essay in Musical Expression* (London, 1752), p. 42.

one of the few movements in his published concertos cast in the form of a fugue (as distinct from others, such as the finale of op. 8 no. 11, which employ fugal techniques). The pamphlet's author was William Hayes, Professor of Music at Oxford. After quoting Avison's contemptuous remarks on the four composers, Hayes goes on:[7]

In truth their style is such as I would not by any means recommend; and yet I think Vivaldi has so much greater merit than the rest that he is worthy of some distinction. Admitting therefore the same kind of levity and manner to be in his compositions with those of Tessarini, etc., yet an essential difference must still be allowed between the former and the latter, inasmuch as an *original* is certainly preferable to a servile, mean copy. That Vivaldi run into this error, I take to be owing to his having a great command of his instrument, being of a volatile disposition (having too much mercury in his constitution) and to misapplication of good parts and abilities. And this I am the more inclined to believe, as in the eleventh of his first twelve concertos, op. 3, he has given us a specimen of his capacity in solid composition. For the generality, in the others, he piques himself upon a certain brilliance of fancy and execution, in which he excelled all who went before him . . . But in the above concerto is a fugue, the principal subjects of which are well invented, well maintained, the whole properly diversified with masterly contrivances, and the harmony full and complete.

That this movement was in reality no isolated exception is proved by the existence of several equally rigorous fugal movements in the concertos (particularly those for four-part strings without soloist) of the Turin collection, as well as the sacred vocal music. When writing fugally, he is admittedly more concerned with the immediately expressive qualities of the texture than with its challenge to his — and the listener's — intellect. Thus he does not deploy the full array of fugal devices as we know them from Bach's works. Augmentation, diminution and inversion of the subject; the separate exposition and

[7] *Remarks on Mr. Avison's Essay on Musical Expression* (London, 1753), p. 39f.

subsequent combination of different subjects: these rarely interest him. However, he evinces a fondness for double and triple counterpoint (like many of his Italian contemporaries he frequently introduces his countersubjects, or additional subjects, together with the principal subject from the outset), for long pedal-points at the climax of the movement, and for stretto. His finest achievement in fugal writing is perhaps the fast section of the *Ouverture* which begins the second part of *La Sena festeggiante*. As a French overture the movement is a very imperfect imitation of the genuine article (for one thing, the initial entries of the fugue subjects work their way upwards from the bass instead of downwards from the first violin; for another, the material is too severe, almost churchly, in character), but as an essay in fugal writing it will stand comparison with anything Marcello or Caldara — perhaps even Handel — wrote. The extract below begins just after the modulation to the relative major, E flat. The three principal subjects, labelled *A, B* and *C*, are first combined and then relieved by the episodic motive *D* (in combination with a form of *B* in the bass). A double stretto (*B* and *C*) leads to a stretto of *A* accompanied — miraculously — by both *B* and *C*, so that at the climax all four parts are strictly motivic. Vivaldi's skill at cadence avoidance is also shown by this passage.

107

He is also exceptionally fond of ostinato. Ground basses, which may either stay in the same key throughout or be transported to other keys, are found in sonata and concerto movements, arias in cantatas and operas, even in one chorus (*Giustino*). One particular chaconne bass well known to his contemporaries (it is present in the first eight bars of Bach's 'Goldberg' Variations) appears in at least five movements. Unlike mid-baroque Italian composers such as Cavalli (and their English emulators including Purcell) Vivaldi and his generation rarely attempt to disguise the regularity of the ground bass by avoiding a perfect cadence at the point of repetition or phrasing the melodic parts over the join. Instead, they diversify the texture or figuration of the upper parts on each restatement of the bass figure after the fashion of sectional variations.

Ostinato figures (groups of notes repeated at the same pitch) are also much used. Vivaldi often grants a repeated figure the harmonic licence of a pedal-note, superimposing it on the texture regardless of any clashes.

Imitation between two or more parts is regularly found in even the most homophonically conceived of his movements. Where there are two parts, they are commonly a fourth or fifth apart (as in the sequence in Ex. 6, p. 103), or at the unison. In either case, each part often plays (a) a motive and (b) a counterpoint to the same motive now heard in the companion part in alternation, producing the effect of straightforward repetition of a pair of motives in continuous voice-exchange. It is as if one hears an altercation between the two parts, growing more intense with each repetition. Vivaldi did not originate this type of imitation — one finds it in trio-sonatas by earlier Italian composers — but the peculiar energy of his lines and the forthrightness of his harmony, often enriched by sevenths, gave it a new lease of life. Such passages are common in Haydn and Mozart, often producing curious echoes of Vivaldi.

It would be a mistake, however, to equate counterpoint — the art of combining melodic lines — with specific contrapuntal devices such as ostinato or imitation, which are certainly less evident in Vivaldi's music, taken as a whole, than in that of Corelli, Couperin, Purcell or Bach. As a contrapuntist Vivaldi unostentatiously achieves excellence when he brings together two or three lines of contrasted melodic and rhythmic character. He has a gift for fresh— which is to say unusual— part-writing, so that even a viola part (in Italian music, generally a receptacle for the harmonic leavings of the other parts) may sparkle. Even more than Bach, he likes to 'drop' his leading-notes when he can thereby obtain an interesting melodic line or effective spacing of the parts.

Nevertheless, his part-writing is not beyond criticism. His liking for parallel movement in several parts, including the bass, often brings him perilously close to consecutive fifths or octaves. The type of passage which once embroiled Corelli in an acrimonious dispute with critics in Bologna[8] occurs again and again in Vivaldi's compositions. Perhaps it was to this short-coming (in the eyes of contemporaries) that Goldoni alluded when he wrote: 'However much connoisseurs claimed that he [Vivaldi] was deficient in counterpoint and did not compose basses correctly, he made his parts sing nicely . . .'[9]

Vivaldi's approach to modulation is characteristically personal. He is apt to short-circuit the normal process of modulation, establishing a new key via its mediant, subdominant, submediant or leading-note chord rather than the conventional dominant. The listener is jerked, not smoothly carried, into the new key. Even when the dominant is the point of entry, it may arrive quite suddenly and entail the chromatic alteration of several notes.

The range of keys visited in the course of a movement is rarely exceptional for the period, though some minor-key movements wander considerable distances up and down the circle of fifths. One of Vivaldi's boldest and most convincing tonal designs occurs in the 'Et in terra pax' of the *Gloria* RV 589. In the schematic representation that follows, major keys are represented by capitals, minor keys by small letters; the keys

[8] The controversial bars occur in the *Allemanda* of op. 2 no. 3.
[9] *Commedie*, vol. xiii, p. 11.

enclosed in parentheses are ones that are passed through, no cadence being made.

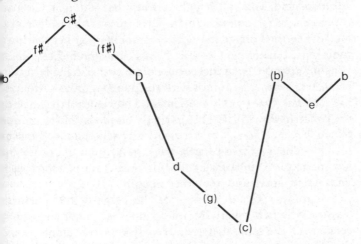

The transition from C minor to B minor is effected by an ingenious piece of enharmonic punning: the ringed bass note F, apparently a dominant seventh in C minor, resolves upwards to F sharp as if it were E sharp, root of a 'German sixth' chord.

Ex. 9

More than any previous composer he exploited with a sure sense of drama the contrast between the major and minor modes. It is normal for many, if not all, of the principal ideas of a movement to appear at some point in the relative key, major or minor, or one of its satellite keys in the same mode, paraphrased

111

if necessary. This is something never found in Corelli and practised only in the most timid and restricted fashion by Albinoni and Torelli, though it must be said that German composers were somewhat more adventurous. Vivaldi is also fond of fleeting visits to the parallel minor key (the key sharing a tonic with a major key), especially as a diversion before a final, clinching phrase. Such enclaves are often pathetic and lyrical in character, making a contrast with the more vigorous surrounding material. One frankly experimental movement, the finale of the concerto RV 159/P.231, jestingly employs this technique to produce a collage of two thematically self-contained movements — one, for three-part *concertino*, in A minor; the other, for four-part *ripieno*, in A major. In this crazy quilt of a form each 'movement' interrupts the other in turn.

Sometimes, Vivaldi anticipates the usage of the Viennese classics, Schubert especially, by juxtaposing major and minor versions of the same material. A well-known example is the fierce minor-key ending of the first movement of the *Concerto alla rustica*, RV 151/P.143, following the normal restatement of the opening material in G major; but there are many other, dramatically less highly-charged instances.

One aspect of Vivaldi's handling of tonality that has received surprisingly little mention in discussions of his style is his readiness to choose as the tonal area next in importance to the tonic a key other than the dominant or (for minor keys only) the relative major. By convention the dominant is usually the first new tonal area to be emphasized; it is the key of the first ritornello outside the tonic key in a concerto movement, or that of the cadence before the first double bar in a binary movement. The proportion of Vivaldi movements that deviate is small, but significant by comparison with other composers. In movements in a major key he sometimes substitutes the mediant minor for the dominant, something familiar only from a few keyboard sonatas by D. Scarlatti. In minor keys, however, one is surprised to see the subdominant used in this function (e.g. in the two slow movements of the cello sonata RV 42). This unusual procedure inverts the normal tonal curve of the movement, since the traditional 'sharp' and 'flat' areas have changed places. It should be added that this tonal bias towards the flat side is paralleled (though not necessarily within the same movement) by a frequent harmonic bias in the same direction, its most typical expression being the plagal (IV-I) cadence.

Vivaldi's attitude to what today's commentators call the 'thematic process' or 'musical unity' is best described as casual and unpredictable. Subtle thematic correspondences between one part of a movement and another (one is not speaking of the repetition and development of ideas inherent in the chosen form) arise, if at all, quite spontaneously. A desire to treat ideas exhaustively, as opposed to merely intensively, is foreign to his nature — not for him the Bachian practice (so expressive of the Protestant ethic) of working material to the limit of its possibilities.

Thematic links between movements of the same work are quite often conspicuous. Here one must be cautious before imputing 'cyclic' intentions to him. Where similarities exist between dance movements in a chamber sonata, they can be explained as vestiges of the old variation suite and equated with instances in the music of many Italian contemporaries. Other, more literal correspondences can be put down to infertility of imagination or, more charitably, an obsession with a particular idea. One example occurs in the violin concerto RV 763 (*L'ottavina*), where the soloist enters in the Largo with a transposition of the phrase with which the preceding Allegro began. Nevertheless, one will find instances of links that are both subtle and purposive, especially among the concertos without soloist, which served Vivaldi as a test-bed for some of his most radical and ingenious experiments in form. The incipits of RV 163/P.410 offer interesting variations on the basic shape $b\,b'''$ —

Vivaldi

$f'' — b^{b\,\prime}$:

Ex. 10

Any view of Vivaldi's music as inherently 'organic' must crumble before the fact of his self-borrowing, which both in incidence and pervasiveness greatly surpasses the showing of Bach and even Handel. To date there has been no comprehensive study of this aspect of his music, though valuable work on individual cases has been published.[10] This mammoth task would in principle require the examination of every bar in every source for over 700 works and would be hampered at every turn by uncertainties of chronology, hence of the sequence of borrowing.

Boundaries of *genre* and form prove no barrier to Vivaldi's raids on his own music: sonata movements are transported to concertos; concerto movements to operas;[11] movements from sacred vocal works to the concerto medium. Binary movements are expanded into ritornello form; movements in ritornello form are redesigned as *da capo* arias.[12]

The portion borrowed is highly variable. Sometimes one or

---

[10] One particularly detailed study is Walter Kolneder, 'Vivaldis Aria-Concerto', *Deutsches Jahrbuch der Musikwissenschaft* (1964), pp. 17–27.

[11] A celebrated instance is the sinfonia captioned *La Fortuna in macchina* (*Giustino*, I, 5), a binary movement based on the ritornello of the first movement of *La primavera*.

[12] Each of the three movements of the recorder concerto RV 442 (better known in its version for flute, RV 434, published as op. 10 no. 5) is found in the shape of a *da capo* aria: the first in *Teuzzone* (I, 14); the second in *Il Tigrane* (II, 4); the third in *Giustino* (III, 7).

114

even two movements are taken over as they stand, or with minimal change of instrumentation. Sometimes the principal but not the subsidiary material is appropriated. This is the case in certain bassoon concertos arranged for oboe, in which Vivaldi troubled to write out only the recomposed (often only lightly paraphrased) solo passages. It happens, though less often, that the subsidiary material is retained, while the principal material is recomposed.[13] The opening movement of RV 210 (op. 8 no. 11) contains much episodic writing in which references to fragments of the ritornello are heard; however, the loss of thematic relevance entailed by the transference of the episodes, slightly pruned, to the first movement of RV 582/P.164, the D major concerto for violin and two orchestras 'per la santissima assontione di Maria Vergine', caused the composer no qualms. Then, what was previously principal material may reappear as subsidiary material, or vice versa. The opening of the *Allemanda* from the violin sonata RV 3 is the basis of the first solo episode in the chamber concerto RV 101 and its later version for flute and strings RV 437 (op. 10 no. 6). When one examines the music at the level of the individual phrase, one discovers that the cadential bars of the ritornello in one concerto (RV 103/P.402, first movement) can resurface as the opening bars of another (RV 156/P.392).

If one is determined to find excuses for Vivaldi's self-borrowing (the fact that so many instances have gone unnoticed speaks for the success of most transplants), it is inadequate to cite the haste with which he had to work, especially in view of de Brosses's testimony to his facility. Vivaldi obviously took pride in his *bricolage* and regarded it as a useful and legitimate part of his art.

A striking feature of his orchestral textures is their spacious-

---

[13] This technique of remodelling was especially favoured by Albinoni. It often goes unnoticed, since thematic incipits do not betray the borrowing.

ness, to which the high tessitura of his violin parts, the wide compass of each part taken separately, and his great tolerance of part-crossing all contribute. When writing homophonically, he favours a texture composed of various strata (each represented by one or more musical lines) differentiated through characteristic figures. Many of these accompanimental stereotypes are recognizable as ones occurring, albeit often in a more sophisticated form, in the Viennese classics; they include the Alberti bass, which in Vivaldi's hands is generally not a bass but an upper part, showing its derivation from the type of arpeggiation found in display writing for violin from the time of Corelli onwards.[14]

He was also one of the first composers for the orchestra to use 'broken' accompaniments, where the 'figure' is assembled from fragments supplied by several instruments. The significance of this innovation is that for the first time in ensemble music (one is not speaking of keyboard or lute music, where free-voicing achieved a comparable result much earlier) individual lines are intelligible only in terms of a larger constituent of the texture, a milestone in the development of orchestration.

When Vivaldi writes in closely-packed textures, they are apt to lie in extreme registers. The luminous aureole of three violins with viola surrounding the soloist in the slow movement of the violin concerto RV 356 (op. 3 no. 6) is a well-known instance; a counterpart in the lower register is Niceno's aria 'Non lusinghi il core amante' in *L'incoronazione di Dario* (II, 19), where the bass is partnered by a solo bassoon and a solo cello, apparently without continuo.

In comparison with the orchestral textures of the previous generation, those of Vivaldi and most of his Italian contemporaries (who may have been to a greater or lesser extent his

---

[14] The arpeggiations on one solo violin heard against a cantabile line on the other in the finale of the double concerto RV 522 (op. 3 no. 8) are an intermediate stage in the removal of this type of figuration from the foreground to the background.

imitators) show in several places the effect of three separate processes, applied singly or in combination. These processes may be called simplification, thinning and lightening.

Simplification entails the reduction of the number of real parts through doubling at the unison, the octave and even the fifteenth. Fluent contrapuntist though he was when working with three or four parts, Vivaldi seems distinctly uncomfortable when their number rises; the seven real contrapuntal parts (one short of the theoretical maximum, there being eight vocal parts) in the 'Sicut erat in principio' fugue of the *Dixit Dominus* RV 594 take him to the limit of his ability. Other practical considerations leading him at various times to double parts may have been to insure against absence of players, to avoid overtaxing the concentration of unsophisticated audiences, and to accelerate the writing of a score (since doubling instruments could be cued in from a fully-notated part). Naturally, genuine artistic reasons are usually present. The ultimate stage of this simplification process, the orchestral unison, is employed to splendid dramatic effect, and two-part textures where both parts are doubled in at least one other octave can produce an evocatively bleak sound, which Haydn was later to make his own.

Thinning the texture entails the removal of doubling instruments normally present. In upper parts its most common form is the reduction to one solo instrument, which introduces a change of timbre. It is, however, the bass which is most often stripped down. Any of the possible constituent parts of the *basso* — the melody instruments cello, double bass and bassoon and the continuo instruments harpsichord, organ and bass lute — can be suppressed or reduced to a single player. Very often, the continuo players are removed *en bloc*, a warning of their eventual demise.

Lightening the texture entails the suppression of the bass register and the transference of the bass part to the middle register, where it is usually played by violins or violas. Vivaldi notates such *bassetto* parts in the bass clef an octave below sounding pitch. High-lying basses of this kind often cross middle or upper parts, producing second inversions of chords, offensive to orthodox theorists (including C. P. E. Bach, who deplored *bassetti*, the introduction of which he attributed to 'a certain master in Italy', by whom he may have meant Vivaldi),[15] but acceptable to many composers, among them Haydn in his early quartets. Vivaldi used the opening movement of his violin sonata RV 12 for the slow movement of the concerto RV 582/P.164, taking the bass up an octave and assigning it to violins. The last two bars show the curious effect produced by chord inversion.

Ex.11

Reserving our main discussion of instrumentation and instrumental technique for later chapters, we can mention here some special effects which are of importance for orchestral texture. Vivaldi is fond of the subdued sound of muted instruments. Normally, muting is prescribed (as far as possible) for the whole ensemble. Thus the *Sinfonia* in the third act of *Teuzzone*, a slow march, is headed 'tutti gl'istromenti sordini'; the instruments include not only strings but two trumpets, two oboes, a bassoon and 'timpani scordati' (which one should probably interpret as muffled rather than mistuned kettledrums). In another, probably later, version of the same movement opening the *Concerto funebre* RV 579/P.385 the muted instruments include a tenor chalumeau and three *viole all'inglese*.

---

[15] *Essay on the True Art of Playing Keyboard Instruments*, trans. and ed William J. Mitchell (London, 1951), p. 173.

Sometimes, a solo violin is exempted from the general muting, so that it may stand out more strongly. As well as normal mutes (*sordini*) Vivaldi employs heavier lead mutes (*piombi*) for his strings; both types are called for in *Orlando*.

His use of *pizzicato* is more often selective than general, however, being found predominantly in bass parts. He does not lack ingenuity: the aria 'Sento in seno ch'in pioggia di lagrime' (I feel in my breast that in a rain of tears) in *Giustino* (II, 1) is picturesquely accompanied by a shower of raindrops on the strings ('tutti pizzicati senza cembalo') except for three instruments — a first violin, a second violin and a double bass — who are instructed to play the same parts with their bows.

Very occasionally, the Cinderellas of the violin family, the viola and the double bass, come into unexpected prominence. One aria in *Giustino* (I, 4), 'Bel riposo de' mortali' (Sweet sleep of mortals), which is very similar in style to the Pastoral Symphony in *Messiah*, has a drone, initially on *C*, for double basses alone. In an 'infernal' scene (II, 6) in *Orlando finto pazzo* all the violinists are instructed to play violas, the better to evoke the lugubriousness of Hades.

Vivaldi's concern for the fine nuances of music in such matters as tempo, dynamics, phrasing and articulation is quite remarkable for its time, as Walter Kolneder has shown.[16] Elsewhere, Kolneder has ventured the interesting suggestion that conditions of performance at the Pietà, where music was heard in silence and the players were well drilled, stimulated the composer's inventiveness.[17] True though this may be, it must be said that his operatic music, written for more boisterous surroundings, yields nothing in refinement of detail.

The basic, universal indications of tempo are frequently qualified for greater precision; thus one finds expressions such as 'Allegro (ma) non molto' or (another example of Vivaldi's

[16] *Aufführungspraxis bei Vivaldi* (Leipzig, 1955).
[17] *Antonio Vivaldi: His Life and Work*, p. 65.

119

humour) 'Allegro più ch'è possibile'. Alternatively, or in addition, he may append a description of the general character of the movement, as in 'Largo (e) cantabile'. Variations of tempo within a movement — as opposed to composite movements like the 'Peccator videbit' from the *Beatus vir* RV 597 — are rare, if one excludes *accompagnato* recitatives and 'motto' statements or cadenzas in arias.

There seems little doubt that from his earliest days as a composer Vivaldi employed both terraced dynamics (instantaneous changes of dynamic level corresponding to the addition or withdrawal of ranks on the organ) and graduated dynamics (crescendo and decrescendo) dynamics. The second type are not indicated by 'hairpins', which came into use somewhat later, but by repetition at intervals of directions such as 'più piano'. In Vivaldi's music this device occurs as early as the *Giga* in RV 79 (op. 1 no. 11), begun by the unaccompanied first violin. De Brosses was struck during his Venetian sojourn of 1739 by the subtlety of dynamic change in orchestral performances. He wrote:

They have a method of accompanying which we do not know but would find easy to introduce into our performance, and which adds infinitely to the value of their music; it is the art of increasing or diminishing the sound, which I could term the art of nuances and shading. This is practised either gradually or suddenly. Besides *forte* and *piano*, *fortissimo* and *pianissimo*, they have a more or less emphatic *mezzo piano* and *mezzo forte*. [18]

Kolneder has identified 13 gradations of dynamic marking in Vivaldi's music, to which one can add a *forte-piano* effect seen in Cato's aria 'Dovea svenarti allora' (I ought to have killed you then) (*Catone in Utica*, II, 11), where the first notes in a series of bowed tremolos receive a sharp attack, presumably to illustrate Cato's bitterness at his daughter's betrayal. Different strata in

[18] Op. cit., vol. ii, p. 332f.

the texture are often contrasted dynamically; thus in the second movement of *La primavera* the dog (viola) barks 'molto forte e strappato', while the leaves (violins) rustle 'pianissimo'.

Vivaldi phrases his string parts remarkably fully, especially where he desires some special effect. Slurs are numerous and vary greatly in the number of notes encompassed. One attractive novelty is a 'syncopated' style of bowing in which the change of bow occurs on a note before (rather than on) the beat, producing a pattern such as ♪♪♪♪♪ | ♪ . Apparent inconsistencies in the phrasing of similar passages abound in the original sources. In some cases, Vivaldi, having made his intentions clear at the beginning of the movement, left the performer to carry on in similar manner; in others, the variation seems deliberate; very often, however, the discrepancy must have arisen through carelessness, abetted by the composer's habit of requoting material from memory without referring back to earlier pages of the score.

Directions referring to articulation are frequent. One meets expressions such as 'arcate lunghe' (long bows) and 'arcate sciolte' (detached bows) — both are especially common in the bass parts of recitatives — 'attacata alla corda' (on the string), 'battute' (such notes being 'beaten', perhaps in *martellato* style) and 'spiccato'. Both dots and vertical strokes are used for staccato; placed underneath a slur, they seem to indicate *portato* and a flying staccato respectively. Different parts written in similar note-values may have contrasted articulation; a *locus classicus* is the B minor section of the slow movement in RV 580 (op. 3 no. 10), where each of the four solo violins phrases and articulates its series of broken chords (the first violin in demisemiquavers, the rest in semiquavers) in an individual way.

Even the improvised continuo realization does not escape Vivaldi's attention. The direction 'Il cembalo arpeggio' appears in the slow movement of *L'autunno*, a picture of dozing inebriates; arpeggiation is also prescribed for Angelica's recitative beginning 'Quanto somigli, o tempestoso mare' (How like you are, o stormy sea) in *Orlando* (i,6).

No discussion of Vivaldi's style can be complete without a fuller mention of his occasional adoption, as a novelty or compliment to a patron, of elements of the French style. Specifically French *genres* appear: the *Ouverture* introducing the second part of *La Sena festeggiante*; minuets found both in concertos and (as dance-songs) in operas; and a few chaconnes, notably the finales of the concertos RV 107/P.360; and RV 114/P.27. In these, and several other movements headed *Alla francese*, he uses dotted rhythms extensively, no doubt intending the length of the dot (and shortness of the ensuing note) to be exaggerated in the manner of the French. Another feature is their homorhythmic character, which contrasts with the differentiated rhythms more typical of the composer.

6 The instrumental music

Vivaldi's music for instruments falls into three broad *genres*: sonata, concerto and sinfonia. If one takes the short version of the Ryom catalogue as the basis of computation, counting variants separately but excluding lost and incompletely preserved works, one arrives at a total of 90 sonatas (including two works with lute entitled 'Trio' and the *Sinfonia al Santo Sepolcro*, which is generically a sonata),[1] 478 concertos and 14 sinfonias. This count omits works recognized by Ryom as spurious and — perhaps rather artificially — sinfonias not preserved independently of the larger vocal work to which all, presumably, originally belonged. Ryom's criteria of authenticity are bibliographical rather than stylistic: provided that at least one original source names Vivaldi as the composer, the attribution is likely to stand regardless of any musical incongruity, unless another composer's name appears in a concordant source whose reliability is thought at least equal. In all probability, several unauthentic works are listed as genuine.[2] Finally, the quartet sonata recently discovered in Dresden should be added.

[1] Until the beginning of the eighteenth century sonatas of the 'church' variety were often termed 'sinfonia', particularly when scored for many instruments. Manfredini's *Sinfonie da chiesa*, op. 2 (1709), and the six sinfonias (individually entitled 'Sonata') in Albinoni's *Sinfonie e concerti a cinque*, op. 2 (1700), fit this description.
[2] These may include the sonatas RV 24, RV 54–59 (*Il pastor fido*) and RV 60, the *Introdutione* (Sinfonia) RV 144/P.145 and the concertos RV 464/P.334, RV 465/P.331 and RV 373/P.335.

THE SONATAS

The impression gained from the statistics given above that Vivaldi cultivated the sonata merely as a sideline to his production of concertos may be a little distorted by the vagaries of preservation; it is remarkable that only eight sonatas, none of them for the 'solo' medium, appear in the Turin manuscripts. Most of the sonatas were probably written not singly (like the concertos for the Pietà) but in groups, and were destined not for institutions but for private patrons.

A classification of the extant sonatas by medium and instrumentation produces the following picture:

1 'Solo' sonatas (one instrument and bass)[3]

violin	40
cello	9
flute	4
recorder	1
oboe	1
musette, etc.[4]	6
TOTAL	61

2 Trio sonatas (two instruments and bass)

two violins	20
two flutes	1
two oboes	1
two unlike instruments	5
TOTAL	27

3 Quartet sonatas (four instrumental lines)

two violins, viola and bass	2
violin, oboe, obbligato organ and chalumeau	1
TOTAL	3

[3] The term 'bass' denotes, according to context, a melody instrument (cello, bassoon, etc.) and/or a harmony instrument (harpsichord, organ, etc.).

[4] Alternatively vièle (hurdy-gurdy), flute, oboe or violin.

VIOLINO PRIMO.

S V O N A T E
DA CAMERA

A Trè due Violini, e Violone ò Cembalo

CONSACRATE

All' Illustrissimo, & Eccelentissimo Signor Conte

A N N I B A L E
GAMBARA

NOBILE VENETO & c.

Dà D. Antonio Viualdi Musico di Violino
Professore Veneto

OPERA PRIMA.

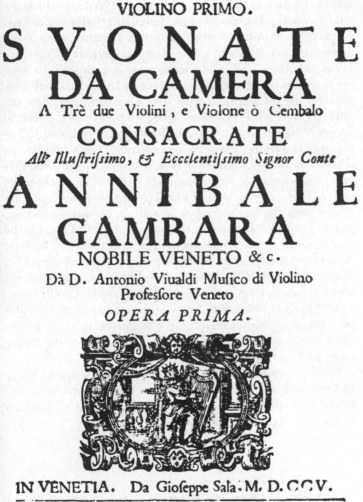

IN VENETIA. Da Gioseppe Sala. M. D. C C V.

Si Vendono à S: Gio: Grisostimo All'Insegna del Rè Dauid.

Title-page of Sala's edition of Vivaldi's op. 1

The twelve *Suonate da camera a tre*, op. 1 (1705), in which the cello (*violone*) and harpsichord are designated (following normal practice in chamber sonatas) alternative rather than complementary instruments, may well be the earliest of Vivaldi's works to have survived. Like many juvenile compositions they oscillate between excessive dependence on a model and striking, often clumsy, attempts to break free. Above all, they show the influence of Corelli, possibly transmitted via the first generation of Venetian imitators (Gentili, Ruggieri, Albinoni). The sequence and stylization of the movements is very Corellian: an abstract movement, generally in slow tempo and entitled *Preludio*, introduces a group of dance-movements all in the same key and invariably in binary form. Two or three movements are chosen from the familiar types: *allemanda, corrente, sarabanda, giga* and *gavotta*.[5] In some of the sonatas one, even two (in the first sonata), abstract movements are interspersed. They are signs of the interpenetration of church and chamber genres (in reality the two had never been sealed off from one another), which one may observe even in the classic models, Corelli's opp. 2 (1685) and 4 (1694). Like many other neo-Corellians, Vivaldi pays the older master tribute by closing the set with a one-movement work consisting of variations on the popular theme *La follía*.[6]

Vivaldi's stylistic debt is evident from the shape of many motives and the presence of certain contrapuntal routines, among them the typically Corellian 'leap-frogging' violins seen in the opening of the first sonata:

[5] Since the Italian dance-movements often differ in tempo and rhythmic character from the cognate French movements, the Italian form of the names will be retained.

[6] Corelli's 'solo' sonatas op. 5 (1700) end with *La folía*.

Ex. 12

While many of the more original passages in these sonatas seem arbitrary, there are signs that a powerful personality is emerging. The lyrical triplets in the *Allemanda* of the seventh sonata, the unaccompanied bass at the start of the *Gavotta* of the tenth sonata and the written-out varied reprises in the *Gavotta* of the eleventh sonata are as inventive as they are effective. *La follía* shows Vivaldi, like Liszt and Ravel in later centuries, to be a composer whose imagination is kindled in musically very fruitful ways by the expansion of instrumental technique.

Two further trio sonatas were published as the last works in his op. 5 (1716).[7] They are mature and fluent, perhaps a little glib. Though not stated to be *sonate da camera* on the title-page, they are on the surface more consistently 'chamber' sonatas than many in op. 1, since they contain no abstract movements other than the *preludio*. The dance titles have become rather a formality, however; the spread of binary form to abstract movements, which gathered pace after 1700, and the stylization of the dances, which permitted more variety of tempo and rhythm, meant that practically any binary movement, other than a slow movement in common time, could acquire (or dispense with) a dance title, as circumstances dictated. The last movement of RV 72 (op. 5 no. 6), an 'Air-Menuet', demonstrates this ambiguity in its style. By 1716 the trio medium was losing ground to the 'solo' medium, which accommodated virtuosity more readily; the

[7] Op. 5 being designated by Roger the 'second part' of op. 2, these two sonatas are numbered 17 and 18.

subordinate rôle of the second violin in these two sonatas (especially appropriate in a set largely consisting of works for the 'solo' medium) acknowledges this trend.[8]

Vivaldi's only other extant sonatas for two violins and bass (two possibly unauthentic works apart) are a set of four, which may be remnants of a larger set, in the Turin collection.[9] The bass part, a *basso seguente* doubling whichever of the violin parts is lower, is stated by the composer to be optional. It is therefore legitimate to regard the sonatas as violin duos in the style of Leclair's op. 3 (1730) and Telemann's *Sonates sans basse* (1727). As Vivaldi's works for the Pietà seem to have been written individually (so many per month), these sonatas were most likely composed to order, perhaps for a visitor from northern Europe. All follow the concerto in having three movements (rather than the four or five more usual in the church or composite church-chamber sonata), but the binary form common to all the movements is typical of the sonata in the closing decades of the baroque period. The virtuosic handling and constant interplay of the violins recalls Vivaldi's double concertos. These fine, unusual works deserve to be better known.

Of the remaining trio sonatas, four are of particular interest: two works for a high and a low instrument with bass, and two trios for lute, violin and bass. Like the sonatas just discussed, RV 86, for recorder and bassoon, and RV 83, for violin and cello, exploit a combination more typical of France than Italy. They move even closer to the concerto, using a version of ritornello form in their fast movements, through RV 86 preserves the traditional four-movement cycle. The lute trios for Count Wrtby, in contrast, approximate to 'solo' sonatas through having non-obbligato violin parts; much of the time the violin doubles the lute, and elsewhere it either presents the

---

[8] Not so radically, however, as the six trio sonatas in Michele Mascitti's op. 4 (1711), where the second violin is marked optional.
[9] RV 68, 70, 71 and 77.

lute line in simplified form (a procedure familiar to *ripieno* violinists in the concerto) or supplies a discreet middle part.

What seem to be the earliest 'solo' sonatas for violin are the twelve in op. 2 (1709). The title-page specifies harpsichord (*cembalo*) as the accompanying instrument, but there is a particularly good case for strengthening the bass line with a cello, for these works, more than any others by Vivaldi, treat the bass contrapuntally, allowing it to take over motives from the violin part or counterpose distinctive material of its own. The idiom is still recognizably Corellian; Pincherle has pointed out the thematic similarity of the *Allemanda* in the fourth sonata (RV 20) and the *Gavotta* of Corelli's tenth sonata.[10] Where Vivaldi is his more expansive self, he exercises far greater control and discretion than in op. 1. He retains the chamber idiom of his earlier opus (corresponding to the second half of Corelli's op. 5) but includes four quick abstract movements, variously entitled *Capriccio, Preludio a capriccio* and *Fantasia,* designed to flaunt the virtuoso.

Discounting the first four sonatas in op. 5, whose characteristics are broadly the same as those already described for the trio sonatas in the collection, the next 'cluster' of violin sonatas is a large group preserved in Dresden. It comprises 12 works: four in the composer's hand and dedicated to Pisendel; seven in copies made by Pisendel himself; and one in an unknown hand. Similar works are contained in isolated manuscripts as far afield as Brussels, Stockholm, Venice and elsewhere.

These sonatas, dating from about 1716, mostly preserve *da camera* outlines, although actual dance titles appear rarely. One very interesting work, RV 25, is laid out as a suite in the French sense of the term, containing seven very short movements, four

---

[10] *Antonio Vivaldi et la musique instrumentale,* vol. i, p. 132. Two other F major works by Vivaldi, RV 69 (op. 1 no. 5) and RV 567 (op. 3 no. 7), have a close thematic resemblance to RV 20 and its Corellian parent.

in G major and three in G minor. Significantly, this is one of the sonatas dedicated to Pisendel; Vivaldi may have thought it appropriate to pay homage to the French style dominant at the Saxon court.[11] In contrast, RV 10 and RV 26 are works in the church idiom, looking back to the first half of Corelli's op. 6. RV 10 features a composite allegro-adagio movement of the sort pioneered in Corelli's first sonata, while RV 26 contains a fugal movement in which the single violin simulates through double stopping the sound of two violins. In comparison with op. 2, the bass parts of these sonatas tend to be severely functional, having almost ceased to interact thematically with the violin part, which has become enriched by varieties of rhythm and virtuosic figuration taken from the concerto.

This process is carried a stage further in the manuscript set of twelve sonatas copied during the 1720s under Vivaldi's supervision. Now in the Central Library, Manchester, these sonatas were probably presented to (or at least acquired by) Cardinal Ottoboni in Rome or Venice, for they seem to have been among a huge job lot, largely consisting of items from the late Cardinal's library, bought by Holdsworth for Jennens in 1742. Comparison is facilitated by the reappearance in modified versions of three sonatas from the Dresden group (RV 3, 6, 12) and two preserved elsewhere (RV 22 in Brussels and RV 758, fragmentarily, in Venice). In places, the violin line has been made smoother and more lyrical (this suggests the influence of operatic *bel canto*), but the bass has been thoroughly reworked to become an unobtrusive prop, more rhythmic (in the manner of the reviled 'drum bass') than harmonic in function. This time, the designation of the accompanying instrument as harpsichord suits the character of the music; the cello can be omitted with advantage. These 'Manchester' sonatas are ostensibly the most purely *da camera* of any group Vivaldi wrote, for they each

[11] The external resemblance between RV 25 and the partitas in Telemann's *Kleine Kammermusik* (1716) is quite striking.

consist of a *preludio* followed by three dance-movements. The effect is different, however, for most of the movements are totally abstract in mood.[12]

The nine extant cello sonatas are, as a group, the best instrumental chamber works works produced by Vivaldi, easily outclassing their nearest rivals, the cello sonatas of Benedetto Marcello.[13] One is tempted to write that the deeper the instrument (this observation applies equally to the bassoon), the more deeply-felt Vivaldi's writing for it. One reason why the cello has always lent itself easily to pathos must be its duality of rôle: in one situation, it is a tenor instrument, a violin playing down an octave; in another, it is a bass instrument underpinning, in plain or elaborated fashion, the entire structure. Vivaldi's cello, like Bach's, switches rôles frequently, sometimes dialoguing with itself. Although the accompanying bass line is generally as simple as that in the sonatas of the 1720s (with which most of the cello sonatas appear, on grounds of style, to be contemporary), enough contrapuntal tension is generated by the solo line itself to prevent a certain static quality which invades some of the violin sonatas.

Six cello sonatas were published in Paris by C.-N. Le Clerc in 1740. Remembering Vivaldi's resolution to send no more works for publication, one must assume that Le Clerc obtained the set in manuscript via a third party. The works are perfect demonstrations of the convergence of church and chamber genres. Their four-movement plan (slow-fast-slow-fast) follows *da chiesa* norms, while the prevalence of binary form is a *da camera* heritage.

The best of the six 'solo' sonatas for wind instruments is the one for oboe (RV 53), which may have been written for the

---

[12] The 'Sarabanda' of the eleventh sonata (RV 756) is even a through-composed movement.

[13] J. S. Bach's sonatas for viola da gamba and harpsichord and partitas for unaccompanied cello are, strictly speaking, not comparable.

Dresden virtuoso J. C. Richter, who accompanied his prince to Venice in 1716.[14] It is an unusually chromatic piece, which, on the two-keyed instrument of the time, must have posed problems of fingering and intonation.[15]

It is ironic that six of the most popular 'solo' sonatas known under Vivaldi's name — those of *Il pastor fido*, so-called op. 13 — are skilful pastiches by a foreign, probably Parisian hand. Their background is briefly the following. During the 1730s the Le Clerc brothers, Jean-Pantaléon and Charles-Nicolas, had virtually cornered the market for Italian music in France: the first was Le Cène's agent in Paris from 1733, while Le Clerc the younger (publisher of the cello sonatas) obtained in 1736 royal letters of patent giving him sole right to publish in France the principal works which the other Le Clerc was importing from Amsterdam. This monopoly seems to have been a pre-emptive move to prevent rival publishers from pirating the Dutch editions. To circumvent it entailed acquiring works not originally intended for publication, arranging music for special instrumental combinations, or outright forgery.

On 21st March 1737 J. N. Marchand, a 'maître de musique', successfully applied for letters of patent, valid for nine years, to bring out Vivaldi's opp. 13 and 14, Albinoni's op. 10 and Valentini's op. 10.[16] All these works were stated to be for

[14] A date of composition around 1716 is also suggested by the thematic connection of the slow movement of the Sinfonia to *L'incoronazione di Dario* with the finale of RV 53.

[15] Zelenka's writing for oboe shows similar boldness, which suggests that Dresden possessed one or more oboists of uncommon ability.

[16] The petitioner was probably one of two half-brothers, both named Jean Noël, from this numerous family of Parisian musicians. Jean Noël the elder (*b* 1689) was a kettledrummer to the Queen of Spain; his younger brother (*b* 1700) was a fife-player and drummer in the Écurie. The same man was presumably the composer and publisher of a *Nouvelle suite d'airs pour deux tambourins, musettes ou vielles*. This undated publication styles him 'Mr. Marchand, Ordinaire de l'Académie Royale' (i.e. a member of the opera orchestra).

the *musette* (bagpipe) and *vièle* (hurdy-gurdy), two mock-pastoral instruments then enjoying a minor vogue in Paris. If one regards as improbable that original compositions for these exotic instruments had already been composed by, or commissioned from, the three Italian composers, one's suspicions are deepened by the coincidence that the cited opus numbers begin exactly where those covered by Le Clerc's monopoly leave off. Marchand evidently did not know at the time of application for his *privilège* that a genuine op. 10 (a set of violin concertos) had appeared from Albinoni in 1735 or 1736, to be advertised in Le Clerc the elder's catalogue of 1737.

It seems that Marchand brought out only two of the promised four volumes: a collection for *musette* and *vièle* under Valentini's name entitled *Musica Harmonica*, [17] and *Il pastor fido*, described on the title-page as 'Sonates pour la musette, vièle, flûte, hautbois, violon avec la basse continue del Sigr. Antonio Vivaldi, opera XIIIa'. [18]

Vivaldi's authorship of *Il pastor fido* can equally be contested on musical grounds. Several borrowings from concertos by not only him but also other masters can be identified. All inner parts are naturally sacrificed, and in many cases the bass line is remodelled. The amount of material actually appropriated varies; it depends on how easily the original ritornello form can be compressed into the dimensions of binary form. The table below shows what borrowings have been identified.

The movements in which no borrowings have been identified include a number of typically French *rondeaux*. Further, they contain several touches of harmony peculiar to the French style. Ironically, these possibly original movements (perhaps by Marchand himself) are generally more attractive than the concerto pastiches. A *Pastorale* in the fourth sonata, where an obbligato

[17] Lost, but listed in C. J. F. Ballard's catalogue of 1742.
[18] The frequent identification of 'op. 14' with Vivaldi's six published cello sonatas is incorrect.

133

no. within set	RV no.	key	movement	source	material borrowed
1	54	C	—	—	—
2	56	C	second	Vivaldi, op. 7 no. 2 (RV 188): third movement	opening ritornello (condensed) and start of first solo
3	57	G	second	Vivaldi, op. 6 no. 2 (RV 259): first movement	opening ritornello, transposed from Eq to G
4	59	A	second	J. Meck, *WV* 18 (= RV Anh.65/P.217): first movement[20]	opening 4 bars
			fourth	G. M. Alberti, vn4A$_1$: first movement[20]	opening $3\frac{1}{2}$ bars, some subsequent material paraphrased
5	55	C	second	J. Meck, *WV* 18: third movement	bars 1-14 and 69-76, transposed from A to C[21]
6	58	g	fourth	Vivaldi, op. 4 no. 6 (RV 316a): first movement	entire movement, with two small cuts

cello joins the upper instrument, is especially memorable. It would be sad if the dubious origin of these sonatas were allowed to obscure their fine musical qualities.

It remains to discuss the three quartet sonatas. Two of them, the sonata 'al Santo Sepolcro' (RV 130/P.441) and the similarly-titled sinfonia (RV 169), both for four-part strings, must have been written as occasional works for the Pietà's chapel. Oddly, they consist of only two movements, a contrapuntal slow introduction and a fugue, but their intensity belies their brevity.

The *Suonata a violino, oboè et organo, et anco se piace il salmoè* (sonata for violin, oboe, organ, and chalumeau *ad libitum*)[22] can be regarded as a quartet even if the chalumeau, which merely doubles the organ bass in the upper octave, is omitted, since the obbligato organ part is written on two staves and normally consists of one part in each hand; the player should supply a continuo realization when there are rests in the upper stave, and possibly elsewhere, if the hands are not too occupied. Originally, the work was composed for the Pietà, as one sees from the

---

[19] The numbering of the concerto is taken from the thematic catalogue in Klaus Beckmann, *Joseph Meck (1690–1758): Leben und Werk des Eichstätter Hofkapellmeisters* (doctoral dissertation, Ruhr-Universität, 1975). Interestingly, the concerto was published as the final work in an anthology (publisher's catalogue no. 448) issued under Jeanne Roger's imprint (where Vivaldi is named on the title-page as one of the composers represented but not identified with any individual work), and later in an all-Vivaldi anthology, *Select Harmony*, issued by Walsh in 1730. Beckmann argues persuasively for Meck's authorship on the basis of other sources: what is important here is that Marchand may have believed the work to be Vivaldi's.

[20] Numbering from M. Talbot, 'A Thematic Catalogue of the Orchestral Works of Giuseppe Matteo Alberti', *R.M.A. Research Chronicle*, no. 13 (1976). Manuscripts of this concerto survive in Paris and Manchester.

[21] See Beckmann, op. cit., p. 76.

[22] A discussion of the chalumeau appears on p. 161f.

names of girls appearing alongside the instrumental specifica-
tions before the first system: Prudenza (violin); Pelegrina
(oboe); Lucietta (organ); Candida (chalumeau). All four girls
were among theose granted permission on 5th June 1707 to
teach private pupils (Prudenza is described as a contralto, and
Candida as a player of the *viola*).[23] Candida also sang in Vivaldi's
Moyses Deus Pharaonis (1714). It is thus reasonable to assign a
date of *c* 1710 to the sonata.

The word 'pedale' appears under the organ bass in two places
in the second movement. Italian organs of Vivaldi's day usually
had only rudimentary pedal-boards capable of doing little
beyond sustaining a low note, thus freeing the left hand for solo
work. Vivaldi later revised the instrumentation of the score,
perhaps just prior to its departure for Dresden, its present
home, substituting a second violin and *basso* for the organ and
amplifying the figuring of the bass.

The organ was used as a continuo instrument in the Pietà's
chapel in conjunction with at least two harpsichords (the *cembali*
referred to in the score of *Juditha triumphans*).[24] Instances of its
use as an obbligato instrument in Vivaldi's sacred vocal music
are few, but one may cite the arias 'Noli o cara te adorantis' in
Juditha triumphans and 'Jucundus homo' in the *Beatus vir*, RV
597. The organ part in this sonata is remarkable for the presence
of long cadenzas over pedal points in the first two movements,
and still more remarkable for the way in which figures are spread
between the hands in the third movement; for once, Vivaldi
achieves a keyboard texture that cannot be reduced to a right
hand and a left hand operating independently, and would defy

[23] *ASV*, Pietà, Busta 688, f. 181; transcribed in Giazotto, op. cit.,
p. 354.
[24] Where 'organo' appears on published continuo parts, however, it is
used as a generic term for *all* keyboard instruments, not specifically the
organ. This wider meaning is regularly mentioned in contemporary
dictionaries.

transference to other instruments (which may be why he abandoned his final revision). At the beginning of the movement the organist is instructed to 'accompany' (i.e. improvise chords) on the strong beats ('la prima nota del battere e levare') only, so as not to obscure the delicate fingerwork.

Ex. 13

Vivaldi

THE CONCERTOS
Vivaldi's extant concertos can be grouped in six classes according to their instrumentation.

1 Solo concertos (one solo instrument, string orchestra and continuo)

violin	220
viola d'amore	7
cello	27
mandolin	1
flute	13
recorder	2
flautino	3
oboe	19
bassoon	37
TOTAL	329

2 Double concertos (two solo instruments, string orchestra and continuo)

2 violins	25
2 cellos	1
2 mandolins	1
2 flutes	1
2 oboes	3
2 trumpets	1
2 horns	2
2 unlike instruments	11
TOTAL	45

3 Ensemble concertos (more than two solo instruments, string orchestra and continuo)	34
4 Concertos for two string orchestras and soloist(s)	4
5 Chamber concertos (three to six solo instruments and continuo)	22
6 Concertos for string orchestra and continuo	44

As a musical term 'concerto' enjoyed a variety of meanings during the seventeenth and eighteenth centuries, all of which conveyed either the notion of joining together or that of competing in friendly rivalry. The first connotation predominated during the seventeenth century, the second (which we retain today) during the eighteenth. Around 1710 both were current, as the following definition by Mattheson shows:[25]

Concertos, broadly speaking, are [musical] gatherings and *collegia musica*, but in a strict manner of speaking, this word is often taken to mean chamber music for both voices and instruments (i.e. a piece actually so named),[26] and, more strictly still, pieces for strings [*Violin Sachen*] composed in such a way that each part in turn comes into prominence and vies, as it were, with the other parts; hence also in such pieces and others where only the uppermost part is dominant, and where among several violins one, called *Violino concertino*, stands out on account of its especially rapid playing.

Concertos in Mattheson's 'strictest' sense came into being at the very end of the seventeenth century as offshoots of the sonata tradition. Leaving aside the problematic case of those works by Corelli published posthumously in 1714 as concertos,[27] but whose pre-1700 prototypes may have functioned as sinfonias or sonatas, and which represent in any case a subsidiary current, it is possible to discern three distinguishing characteristics of the concerto up to about 1710: its tolerance of— indeed, preference for — orchestral doubling; its fondness for display writing on violin or cello (not necessarily allotted to a soloist); its generally homophonic texture and receptivity to influence from the operatic sinfonia. After about 1710, largely as a result of Vivaldi's work, other criteria became dominant: the presence of solo

---

[25] *Das neu-eröffnete Orchestre* (Hamburg, 1713), p. 193f.
[26] Mattheson's term 'Cammer-Musik' would include music for private devotions.
[27] *Concerti grossi*, op. 6.

parts; the preference for a three-movement cycle, and the use of ritornello form in outer movements.[28]

It was only during the second half of the seventeenth century that composers began to write with orchestral timbre specifically in mind, the Papal cities of Rome and Bologna becoming leading centres of this new fashion. The addition of one or two viola parts helped to fill the music out, but what was needed was a new style capable of giving expression to the power and richness of orchestral sound. The sonata for one or more trumpets and strings, cultivated in Bologna from the 1660s, became an important catalyst in this stylistic transformation; indeed, the characteristic figures of trumpet writing — note repetitions, fanfare-like arpeggios and tight clusters of stepwise-moving notes — left an imprint on violin writing that lasted for over a century.[29] Whereas the more substantial movements of an instrumental composition had previously relied for their coherence on imitative counterpoint, the unifying factor was now the statement, and restatement at strategic points, of pithy mottoes. The earliest concertos, including those of Torelli's op. 6 (1698) and Albinoni's op. 2 (1700), retain and develop this motto technique. A fast movement will consist of upwards of three periods,[30] each of which will be introduced by the motto, usually delivered in the key of the previous cadence.

Torelli's mottoes often preserve a dash of imitative counterpoint, even fugato; Albinoni's, however, are markedly similar to those in his operatic sinfonias — resolutely homophonic and rhythmically insistent. A comparison of the motto in the open-

---

[28] Because of this shift in emphasis, chamber concertos without orchestra — even a concerto for harpsichord alone like Bach's 'Italian Concerto', BWV 971 — ceased to be a contradiction in terms.

[29] The 'violino in tromba' appearing in three concertos acknowledges this stylistic indebtedness in exaggerated form.

[30] A period is to music what a sentence is to prose, cadences acting like marks of punctuation.

ing movement of the second concerto in his op. 2 with the opening bars of Vivaldi's op. 4 no. 2 (RV 279) reveals one aspect of the strong influence he exerted on the Vivaldi concerto in its formative stage.

Ex. 14

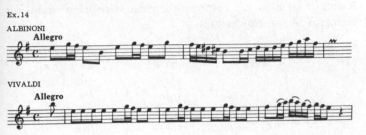

Display writing in these early concertos is generally sandwiched between the motto and the cadential phrase ending the period, and consists of thematically rather nondescript passage-work. Occasionally, as in three instances in Torelli's op. 6, these bars are entrusted to a solo violin or pair of violins, sometimes partnered by a solo cello. However, the use of solo players, often associated (as one would expect) with advanced technical requirements, affects the movement's form very little. It took a widening of the contrast between solo and tutti material to propel the form forward. In comparison, the Corellian type of concerto, where the alternation of *concertino* (ensemble of soloists, comprising two violins, cello and continuo) and *ripieno* (full ensemble) produced effects of light and shade but little contrast of material, was stagnant.

Torelli's later concertos begin the move towards segregating tutti and solo in separate, alternating periods, leaving Vivaldi to clinch the new form. The motto is expanded to become a period made up from a number of elements which is requotable in whole or part: the ritornello. The scoring is generally tutti throughout, and it is usual for the ritornello on any of its statements to begin and end in the same key. The connecting

141

periods or episode, which commonly lead to a new key, are dominated by the soloist and introduce new thematic material freely. The third movement of the *flautino* concerto RV 443/P.79 exemplifies these principles particularly well (the letters A to E in the column 'thematic derivation' stand for elements of the ritornello):

no. of bars	key centre	type of scoring	thematic derivation
$8\frac{1}{2}$	C	tutti	ABCDE
9	C — G	solo	free
6	G	tutti	ABCE
13	G — e	solo	free
3	e	tutti	DE
13	e — a	solo	free
5	a	tutti	ABE
$12\frac{1}{2}$	(a) — C	solo	free
$6\frac{1}{2}$	C	tutti	BCDE

In practice, this schema was adhered to far less rigidly by Vivaldi than many of his imitators. Some common ways in which it is modified can be instanced.

1. The first ritornello is preceded by an episode in the home key. This arrangement has great dramatic potential, for the soloist enters immediately and builds up towards the entrance of the tutti. Good examples occur in the opening movements of RV 249 and RV 204 (op. 4 nos. 8 and 11).

2. The second ritornello, like the first, is in the home key. This device is common in, though not restricted to, movements on a particularly grand scale.

3. The penultimate ritornello is in the home key. Inevitably, the episode which follows is centred on the tonic; Vivaldi often gives it the character of a cadenza (arpeggiation over a continuo pedal-point is a common feature here), or indicates an actual cadenza, as in the finale of RV 556/P.84, the

Concerto per la solennità di S. Lorenzo. Very often, the concluding ritornello begins exactly where its predecessor left off, producing the effect of a single ritornello interrupted midway by an episode.

4. Some of the ritornellos modulate. By thus absorbing one of the functions of the episode in the ritornello, Vivaldi is able, when the other function (solo-tutti contrast) is not required, to dispense with episodes altogether, as one sees in several of the concertos without soloist. Superficially, the result may seem like a reversion to the methods of Torelli and Albinoni; the difference is that Vivaldi brings back and develops all the elements of the ritornello, not just an initial motto.

Most of Vivaldi's movements in ritornello form go beyond the necessities of the form in unifying the diverse parts, though never as systematically and ingeniously as in Bach's concerto movements. Episodes are often punctuated by brief ritornello fragments, and the melodic substance of many episodes can be traced back to an element of the ritornello. One device taken over by Bach is to begin the first episode with a quotation, often ornamented, of the ritornello opening. Another is to lead off with a repetition of the ritornello's cadential phrase. The first and last episodes are often thematically linked, as in the first movement of the Concerto for Three Violins RV 551/P.278; this supplies a welcome element of reprise in the solo part. The internal organization of some ritornellos (one is speaking primarily of opening ritornellos, as later statements tend to be curtailed) reveals a desire to produce a well-rounded musical entity, almost a piece within a piece, whose own pattern of modulation may paraphrase in miniature that of the whole movement. As Vivaldi's opening phrases so often present the harmonic outline of a perfect cadence,[31] nothing could be more

---

[31] Walter Kolneder has coined the excellent term 'Kadenzmelodik' (cadential melody) to characterize this feature of Vivaldi's style.

natural than to recapitulate them, perhaps in condensed form, at the very end of the ritornello.

Ritornello form is the quasi-automatic choice for the first movement in a Vivaldi concerto. It is the most common choice for finales, and appears in a few slow movements, where it may be reduced to a simple frame around what would otherwise be a through-composed movement for the soloist, lightly accompanied.

Four alternatives to ritornello form are employed: fugue, unitary (or through-composed) form, binary form and variation form. Most of the fugues occur as fast movements in the concertos without soloist, but a few examples can be found in each of the other kinds of concerto. Where a soloist is employed, many of the episodes consist of conventional passage-work only tenuously related to the subject and countersubjects, a feature perhaps inherited from the fugal finales of Albinoni's op. 5 (1707). Unitary slow movements are of two main types: a series of modulating chords, or an arioso for the soloist. The first type, inherited from Torelli and Albinoni, serves to bridge the two fast movements (in its most condensed expression it appears in Bach's third 'Brandenburg' Concerto). The chords may be patterned in several ways: in flowing, quasi-vocal counterpoint replete with suspensions; in brief phrases, articulated by rests (during which the soloist may have bursts of lyricism, as in the second movement of op. 4 no. 9 (RV 284), hypnotic in its reiterative quality); in gently chugging quavers, like an accompaniment divested of its melody. The second type generally approximates to a binary movement without repeat signs. Binary movements, which include some finales, range from the brief and symmetrical to the extended and markedly asymmetrical. A movement such as the finale of RV 158/P.235 stands on the very threshold of sonata form. Vivaldi wrote few variation movements of sectional type (i.e. where there is a break between the end of one variation and the start of the next);

one example is the minuet finale to the oboe concerto RV 447/P.41. He was fond, however, of the continuous type over a ground bass discussed in the previous chapter.

The vast majority of the concertos retain the three-movement cycle popularized by Torelli and Albinoni, but a group of almost 30, by no means all early works, have an additional slow opening movement or slow introduction to the first fast movement. Several concertos in this group are linked through their titles with the Pietà (e.g. the two concertos for the feast of St Lawrence and the *Concerto funebre*); one can well imagine that Vivaldi hoped to add an extra touch of grandeur and solemnity by reverting to the four-movement cycle of the church sonata.

His choice of key for the 'interior' slow movement shows a rather unexpected distribution. Whereas most of his contemporaries favour the relative major or minor key, Vivaldi resorts to it rather infrequently; instead, he most often plumps for the key of the whole work, sometimes its parallel minor key. This bias to homotonality does not seem to be an echo of the *sonata da camera*; perhaps Vivaldi, like Haydn later, retained a single key centre to give the work a more uniform character. Other choices of key are the dominant, the subdominant and (in major-key works) the mediant minor. Where more distant relationships are found, they must often owe their origin to the borrowing of a slow movement from another work. Compared with Locatelli, who liked to place his slow movement in a 'mediant' relationship with the outer movements (e.g. B flat major, for a work in D major), he is almost conservative.

Approximately one in five of Vivaldi's known concertos was published during his lifetime. Discounting 13 concertos published individually or in unauthorized collections, 84 appeared at intervals between 1711 and 1729 in sets bearing an opus number. Of these 60 were for a single violin soloist, reflecting the dominance of this type in the published repertory. The distribution of other types shows the influence partly of changing fashion, partly of the circumstances in which each opus came into being.[32]

op. 3 (1711)	nos. 5 and 8 for two violins
12 works	nos. 2 and 11 for two violins and cello
	no. 4 for four violins
	nos. 1, 7 and 10 for four violins and cello
op. 4 (c 1714)	nos. 1, 4, 9 and 11 for two violins
12 works	no. 7 for two violins and cello
op. 6 (1716–17)	(all for one violin)
6 works	
op. 7 (1716–17)	nos. 1 and 7 (= libro II no. 1) for oboe
12 works	
op. 8 (1725)	nos. 9 and 12 optionally for oboe
12 works	
op. 9 (1727)	no. 9 for two solo violins
12 works	
op. 10 (c 1728)	all for transverse flute
6 works	
op. 11 (1729)	no. 6 for oboe
6 works	
op. 12 (1729)	no. 3 without soloist
6 works	

Through these nine collections we can gauge Vivaldi's development as a composer, allowing for the fact that several works, in their original versions, at least, must have been composed many years previously. Ryom has proposed, for instance, that the oboe concerto RV 460 (op. 11 no. 6) is an earlier version of the almost identical work (RV 334) published a few years before as op. 9 no. 3.[33] Opp. 3 and 4 show the

---

[32] In the concertos with additional solo instruments in opp. 4 and 9 only the first solo violin has its own partbook; the other solos are indicated by cues in the *ripieno* parts.

[33] 'Les catalogues thématiques et *La cetra*', *Vivaldi Informations,* vol. ii (1973), p. 47.

composer groping his way towards the definitive shape of the Vivaldian concerto, realized most perfectly in opp. 8 and 9. The other five collections are less homogeneous stylistically and less even in quality; this, and the fact that they were not dedicated to a patron, suggests that Vivaldi or his publisher put them together hurriedly with commercial considerations uppermost. Vivaldi's powers did not decline with advancing years, as the four works composed for the Saxon prince's visit in 1740 attest convincingly, but it cannot be denied that it became increasingly easy for him to repeat himself (often, as we have seen, quite literally). Only op. 8 (which includes *The Four Seasons*) recaptured the success of *L'estro armonico*. Quantz, who acknowledged that Vivaldi, together with Albinoni, had given the concerto a better form and had provided excellent models, seems to be using him as a stick with which to beat other Italian composers (particularly those concerned with opera, for whom he had little regard) when he writes: 'But finally, as a result of too much daily composing, and especially after he began to write operas, he sank into frivolity and caprice both in composition and performance, for which reason his last concertos earned less approval than his first.'[34]

Opp. 3 and 4 require separate discussion, not only because of their complex organization and stylistic indebtedness to other composers but also because they supplied the bulk of the concertos transcribed for keyboard by Bach. Op. 3 is an example of a composite set (like Torelli's op. 8 or Albinoni's opp. 2, 7 and 9) in which works of varying specification are grouped symmetrically. Discounting the solo cello, which appears irregularly, one finds the twelve concertos made up of four groups, each comprising in turn a work for four solo violins, one for two solo violins and one for a single violin. Four separate violin partbooks are provided. In the concertos for four violins no distinct *ripieno* parts exist, though orchestral doubling can be used in

[34] *Versuch*, p. 309.

passages marked 'tutti'. The third and fourth violins in those with two solo parts constitute the *ripieno*. In those with one soloist there are potentially three *ripieno* violin parts, though doubling reduces their number to two or even one (save in the slow movement of the sixth concerto). There are two viola partbooks, five concertos requiring divided violas at least part of the time. Venice was later than Rome or Bologna to accept one viola part rather than two as the norm; even so, *L'estro armonico* is one of the last published set of concertos to call for two violas.[35] One should not infer, as Kolneder does,[36] that when the viola partbooks contain an identical part (similarly with the violins) antiphonal performance was intended. The eight partbooks serve to accommodate the maximum number of independent parts; when fewer than the maximum are needed, any 'redundant' part simply doubles the most appropriate of the others.

La stravaganza, op. 4, is nominally a collection of solo concertos for violin, though five works echo op. 3 by co-opting additional (violin or cello) soloists.

What distinguishes these two *opera* from their successors is their spirit of experimentation (suggested by their very titles) on the one hand and their open reminiscences of Corelli, Torelli and Albinoni on the other. Except in some programmatic concertos, one does not see again such an assorted succession of movements, some very short, as in RV 565 (op. 3 no. 11): 1. Allegro (31 bars, soloists only). 2. Adagio (3 bars, tutti). 3. Allegro (70 bars, fugue). 4. Largo (20 bars, simple ritornello form). 5. Allegro (73 bars, ritornello form).

The most Corellian feature in them is the treatment of two solo violins and solo cello as a *concertino* group in dialogue with the tutti, most noticeably in the finale of RV 185 (op. 4 no. 7). Torelli's influence is seen in the rapid semiquaver passages for

---

[35] Vivaldi used divided violas again in the aria 'Siam navi all'onde algenti' in *L'Olimpiade* (II, 6).

[36] *Antonio Vivaldi: his Life and Work*, p. 97.

	BACH TRANSCRIPTION		VIVALDI ORIGINAL			
BWV	key	instrument(s)	RV	identification	key	solo instrument(s)
593	a	organ	522	op. 3 no. 8	a	2 violins
594	C	organ	208	variant of RV 208a (op. 7 no. 11)	D	1 violin
596	d	organ	565	op. 3 no. 10	d	2 violins and cello
972	D	harpsichord	230	op. 3 no. 9	D	1 violin
973	G	harpsichord	299	op. 7 no. 8	G	1 violin
975	g	harpsichord	316	variant of RV 316a (op. 4 no. 6)	g	1 violin
976	C	harpsichord	265	op. 3 no. 12	E	1 violin
978	F	harpsichord	310	op. 3 no. 3	G	1 violin
980	G	harpsichord	381	variant of RV 383a (op. 4 no. 1)	B♭	1 violin
1065	a	4 harpsichords and orchestra	580	op. 3 no. 10	b	4 violins and cello

two violins over pedal-notes (a kind of display writing known to contemporaries as *perfidia*). Albinoni is recalled in the sharply-etched rhythms, the fondness for unison violins and the use of a tutti motto in the opening movements of RV 383a and RV 347 (op. 4, nos. 1 and 5).

The ten concertos (six from op. 3) transcribed by Bach can be identified from the table on page 149.

Some of the changes introduced by Bach are ones which any imaginative or even merely competent transcriber would have made. In the harpsichord transcriptions (which lack the convenience of a pedal-board) middle parts are drawn closer to the outer parts or sacrificed altogether; intertwining parts are separated by octave transposition; long notes (many of which would have been ornamented extempore in the original medium) are broken down into shorter notes or embellished. But Bach goes beyond such alterations, adding or subtracting bars to produce a symmetry more characteristic of his own music than that of Vivaldi, and devising new counterpoints. It is instructive to compare the closing bars of the first movement of BWV 972 with the equivalent bars in an anonymous English transcription of the same concerto (RV 230) made around the same time.[37]

Ex. 15

ANON. c. 1715

(Allegro)

[37] This version is one of twelve transcriptions for harpsichord of works in Vivaldi's opp. 3 and 4 contained in *Anne Dawson's Book*, an anthology preserved in Manchester, Central Library, B.R.M710.5.CR71.

J.S.BACH c.1715
(Allegro)

It would be perverse not to concede that Bach's retouchings help to make the works come alive in their new medium and often improve the musical substance into the bargain. Nevertheless, a streak of pedantry sometimes makes Bach gild the lily. One can see why he chose to insert an extra note (ringed) in the second bar of the finale of RV 580. What Vivaldi wanted, however, was not a smooth downward progression from e' to a ($f\sharp'-b$ in the original) but a gap drawing attention to the symmetry between bars 1 and 2.

Ex. 16

Allegro

Most of Vivaldi's concertos published subsequently, as well as those remaining in manuscript, are for solo violin. No full discussion of the technical aspect of his writing for violin will be attempted here, but attention should be drawn to the importance of the open strings in his violin parts. In Vivaldi's day vibrato was a special effect, not a natural part of technique, so the difference in sound between an open and a stopped string was more one of power and resonance than of timbre. One is not surprised to find, therefore, that the favourite keys for virtuosic violin writing are those in which open strings can contribute to the chords most likely to require special emphasis: the tonic and dominant chords. In the solo violin concertos D major leads the

151

table of popularity with 33 appearances, while C major and B flat major each have 25. Multiple-stopped chords tend to include one or more open strings, not merely for their sound but because an open string releases fingers for employment on other strings. Another facility of open strings may be less familiar: as baroque violinists used no chin-rest, shifts of hand position were liable to produce a portamento, which could be avoided, however, if the shift took place after an open note.

Five concertos revive the obsolete technique of *scordatura*, a mis-tuning of the solo violin's strings whose main function is to make new combinations of notes possible in chords and *brisures* (rapidly-broken chordal figures). Violin *scordatura* had never been popular in Italy — its foremost exponents were Germans and Austrians, such as Biber and Strungk — and Vivaldi's espousal of it is a reminder (like some of the more exotic instruments played at the Pietà) of Venice's close ties with northern Europe. The mis-tuned strings are written for like transposing instruments, the player fingering as if the violin were normally tuned. In interpreting the first two bars of RV 391 (op. 9 no. 12) as reproduced in (a) below, we must remember that the *e″* string has been tuned down to *d″* and the *g* string up to *b*, giving a sound shown in (b).

Ex. 17

In a few concertos the solo violin is treated in other special ways. RV 221/P.179, RV 311/P.117 and RV 313/P.138 all feature a 'violino in tromba' (violin imitating a trumpet); RV 558/P. 16 calls for two 'violini in tromba marina', which simulate that instrument (a kind of bowed monochord played entirely in natural harmonics) by confining themselves in solo passages to notes consistent with a fundamental C'. In RV 243/P.310 the soloist forgoes the use of his 'cantin' (E string).

A handful of authentic cadenzas to Vivaldi's violin concertos (and others by Pisendel which may be based to a greater or lesser extent on the composer's originals) have been preserved. But for their length and the fact that they are entirely unaccompanied they are not very different from several concluding episodes in fast movements; they remain in the home key and do not refer obviously to the principal material of the movement.

The seven solo concertos (including one variant) for viola d'amore are very similar in style to the violin concertos.[38] Vivaldi's instrument has six bowed strings and most probably six sympathetic strings under the fingerboard. Normally, the strings are tuned to a chord of D minor (*d-a-d'-f'-a'-d''*), but for other keys *scordatura* (without effect on the notation) is indicated. Two concertos (RV 393/P.289 and RV 397/P.37) conceal in their title the name of the person for whom they were written, 'amore' (how appropriately, perhaps) being spelt 'AMore' with obvious reference to Anna Maria.

Vivaldi's cello concertos tower above those of his contemporaries (Leonardo Leo perhaps excepted) no less than his cello sonatas. Some, as we saw, are very early works; others seem to date from the 1720s, when the Pietà employed Vandini and Aliprandi as cello teachers. It is noticeable how the concertos for low instruments, bassoon as well as cello, favour a fuller, motivically more complex accompaniment than those for high

---

[38] The viola d'amore also appears as a solo instrument in the double concerto (with lute) RV 540/P.266, the chamber concerto RV 95/P.286, and individual arias in *Juditha triumphans*, *Nisi Dominus* RV 608 and the original version of *Tito Manlio*.

instruments. This feature is quite general in music of the period; one also finds it in arias for low voice.

The earliest concertos for wind instruments that Vivaldi is likely to have written are those for oboe. The Pietà appointed its first oboe master, Lodovico Erdmann (or Ortoman), in 1707. Erdmann left quite soon afterwards to serve the Grand Prince of Tuscany, however, and his replacement, Ignazio Siber, arrived only in 1713. In late 1716 he was succeeded by Onofrio Penati, a member of the St Mark's orchestra, who was reappointed annually until 1722. The fact that two out of these three names are German underlines the slowness of the instrument's assimilation into Italian music. The earliest published oboe concertos are those of Albinoni's op. 7 (1715), although it is probable that German composers such as Telemann and Handel had already written examples. Ostensibly, the two oboe concertos in Vivaldi's op. 7 are the earliest by him on which one can place an approximate date (1716–17). Their style, very reminiscent of Telemann, is so uncharacteristic of him, however, that their genuineness must be questioned. They are so much more concertos 'with' oboe, after Albinoni's manner, than concertos 'for' oboe, and segregate solo and tutti scoring much less rigorously than Vivaldi's other oboe concertos. Perhaps Roger, wishing to repeat the success of Albinoni's works, could not wait for the genuine articles to arrive.

This would leave op. 8 nos. 9 and 12 as the earliest of his oboe concertos to appear in print. Whereas Albinoni models his solo oboe parts on vocal writing, eschewing rapid leaps, Vivaldi takes his own style of writing for the violin as the basis of all his virtuosic woodwind parts, making some allowance for the player's need to draw breath and avoiding unobtainable or weak notes. Only the close spacing of the broken-chord figures in the next example (from the first movement of RV 463, a version for oboe of the bassoon concerto RV 500/P.89) and the thoughtful insertion of a rest suggest a part for oboe rather than violin.

Ex. 18

(Allegro)

It remains a mystery why Vivaldi wrote so many bassoon concertos (39, including two incomplete works), for there was no recent tradition of solo bassoon writing in Venice. One concerto (RV 502/P.382) is inscribed with the name of Giuseppe Biancardi, a local musician, and another (RV 496/P.381) with that of Count Morzin, but most were probably composed for the Pietà. Were a bassoon concerto even today less of a curiosity, they would be among the most highly prized of Vivaldi's works. In matters of style they relate to the oboe concertos rather as the cello concertos relate to those for violin. Just like his cello (but remarkably for a wind instrument), Vivaldi's bassoon often skips between the bass and tenor registers to produce the effect of a duet or dialogue. The passage in RV 500 (qouted above in its paraphrase for oboe) exemplifies this quirky style of writing very well.

Ex. 19

(Allegro)

Elsewhere, Vivaldi gives the bassoon dreamily lyrical passages that belie the instrument's reputation for jocularity.

The Ricordi edition advertises indiscriminately as flute concertos works which the sources show to be for two distinct instruments: *flauto* (alto recorder) and *flauto traversiere* (flute). The flute concertos proper are in a large majority (thirteen against two). Vivaldi probably did not write any before the late 1720s; Siber's reappointment at the Pietà as flute master dates from 1728, and Vivaldi's first known use of the flute in an opera occurs in *Orlando* (Autumn 1727). One would expect the works

155

for recorder to be earlier, for the flute rapidly ousted the recorder, first in France and later in Germany and Italy, rather as the piano superseded the harpsichord 50 years later. The recorder was certainly in use at the Pietà in 1706, when Penati was paid for repairs to four instruments.[39] Significantly, five of the six works comprising op. 10 are arrangements for flute and strings of earlier recorder concertos or chamber concertos including a recorder or flute. They contain the three programme works *La tempesta di mare* (RV 433, op. 10 no. 1), *La notte* (RV 439, op. 10. no. 2) and *Il gardellino* (RV 428, op. 10 no. 3), all originally chamber concertos. RV 434 (op. 10 no. 5) is the recorder concerto RV 442 with its slow movement transposed from F minor to G minor. This alteration was needed, as the flute, whose natural scale was that of D (the recorder's is F), could not play satisfactorily in the original key.[40]

The instrument called *flautino* required in three concertos can hardly be the piccolo (whose existence is not attested until the 1730s) or the flageolet, which Vivaldi terms *flasolet(to)* and uses in the aria 'Di due rai languire costante' from an unidentified opera;[41] instrumental compass and etymology identify it as the sopranino recorder playing an octave above notated pitch. Obbligato parts for *flautino* also occur in the operas *Tito Manlio* (1719) and *La verità in cimento* (1720). Vivaldi's parts for *flautino* are often quite fiendishly difficult, requiring the agility of a violinist rather than a wind player, and the rich musical substance of the concertos dispels any idea that he regarded this tiny instrument as an ear-tickling toy.

Most of Vivaldi's concertos with descriptive titles belong to

[39] Arnold, op. cit., p. 76f. The author has translated the word as 'flutes', but the transverse flute is out of the question at this early date.
[40] The Turin score of RV 442 contains Vivaldi's direction to a copyist to write the movement out a tone higher, perhaps in preparation for the work's publication as a flute concerto.
[41] Foà 28, ff. 104–6, 90–1.

the solo category. If one discounts immediately references in the titles to performers, patrons, occasions of performance and technical features, some 25 works, several existing in more than one version, are left. The titles often indicate no more than the general mood or style of the piece: thus 'rest' (*Il riposo*, RV 270/P.248) or 'pleasure' (*Il piacere*, RV 180, op. 8 no. 6). In concertos like *La caccia* (RV 362, op. 8 no. 10) or *Il gardellino* the description is lent concreteness by onomatopoeic touches in the music. Only seven concertos justify the label 'programmatic' by including a narrative element — slight in the three versions of the concerto *La tempesta di mare* with flute (not to be confused with a similarly-named violin concerto in op. 8) and the two different concertos, for flute (RV 439/P.342 and the earlier RV 104) and bassoon (RV 501/P.401) respectively, entitled *La notte*, but well worked out in *Le quattro stagioni*, assisted by their descriptive sonnets.

Programme music, whose history stretches back to the middle ages, was less popular in eighteenth-century Italy than in France, where the view of Art as an imitation of Nature was taken more literally. Nature was still man-centred, however; not the least modern aspect of *The Four Seasons* is their subordination of human activity to the uncontrollable play of the natural elements. The uninhibited and sometimes remarkably original way in which Vivaldi depicts situations permits use of the epithet 'romantic', both as a statement of general musical outlook and as a reminder that these four concertos inaugurated a tradition which continued right through to the nineteenth century. Works standing wittingly or otherwise in the line of descent from them include Telemann's secular cantata *Die Tageszeiten* (1759), Haydn's symphonic trilogy *Le matin — Le midi — Le soir* (1761) and, naturally, his oratorio *The Seasons* (1800), Beethoven's *Pastoral Symphony* (1808), and even Berlioz's *Symphonie fantastique* (1830).

Vivaldi solves the problem of combining programmatic content with ritornello form in a manner both simple and satisfying. The underlying mood of the movement is captured by the ritornello, while successive events are portrayed in individual episodes. In the opening movement of the Spring concerto the ritornello, a heavy-footed dance, represents joy at the advent of Spring — 'Giunt'è la primavera'. The remainder of the two quatrains is parcelled out among the four episodes as follows:

1. '. . . and joyfully the birds greet her [Spring] with merry song.' Vivaldi's avian chorus, based entirely on the tonic chord (E major), employs three solo violins, the orchestral parts being reduced to a single player.

2. 'While the brooks, fanned by gentle breezes [Zephyrs], murmur sweetly as they course along.' Slurred pairs of conjunct semiquavers in thirds conjure up the rippling brooks, similar motion in minims the wafting breeze.

'Thunder and lightning, chosen to proclaim her, envelop the air in a black shroud.' Bowed tremolos depict the thunder, rapid ascending scales and flashing arpeggios the lightning.

3. 'The birds, having meanwhile fallen silent, resume their melodious singing.' Vivaldi begins with a motive often found in his works in association with sleep and then reproduces in subdued form some of the bird motives.

4. An uncaptioned episode, in which the chirruping of a bird is nevertheless audible.

In slow movements, whose smaller dimensions almost preclude the narrative element, Vivaldi is content with a tableau-like depiction of a scene, of which different constituents may be represented by different layers of texture. In the Winter concerto, for example, the soloist and lower strings paint a picture of fireside comfort, while the violins supply the raindrops outside.

The special case of opp. 3 and 4 apart, Vivaldi's double concertos, whether for like or unlike instruments, are closely related in form and style to his solo concertos. The manner of interaction of the soloists is very varied: at one extreme, they may perform more in dialogue than as a pair, one instrument repeating immediately whatever the other plays; at the other, they may move in endless chains of thirds as if unable to escape from one another. Both devices become tiresome through over-use, and Vivaldi's record is not spotless in this regard. Against this, one is glad to find in several works, particularly those for two solo violins, a contrapuntal interplay worthy of his best trio sonatas.

The double concertos for like instruments comprise 25 for violins, three for oboes, two for horns and one each for cellos, mandolins, flutes and trumpets. Those for unlike soloists include four (RV 541/P.311, RV 542/P.274, RV 766 and RV 767) for violin and organ and two for violin and oboe (RV 548/P.406 and RV 543/P.301); the last work is curious in having the soloists in unison throughout. RV 544/P.308 and RV 547/P.388 combine violin and cello most effectively. Vivaldi later redesignated RV 544 for solo *viole all'inglese* of equivalent sizes, making no alteration to the actual notes in either the solo or *pipieno* parts. The *viola all'inglese* appears in four other Vivaldi works: the ensemble concertos RV 555/P.87 and RV 579/P.385 (*Concerto funebre*), the oratorio *Juditha triumphans* (1716), where a five-part 'concerto' (consort) accompanies the heroine's prayer and subsequent aria, and the opera *L'incoronazione di Dario* (1717), where the bass member of the family has a difficult obbligato part in Statira's 'Cantata in scena' in Act I. Besides the sizes corresponding to the violin and the cello the *viola all'inglese* has a middle size, identifiable as the 'englisches Violett' mentioned by Leopold Mozart in his famous treatise. From Mozart's description and the very few surviving instruments[42] one learns that the *viola all'inglese* broadly resembled the viola d'amore, but had two or three times the number of sympathetic strings. One can establish from the layout of the chords in the *Dario* obbligato that the instrument used there had six strings tuned *D-G-c-e-a-d'*.

The catch-all phrase 'ensemble concerto' is a convenient way of referring to Vivaldi's numerous concertos for single orchestra with more than two solo instruments. It includes concertos for three and four violins, which reveal few features not already present in the double violin concertos, as well as works for a large, heterogeneous ensemble, which Vivaldi, lacking the patience or space to list the names of all the instruments in the title, liked to call 'concerto con molti istromenti'. At least two of the latter (RV 576/P.359 and RV 577/P.383) were supplied to the Dresden orchestra, as befitted its large complement of wind instruments, but most were clearly destined for the Pietà. If, as the English traveller Edward Wright averred,[43] its female performers were hidden from public view by a lattice, the revelation in brief solo passages of one rare specimen after another from the Pietà's menagerie of instruments must have both surprised and delighted the audience. Like animals in the Ark, these instruments, which include mandolins, theorboes, chalumeaux, clarinets and *tromboni da caccia*, usually come in

---

[42] Anthony Baines, *European and American Musical Instruments* (London, 1966) describes and provides illustrations of *viole all'inglese* dated 1712 and 1737 in the Nationalmuseum, Nuremberg, and the Royal College of Music, London. From Pincherle onwards, many writers have identified Vivaldi's 'English viol' with the family of viols proper, which enjoyed a late florescence in seventeenth-century England; but the English connexion can be explained just as well by the presence of sympathetic strings, whose introduction (in the lyra-viol) has been credited to the English.

[43] *Some observations made in travelling through France, Italy . . . in 1720–1722*, vol. i (London, 1730), p. 79.

pairs. Vivaldi makes no pretence of equality between his soloists, a violin or pair of violins often taking the lion's share of solo
material. Sometimes, solo instruments are featured in certain
movements only, like the lute in the slow movement of the
original version of RV 556/P.84 and the two trumpets in the
finale of RV 555/P.87.

Although the chalumeau was known in Italy — F. Bonanni
includes it in his *Gabinetto armonico* of 1722 — the five works by
Vivaldi in which it appears (three concertos, one sonata and
Juditha triumphans) are the only ones so far discovered south of
the Alps. Elder cousin (or perhaps parent) of the clarinet, the
chalumeau first appeared towards 1700 in France or Germany as
a more powerful type of recorder in which the usual mouthpiece
was replaced by one housing a single reed on top.[44] The instrument could not overblow, but one or two keys located between
the row of seven holes and the mouthpiece extended its compass
by a few notes. Although its tone was reputed harsh, the
chalumeau, built like the recorder in various sizes, achieved a
degree of popularity as a 'pastoral' instrument in Germany and
Austria during the first half of the eighteenth century; it appears
in instrumental works, including some concertos, by J. L.
Bach, Fasch, Graupner, Hasse, Molter and Telemann, and
operas by Ariosti, Bononcini, Fux, Keiser and even Gluck (*Orfeo*
and *Alceste*). Handel's *Riccardo primo* (London, 1727) contains an
aria with parts for two soprano chalumeaux. Vivaldi calls the
instrument 'salmòe' or 'salmò' (a more orthodox Italian form is
'*scialmò*', as used by the Viennese composer Bonno). He employs
the smallest (soprano) size in Judith's aria 'Veni, veni me

---

[44] On the chalumeau see especially Heinz Becker, 'Das Chalumeau
im 18. Jahrhundert', ed. H. Becker and R. Gerlach, *Speculum musicae
artis. Festgabe für Heinrich Husmann* (Munich, 1970), pp. 23–46. In the
light of recent research it is surprising that the hypothesis, first stated
by Pincherle, that the *salmoè* was some kind of obsolete double-reed
instrument continues to be widely believed.

Vivaldi

sequere' (in which the cooing of a turtle-dove is evoked), confining the solo part to the notes between a' and bb'', which suggests an available compass f'-bb''. As tenor instrument, pitched an octave lower, is used in the *Concerto funebre*. In both cases the instrument is muted. Tenor chalumeaux in C (compass g-c'') are required in RV 555/P.87, RV 558/P.16 and the Dresden quartet sonata. Vivaldi writes tenor chalumeau parts an octave lower in the bass clef, quite appropriately, as the instrument often has to supply a *bassetto* or double the bass line an octave higher.

He uses clarinets in C in three concertos (RV 556/P.84, RV 559/P.74 and RV 560/P.73), partnering them with two oboes; and in RV 556 with two recorders, two violins and bassoon in addition. The simple two-keyed clarinet is treated almost as two instruments in one, the first corresponding to the register of fundamentals (f-f') and the second to that of twelfths (c'-c'''), the 'open' note g' being common to both. As the clarinet had yet to acquire its long B key, producing e and b', the two registers are separated by a gap which coincides with that between the sixth and eighth harmonics (the seventh, lying outside the diatonic scale, is unusable) of the natural trumpet.

Vivaldi shows a prescient awareness of the aptness of the low 'chalumeau' register for eerie or lugubrius effects, as the following passage from the first movement of RV 560, with its typical minor inflexions, demonstrates:

Ex. 20

Much of the writing for the clarinet in its higher register is stylistically indistinguishable from that of the trumpet in its 'clarino' register, a resemblance which the bold, strident tone of early instruments must have heightened. The following passage from the same movement is a good specimen:

Ex. 21

This identity of style (restricted, of course, to the range g'-c''') induced some scholars to believe that the instruments Vivaldi called not only 'clarinet(ti)' (in RV 559 and 560) but also 'claren(i)' (in RV 556 and also in *Juditha triumphans*, where two instruments in B flat play in unison) and even 'clarini' (in the slow movement of RV 556) were in fact really trumpets.[45] It must be remembered, however, that it was Germans, not Italians, who used the term 'clarino' to refer to an instrument (trumpet) as well as a specific register; also that Bonanni's name for the clarinet is 'clarone'. The appearance of clarinets in *Juditha* (1716) is the earliest known instance of the instrument's orchestral use.

The identity of the two *tromboni da caccia* in RV 574/P.319 (and also in two numbers in *Orlando finto pazzo*) remains elusive. Nothing in the notation (in the treble clef, an octave above sounding pitch), the notes employed or the general style is uncharacteristic of *corni da caccia* in F; these 'hunting trombones' must be close relatives of the horn, if not the same instrument.

Five concertos (one incomplete) requiring double orchestra have survived. Three attach a solo violin to the first orchestra, while the other two are laid out symmetrically with an identical group of soloists for each 'coro'. All were probably intended for the Pietà's chapel services, two being inscribed 'per la santissima assontione di Maria Vergine' (RV 581–2/P.14 (Turin version) and 164). The remarks in the next chapter on Vivaldi's vocal works 'in due cori', which were presumably performed at the same services, largely apply to these concertos.

[45] The most lengthily argued presentation of this case occurs in Walter Lebermann, 'Zur Besetzungsfrage der Concerti grossi von A. Vivaldi', *Die Musikforschung,* Jg. vii (1954), pp. 337–9.

The chamber concertos, written for three to six instruments and continuo, number 22. Several are for wind instruments only; in fact the only example not to include at least one wind instrument is the lute concerto RV 93/P.209 (discounting possible substitutions of wind by stringed instruments indicated by the composer in some scores). The instruments usually appear individually, but in a few cases paired instruments — violins, oboes or horns — are featured. The bassoon is required in 16 concertos, the flute and oboe each in 12 and the recorder in nine.

All are apparently mature works, but the purpose for which they were written remains obscure. Their conception is unique for Italy, though similar works, of which Bach's Third and Sixth 'Brandenburg' Concertos are elaborate but valid examples, were composed by a number of German and French composers, who often termed them 'sonatas', obviously thinking more of the medium than the musical forms employed.

In a chamber concerto all the parts (except the continuo, which doubles the lowest instrument) are obbligato, playing in unison only for special effect. In some instances the distinction between ritornello and episode is not reflected in the pattern of the scoring, which varies independently, so that tonal and thematic criteria alone establish the formal outlines — this occurs in RV 107/P.360, for flute, oboe, violin and bassoon. Elsewhere the texture lightens in the episodes as one or more instruments drop out, leaving behind a 'soloist'. The choice of such a soloist may vary between episodes or even within a single episode, but in many cases the same solo instrument appears during a movement, even a work. A disguised solo concerto of this type is RV 106/P.404, where the flute is partnered by violin and bassoon.

The most admirable qualities of Vivaldi's chamber concertos, scarcity value apart, are their exquisite tone colour and feeling for the natural idiom of each instrument. They are closer to the modern spirit of chamber music than any other of his works.

Vivaldi's 44 concertos without soloist for four-part strings and continuo (the ones Pincherle so aptly describes as being 'in symphonic style') show him in his best light as a composer pure and simple, freed of the necessity to engage in display for its own sake. The distinction between these *concerti a quattro* (in three works he employs the designation 'concerto ripieno' — concerto for orchestra) and operatic or operatic-style sinfonias is one of stylistic and formal tendency rather than something clear-cut. We thus find certain works, whose allegiance to one *genre* rather than the other is not pronounced, used *in toto* (and even more often in part) in both guises, or at any rate under both titles; RV 134/P.127, originally entitled 'Concerto' in the composer's autograph manuscript, later received the additional, presumably substitute, title 'Sinfonia'. The concerto RV 117/P.64 also appears, with another slow movement, as the sinfonia to *La sena festeggiante*.

Typically, sinfonias are written in a homophonic, treble-dominated style, for which the violins are often in unison. The opening movement, traditionally by far the longest, tends to aim at sheer weight of sound (perhaps needed to silence a chattering audience) with multiple-stopped chords, *brisures* and prominent open strings, as illustrated by the beginning of RV 116.

Ex. 22

The slow movement is customarily in cantabile style, while the binary finale, a mayfly of a movement, leads a merry but brief dance. Major tonality is greatly preferred.

The concertos are written in a severer, often contrapuntal vein, where one violin part is often set off against the other through imitation or dialogue. Their slow movements are more varied in type, and the disparity in length and weightiness between the outer movements is less marked, even absent. A normal incidence of minor tonality is found. An opening movement such as the one in RV 157/P.361, constructed over a ground bass, would be inconceivable in a sinfonia, as it lacks the vital ingredient of panache.

It is strange that only one of these 'symphonic' concertos — RV 124 (op. 12 no. 3)— was published in Vivaldi's lifetime, when so many less distinguished examples by Albinoni and Alberti were printed and reprinted. In statistical terms, *concerti a quattro* fared badly beside solo concertos almost everywhere. De Brosses, hearing some in Venice in 1739, thought them uniquely appropriate for concerts in small gardens and regretted the ignorance of them in France.[46] Perhaps the manuscript set of twelve such concertos by Vivaldi preserved in the Paris Conservatoire Library represents De Brosses's attempt to repair the omission.

The foregoing survey of Vivaldi's concertos has neglected to discuss in as great detail as many earlier studies the extent of their influence on the course of development of the concerto and the nascent pre-classical style. One problem is that after those crucial years in the second decade of the eighteenth century when the imitation of *L'estro armonico* was almost *de rigueur* among German and Italian composers, it becomes hard to distinguish between the continuing personal influence of Vivaldi and that retransmitted and often refracted by his disciples. By the third decade one encounters concerto composers like Locatelli and Tartini whose music is both stylistically and formally in advance of Vivaldi's in many respects. Vivaldi is henceforth their beneficiary as well as one-time mentor. (Albinoni's relation to Vivaldi shows the same reversal of rôles.) Where Vivaldi continued longest to be a vital influence on his

[46] Op. cit., p. 194f.

contemporaries was perhaps in matters of instrumental technique and nuances of performance. His importance for the history of orchestration may have been exaggerated. In his search for novelty he introduced dozens of incidental innovations, but it was not his intention to consolidate them into a distinct practice which others could imitate. Taken as a whole, however, Vivaldi's achievement in the concerto is as remarkable as that of Monteverdi in opera or Haydn in the symphony.

7 The vocal music

'Vivaldi, who wanted to be active in both fields [vocal and instrumental], always got himself hissed in the first, though he enjoyed great success in the second.' Thus Tartini, arguing his case that vocal and instrumental composition, being so different in character, could not be mastered equally by one man.[1] This opinion, which smacks of sour grapes, is belied not only by the facts of Vivaldi's career but by remarks of other contemporaries, notably Mattheson, who, having observed that vocal writing does not tolerate the leaps found in instrumental writing, states: 'Vivaldi, albeit no singer, has had the sense to keep violin-leaps out of his vocal compositions so completely that his arias have become a thorn in the flesh to many an experienced vocal composer.'[2]

The sheer mass of Vivaldi's vocal music, sacred as well as secular, would not disgrace a composer who never wrote a note of instrumental music: over 45 operas, of which 16 survive in their entirety and four (including Vivaldi's contribution to *Il Tigrane*) in sufficiently complete form to merit analysis; eight shorter stage works (three extant); 39 cantatas; over 60 sacred works, including three oratorios (one extant).

Although the knowledge of Latin and of Catholic ritual acquired during ten years of training for the priesthood must have served Vivaldi well in his sacred works, he cannot have found much time — nor can his humble origins have afforded

[1] As reported in Brosses, op. cit., vol. ii, p. 316.
[2] *Der vollkommene Capellmeister* (Hamburg, 1739), p. 205.

him much opportunity — to gain more than a rudimentary acquaintance with vernacular literature and the classical tradition by which it was still so heavily influenced. One must remember, of course, that true literary connoisseurs like the Marcello brothers were a minority among composers. From Vivaldi's original drafts we can see how often a hasty or superficial reading of a text to be set led him into error. For example, the first (1727) version of *Farnace* misreads 'schiva' (shy) as 'schiava' (slavish) — (the object of reference being an aloof princess — and a few lines later turns the 'essa' (it) of the libretto into a syntactically inexplicable 'esca' (goes out).[3] In the score of *Orlando,* where the text in the recitatives corresponds not to the 1727 libretto but to that published in 1714 for Ristori's setting, Vivaldi betrays his unfamiliarity with French at the point when the delirious paladin begins to speak in that language.[4] Through a typographical error the earlier libretto appears to split the oath 'ventrebleu' into two words: *ventreb leu.* In his innocence, Vivaldi follows suit.

Literary novice though he was, Vivaldi did not lack confidence. The operatic scores abound in petty alterations to the text in his own hand. Since these revisions are often so inconsistent — they may be lacking, for example, when a portion of text is repeated — they can hardly all have been introduced at the bidding of a literary collaborator. One case establishes beyond doubt that he was capable of writing serviceable, if trite, verse. The central recitative in *Nel partir da te, mio caro,* a solo cantata for soprano, achieved its final form only at the fourth attempt. In his first two attempts Vivaldi gave up after sketching the notes of the vocal line up to the third bar and taking the text only as far as the third word. Five bars were completed in his

---

[3] Act II, Scene 2, lines 2 and 9. In the later (1739) version of *Farnace* Vivaldi corrects the first error.

[4] Act III, Scene 5. The 1727 libretto paraphrases the French passages in Italian.

third attempt. By now, he must have become dissatisfied with
the words, for the final, successful version has a new text,
paraphrasing the old, which only he can have supplied.

Original text
Parto, sì parto lungi da te, mio bene,
Ma in pegno del mio amor ti lascio il core.
Tradiscilo, ti priego,
Perch'un dì lo gradisti
. . . .[5]

New text
Parto, mio ben, da te, io parto, addio,
Ma il cor qui resta in ossequioso pegno.
Di gradirlo ti priego,
E all'afflitto mio core
Donali in premio almeno un dolce amore.[6]

These texts are written in the form known as *versi sciolti*, in
which lines of seven and eleven syllables are mingled freely and
rhyming is usually confined to a final couplet. Such verse was
standard in recitatives, the length of line corresponding excellently to the length of phrase a singer could sustain in a single
breath. The twelve-syllable opening line of the original text
(presumably also by Vivaldi) is a blemish not entirely removed
in the new version, where, although the syllable-count is now
correct, the flow is very halting (note the clumsy hiatus between
'te' and 'io'). But perhaps one should not expect a composer to be
too scrupulous about prosody; like many of his colleagues,
Vivaldi often chose to ignore elisions essential to the poetic
rhythm but irrelevant, even awkward, in a musical setting.

[5] 'I am going, yes, I am going far from you, my sweetheart; but I am
leaving you my heart as a pledge of my love. Deceive (?) it, I beg you,
for once you welcomed it . . .'
[6] 'I am going, my sweetheart, from you; I am going, farewell! But my
heart is remaining here as a humble pledge. Accept it, I beg you, and
deign to reward my suffering heart with sweet affection.'

In regard to accent and length his word-setting is generally irreproachable. When writing in declamatory style, either block-chordally as in the outer movements of the *Credo* RV 591 or imitatively as in the 'Sicut erat in principio' concluding *Lauda Jerusalem*, he often achieves that compromise between fidelity to the spoken word and imaginative artificiality that results in true memorability. Like Handel, he uses dotted rhythms to impart zest and lend emphasis. It would be unfair to judge the melismatic style of his arias by the same standards, for the extension of one syllable over several bars is an artificiality so blatant as to mask most other deviations from the natural, but he selects the syllables so treated intelligently, with due regard to their vowel quality. The following example, from Emilia's aria 'Come invano il mare irato' (As in vain the angry sea) (*Catone in Utica*. II, 14), illustrates the exuberance of his bravura writing in the later operas. Vivaldi does not take Mattheson's advice so literally as to spurn all leaps, but such as occur are eminently singable.

Ex. 23

Instances of bad word-setting are most numerous in *contrafacta*, old pieces furnished with new texts. Even in lines with the same number of syllables, variations in the stress pattern and a different placing of diphthongs, hiatuses and elisions can have adverse effects. The great quartet 'Anima del cor mio' from *La Candace* (II,9) begins with a phrase which accommodates the diphthong in 'mio' very happily with a feminine cadence. Later in the same year (1720) Vivaldi adapted the movement as a quintet in *La verità in cimento* (II,9), where its first line is amended to read 'Anima mia, mio ben'. The feminine cadence on 'ben' sounds unnatural, especially as the syllable is closed. Minor infelicities of this kind were more or less inherent in the technique of *contrafactum*; we find them, too, in the music of Bach and Handel.

Vivaldi's ability as a word-painter is unrivalled for his period. It is remarkable how pictorial significance can permeate the whole of the texture, bringing simple accompanimental figures into relief. The obsessional quality of Vivaldi's natural musical thought, which can, in extreme cases, sustain a single idea for the duration of the entire movement, helps to establish a basic 'affection' (*affetto*) for the movement; supplementary motives and figures suggested by individual words and phrases of the text increase the richness of allusion. No finer example can be found than Tito's aria 'Se il cor guerriero' in *Tito Manlio* (I,2). The rhythmic ostinato ♩♩ ♩ ♩, usually on a monotone, sets the warlike mood in a manner reminiscent of Monteverdi's *stile concitato* as featured in *Il combattimento di Tancredi e Clorinda*. Abrasive, tardily resolving dissonances evoke the clash of arms in the A section, while in the B section rushing semiquavers on the violins accompany Tito's stern command to his son: 'Flee the tumult of battle'.

The allusive significance of a motive is usually clear from the words with which it is initially heard. Once announced, the motive tends to be developed autonomously, almost as in a purely instrumental composition. When the motives appear in contrapuntal combination, there is little risk of inappropriateness, since one or other of them is likely to be relevant to the

Ex. 24

(a) (**Allegro**)

Se il cor guer - rie - ro T'in - vi - ta al - - l'ar - mi, t'in - vi - ta al - l'ar - mi,

Strings   vla.   vn.2   vn.1

(b)

Sfug - gi il ci - men - to Del - la bat - ta - glia,

words as they occur and recur. This is the case in Holophernes's aria 'Agitata infido flatu' in *Juditha triumphans*, which describes a swallow's flight to its nest, buffeted by stormy winds. Three important motives, mostly heard simultaneously, occur in the voice and the upper instrumental parts (the bass underscores the restlessness with pounding quavers and some tortuous inter-

173

vals): a chromatically descending line in semibreves or minimims expressive of the soughing of the wind; a semiquaver figure representing the flapping of the swallow's wings; a jagged figure in dotted rhythm evocative of weeping.

Ex. 25

This is in essence the 'tableau' manner of representation as found in the slow movements of programme concertos. Where the style is more homophonic, however, and the motives appear one by one, Vivaldi sometimes cannot — or will not — maintain the strict correspondence of word and motive observed at the outset. His setting of Metastasio's famous comparison aria 'Qual destrier ch'al albergo è vicino' (*L'Olimpiade*, I,3) bears this criticism out. In the A section Vivaldi illustrates the whinnying of a stallion with trilled appoggiaturas, and the commanding voice of his rider with a high-pitched monotone in even crotchets.

174

These onomatopoeic touches recur in the B section, where their presence, justifiable on purely musical grounds, is no longer textually apposite, since Metastasio has abandoned the simile of a headstrong horse to describe the object of comparison: a man intoxicated by the vision of his impending happiness. To regard the motives as a subtle reminiscence-cum-anticipation of the A section would be mistaken. Impulsive rather than reflective, Vivaldi was apt to let such a movement take its own course once he had set it on its path— a slightly risky prescription for vocal composition.

THE CANTATAS

After opera, the cantata was the most important new vocal form forged in the early Italian Baroque. It is generally conceived as a monologue (the singer sometimes also acting as narrator), less often as a dialogue. With rare exceptions, the Italian cantata, unlike the Lutheran church cantata, is a setting of secular verse in the vernacular. The most modestly scored type, that for solo voice and bass (realizable on harpsichord or cello, or the two combined), was by far the most popular, rivalling the solo sonata in the number of works composed if not in depth of social penetration. Alessandro Scarlatti and Benedetto Marcello, the two most accomplished composers of cantatas contemporary with Vivaldi, each produced hundreds. The currents of reform associated with the Arcadian Academy in Rome, whose purifying and disciplining effect on opera cannot be denied, restricted the scope and imagery of the cantata to a stultifying degree. The setting is invariably Arcady, peopled by lovelorn shepherds and fickle nymphs (the epithets are reversible), with whose vulnerable hearts Cupid plays havoc. Invariable, too, the form of the poem: alternating strophes of *versi sciolti* (generally set as recitative, though a few lines may receive arioso or fugato treatment) and rhymed verse for the arias. *Da capo* form— as much a poetic device as a musical one— is normally prescribed for the latter.

The main sources for Vivaldi's cantatas are two volumes (nos. 27 and 28) in the Foà collection, though a few are preserved elsewhere. Twenty-two of the solo cantatas are for soprano, eight for alto, a ratio quite normal for the time. The absence of 'natural' male voices is not surprising: works for high voice, which could be sung either by women or castrati (the sex of the character portrayed by the singer was not a restricting factor), had greater versatility; also, it is uncommon for arias, whether in cantata or opera, to be written for a low voice unless there is an instrument in an upper register to act as a foil. On his scores, some of which are very rough drafts, Vivaldi left several instructions for transposition or change of clef. Such directions, often misunderstood when occurring in the instrumental works as afterthoughts or corrections, enabled a pre-existing score to be used as a copyist's exemplar when a work (or individual movement) was arranged to suit new circumstances. Several works contain more than one 'generation' of instructions, testifying to their popularity either with the composer or his customer. The cantatas with instrumental accompaniment comprise five for soprano and four for alto.

Vivaldi is at his least original in terms of form when working in the cantata *genre*. It is interesting, however, that whereas most contemporaries, including Albinoni, whose 40-odd solo cantatas offer the closest comparison with Vivaldi's, preferred a four-movement cycle (recitative — aria — recitative — aria) related in scale and the pattern of movements to the traditional church sonata, Vivaldi shows a slight preference for a three-movement cycle (aria— recitative— aria) after the fashion of his concertos. The older plan possesses an advantage in that the first of the arias, being enclosed within the work, can be in a new key, but Vivaldi guards intelligently against the danger of making the second aria too much like the first, varying the rhythmic character and the pattern of modulation.

The structure of the *da capo* aria, which varies very little, can be summarized thus:

1. Introductory ritornello.
2. First vocal period, modulating to the dominant or alternative key.
3. Ritornello in the new key (vestigial in solo cantatas).
4. Second vocal period, leading back to the home key. Sometimes capped by a coda.
5. Reprise of introductory ritornello, often abridged.
6. One or two vocal periods cadencing in new keys.
7–11. Recapitulation of 1 to 5, ornamented *ad libitum*.

The ritornello, no doubt often added after completion of the vocal portion, may either paraphrase the opening of the vocal melody or (particularly in works where the bass has a strongly instrumental character and uses ostinato figuration) its accompaniment. That the A section (1–5) is so much longer than the B section (6) is due, first, to the presence of ritornellos and, second, to the twofold presentation of the text, once in each vocal period. The most extended melismas are usually reserved for the second vocal period, an appropriate point for the climax.

Like Albinoni and other Venetians, Vivaldi tends to differentiate the idoms of the voice and the bass sharply; the first is sinuous and flowing, the second jagged and assembled from short motives. He is less of a natural tunesmith than Albinoni, but the rhythmic invention and frequently highly virtuosic conception of his cantatas amply compensate. His recitative, though lacking in the more extreme dramatic effects found here and there in the operas, is subtle and imaginative, especially in flights of arioso.

Two of the instrumentally-accompanied cantatas, *All'ombra di sospetto,* with flute, and *Lungi dal vago,* with violin, require a single obbligato partner; the remainder, operatic in style if not in spirit, call for a full complement of strings (*Qual in pioggia dorata* for two horns in addition). Vivaldi handles his obbligato instruments with great sensitivity and discretion, never forgetting that outside the ritornellos the voice must reign supreme. Of the orchestral cantatas *Amor, hai vinto* should be singled out for the contrapuntal complexity of its first aria.

The popularity of Vivaldi's cantatas will depend on that of the *genre* as a whole, which, being more limited by period than its instrumental equivalent, the violin sonata, has so far failed to establish itself strongly in the concert repertory. Given the opportunity to hear the best of them, many listeners will concur with the opinion of Charles Burney (a severe critic of the instrumental music) that 'D. Antonio Vivaldi merits a place among the candidates for fame in this species of composition'.[7]

THE SERENATAS

Giovan Maria Crescimbeni, historian of the Arcadians, explained the meaning of *serenata* thus: 'Nowadays, cantatas of this sort [i.e. as opposed to other poetic *genres*], when performed before an audience, are customarily put on at night, and are called *serenate*.'[8] He might have added that most serenatas have solo rôles for between three and six singers, and a few include a chorus. It remains unclear whether serenatas were normally performed in costume on a stage (Crescimbeni implies this in speaking of the 'consummate magnificence and splendour' of certain productions), but they can easily be distinguished from operas proper by their compact dimensions, division into two 'parts' (without subdivisions corresponding to the operatic scene) and subject-matter. As in a masque or an operatic prologue, the *dramatis personae* of a serenata are allegorical, gods or stock figures from Arcady, whose sole purpose is to unite in praise of the potentate to whom the work is addressed.

[7] *A General History of Music*, vol. iv (London, 1789), p. 178.
[8] *Dell'istoria della volgar poesia*, vol. i (Venice, 1731), p. 300.

A serenata unites the lyricism of a cantata with the resources of opera.

Of Vivaldi's three preserved serenatas by far the most interesting, as well as the longest, is *La Sena festeggiante*, whose circumstances of composition have been discussed earlier.[9] It has three characters: La Sena (the Seine — bass), L'Età dell'ora (the Golden Age— soprano) and La Virtù (virtue— alto). If the optional tenor part is included in the final ensemble (borrowed from *Giustino*), it would be logical to use a chorus (Vivaldi's description 'Coro' is ambiguous, as the word can apply to any ensemble, including one comprising merely the soloists). In the first part there are 21 numbers, headed by a *Sinfonia*; in the second, 15 numbers, headed by an *Ouverture*. The distribution of movement types is unexpected: seven simple recitatives against ten *accompagnati*; three duets and three terzetts ('cori') against eleven solo arias. These statistics, which reveal an unusually high incidence of 'complex' settings (*accompagnato*, ensemble numbers), hint at a quality fully realized in the music. In many movements Vivaldi captures the wistful tenderness at the heart of 'le goût français', as in Età's aria 'Al mio seno il pargoletto' (no. 14). The direction 'alla francese' refers not so much to the minuet character as to the dotted rhythms, which should be exaggerated where appropriate.

Ex. 26

Largo alla francese

ings

[9] See p. 73f.

179

Of all Vivaldi's large-scale secular vocal works *La Sena festeggiante* is the most varied and most carefully wrought. As it is also the one most likely to appeal at a purely musical level, it deserves to join works like Handel's *Alexander's Feast* in the modern repertory.

THE OPERAS

In Vivaldi's day Italian opera was less an amalgam of its various components — music, literature, acting, dancing, scenery and machinery — than a loose conjunction where smooth co-ordination was rendered possible only by the adherence of each to universally-recognized conventions. The autonomy of the principal contributors, the composer and the librettist, was respected, so that no librettist would think ill of a composer for omitting to set part of his drama, provided that its integrity was preserved in the published libretto, where such passages would be identified by double commas (*virgolette*). The librettist had no lien on the music, which could reappear with or without its original words in opera after opera; and the composer had no lien on the libretto, which successive operatic managements would obtain, have revised to suit their needs, and entrust to the composer of their choice. The scenery would offer permutations of the same settings: palace antechambers, open fields, sacred groves, riversides, and so forth. Whereas in modern times a cast of singers is chosen for a particular work, it was more normal then for a work, selected for its literary merits, to be adapted to the cast already engaged. Since the services of the singers cost the impresario considerably more than those of the composer, they were in a position to insist on alterations that went beyond the strictly necessary (such as the inclusion of favourite items from their repertory). In his penetrating study of Italian operatic arias in the early eighteenth century[10] Reinhard Strohm argues convincingly that only two fixed musical entities can be recognized in the opera of that time: the individual aria (or ensemble) at the lower level and, at the higher, the individual production for a specified place and season. The 'work' is something elusive and intangible.

When adapting one of his operas for a new production (or even in the course of a production) Vivaldi liked to retain as much as possible of the score in the form in which he had previously left it — crossing out, writing in, pasting over, removing and inserting material with an ingenuity born of long experience. If the result of these metamorphoses often looks untidy, we must remember that, once completed, a score's only function was to serve as an exemplar for copyists. Some detective work is often needed to unravel the previous history of a work. Naturally, one should check the score against librettos, but since divergences between scores and librettos for the same production are common, the physical structure of a score needs careful examination. With typical self-confidence Vivaldi

[10] *Italienische Opernarien des frühen Settecento,* vol. i (Cologne, 1976), p. 11f. This work includes the best evaluation of Vivaldi's operatic music yet to have appeared as well as a detailed catalogue (in vol. ii) of the operas and their surviving fragments.

nearly always wrote the recitatives, and sometimes the arias, straight into score, accepting the probability of errors and changes of mind that would result in deletions. He wrote on four-leaf sections of paper (one bifolium being enclosed within another), numbering them consecutively within each act and identifying the act by the number of stokes (one to three) under the number. Generally, he left no unnecessary gaps, so that an aria or recitative often straddles two sections. The same procedure is followed by copyists working under his direction, as in the earlier *Farnace* score (Giordano 36), where three different hands besides his own appear. When Vivaldi later came to remove material, either outright or with the intention of making a substitution, he had many methods at his disposal: he could take out an entire section or one of its bifolia, or cut down any number of leaves to stubs (these measures would normally entail the subsequent restoration of some of the material); he could cross out material (when a number spreads over two sections, it is noticeable that Vivaldi often deletes only the shorter — hence less re-usable — portion); he could leave it intact, indicating its supersession by inserting the replacement in the middle of the section, so splitting it in two. Inserted leaves may be written out specially or lifted from other scores; in the case of pasticcios like *Rosmira*, which acknowledges borrowings from Mazzoni, Paganelli, Handel, Hasse and Pampani, the insertions can be handy copies of individual arias perhaps acquired through singers. Clues to the presence of 'imported' arias are blank pages at the end of a section or an irregular number of leaves in it. Minor alterations may be entered directly on the score or supplied on a slip of paper pasted over it (the first movement of the overture to *L'Olimpiade* was slightly lengthened in this way). Special problems arose when, in a revival, a rôle was allotted to a singer in a different vocal range. Inevitably, the arias for that character were replaced, as well as his more extended passages of recitative, but in recitatives where the character was only one of several participants Vivaldi saved himself labour by merely inking in note-heads in vertical alignment with the original notes. In this way Medoro's part in *Orlando* was changed from alto to soprano, and Aminta's in *L'Olimpiade* from bass to soprano.

The themes of baroque opera were most often taken from the history and mythology of the ancient world, which were embroidered and adapted with little restraint. Medieval romances, such as form the basis of the librettos of Vivaldi's *Orlando* and *Ginevra*, were also popular. Lastly, a vogue for the exotic caused operas to be situated in places as far-flung as America (*Motezuma*) or China (*Teuzzone*). The Moslem east was also a favoured locale, as we see in *La verità in cimento*. In their prefaces librettists normally stated the sources from which they had directly or indirectly culled their story, only to expound the various licences they had permitted themselves 'for the convenience of the modern stage'. Metastasio himself did not scruple to change the names of Cornelia and Juba, historical characters in *Catone in Utica*, to Emilia and Arbace for the sake of euphony.

Although there was a fashion for five-act operas, in the style of classical models and the French tragedies patterned on them, at the start of the reform movement associated, perhaps too exclusively, with Apostolo Zeno (1668–1750), three acts continued to be the norm (discounting intermezzos and ballets inserted between, sometimes inside, them). Each act was divided into a number of 'scenes', generally between ten and twenty. The criterion of a scene change was not, as in modern usage, a *mutazione*, or change of set— this occurred only three or four times during the act — but the exit of one or more characters. Since it was customary for singers to sweep off the stage, having acknowledged the audience's applause, at the end of their aria, most arias inevitably occur at the end of a scene. By no means every scene has an aria or other closed number; as many as four scenes sometimes pass without one.

It was part of the librettist's skill to distribute arias equitably among the approximately five principal singers and perhaps two lesser singers, to vary the character of each singer's arias, and to space them well out so that no one singer held the centre of the stage for too long. Theorists devised rules for the guidance of librettists, but practice admitted some flexibility. In its original form, to which Vivaldi's 1734 setting for S. Angelo closely adhered, *L'Olimpiade* was a model libretto, as the table below shows. It is interesting to note that when Vivaldi later revised his score (possibly for the thwarted performance in Ferrara) he ironed out the disparity in the number of arias allotted to the principal and minor characters, perhaps as an inducement to the latter to join his troupe. Figures for this revised version appear within parentheses in the table.

	Act I	Act II	Act III	Total
Aristea	1(1)	2(1)	1(1)	4(3)
Megacle	1(1)	1(1)	1(1)	3(3)
Argene	1(1)	2(1)	1(1)	4(3)
Licida	2(2)	1(1)	0(0)	3(3)
Clistene	1(1)	1(1)	1(1)	3(3)
Aminta	0(1)	1(1)	0(1)	1(3)
Alcandro	0(0)	0(1)	0(1)	0(2)
Meg + Ari	1(1)	0(0)	0(0)	1(1)
Arg + Ari	0(0)	0(1)	0(0)	0(1)
Chorus	1(1)	1(0)	2(2)	4(3)

Plots revolve around palace intrigues, conflicts between love and honour or passion and piety, and the resolution of old vendettas, all enmeshed in complex love-chains. The mainspring of the plot is often wound before the curtain goes up, necessitating a lengthy exposition of the background in the *Argomento* before the libretto. A happy ending (*lieto fine*) was favoured by custom and out of respect for the established order. Dramatically, this was unfortunate, as many otherwise good plots are spoiled by a contrived and over-hasty dénouement. In Lucchini's *Farnace*, for instance, the superbly implacable Berenice quite arbitrarily recovers her maternal instincts in the very last scene. The force of the custom is shown in Vivaldi's adaptation of *Catone in Utica* for Verona. In Metastasio's splendid original libretto Cato dies by his own own hand on stage in the final scene, prophesying Caesar's downfall. This was too strong for contemporary taste, and Metastasio was persuaded to amend the ending so that Cato died offstage. Vivaldi (or his collaborator) goes further: Cato lives to capitulate gracefully to Caesar, leaving the prophesying to Emilia.

The division of function between recitative and aria is absolute: recitatives carry the action forward, while arias and other closed numbers freeze, like a still in a motion picture, thoughts and feelings at one particular point. The dynamics of action or character development are absent from the aria; the most one will find are antitheses between the framing A and central B sections. The self-contained nature of arias and the small variation in their construction and scale make the formation of over-all climaxes within the act — still more within the work — virtually impossible. One can rarely guess from looking at an individual number at what point during the act or the opera it occurs. In this respect contemporary French opera, where numbers were frequently linked to make complexes and which possessed more (and less sharply differentiated) types of musical setting, possessed an advantage.

One should not look for much originality of character portrayal in the world of Vivaldi's operas. It is the traits which are predetermined and then coupled with suitable persons, historical or invented, rather than the reverse. Stock character-types such as the amorous warrior, the faithful wife, the vengeful widow and the blustering tyrant regularly appear (which makes it easier to transport an aria from one opera to another). It is observable, however, that Romans are painted in rosier colours than their barbarian opposite numbers. In *Farnace* Pompey is a more honourable conqueror than his ally, the Cappadocian queen Berenice, and his lieutenant Aquilio is harder to suborn than her captain Gilade. Poor Arbace, in *Catone*, nobly struggles against the handicap of his Numidian background. This ethnic discrimination, inherited, of course, from the classical writers themselves, serves to eulogize those patrons of opera who, like the Viennese court or the Venetian senators, regarded themselves as latter-day Romans.

Vivaldi's recitative is not normally the most dramatic, but it is inventive in the resources it employs. Whereas expressiveness in the cantata recitatives is concentrated in the vocal line, it is the harmonies and sometimes the accompaniment which are most telling in the operas. The marvellous setting of the ninth scene in Act II of *L'Olimpiade* makes appropriate use of all the main varieties of recitative.

The hero, Megacle, bound by a debt of gratitude to his friend (and rival suitor) Licida, bids a last adieu to his sweetheart Aristea. Here, as previously, the most common type of recitative, over sustained pedal-notes, suffices. Aristea's uncomprehending anger.is signalled by violent twists in the harmony, and when she feels cold sweat on her brow, just prior to fainting, the key lurches from B minor to D minor. To express Megacle's bewilderment and shock at seeing her lie motionless, Vivaldi chooses the most extreme form of 'detached' accompaniment: sparse crotchets, doubled at the octave by the entering upper strings. Realizing that she is unconscious, Megacle panics at the thought that she may be dead; the upper strings break into chords, and the unison violins twice evoke horror with searing arpeggios which change chord during their descent:
Resigned to the worst, he gathers his confused thoughts to an accompaniment of detached chords alternately on continuo and the full ensemble. As he bids Aristea farewell, the texture changes to that of the traditional *accompagnato* reserved for

Ex. 27

solemn moments such as a prayer or the reading of a letter: a 'halo' of sustained chords. Finally, he looks around for Licida, and the accompaniment reverts to continuo pedal-notes.

More than any other type of movement, the aria charts Vivaldi's stylistic development over the decades. In his earlier operas, up to about the mid 1720s, he often allows the instrumental parts, much more active than those of most contemporaries, to define the phrase structure, impose thematic coherence and even arrogate to themselves the main melodic interest. A parallel with Wagner's operas is not out of place. In the aria from *Tito Manlio* illustrated in p. 173 the voice starts as an added counterpoint against an orchestral texture which has already been heard by itself as the ritornello. In later operas Vivaldi tends to conform to Neapolitan practice, letting the vocal part (possibly doubled by violins) dominate every aspect of the composition. The busyness of the accompanying instruments is likely to base itself not on a density of motivic play as formerly, but on simple technical devices like the bowed tremolo. In the early operas arias tend to be compact — of necessity, since the librettists were more lavish with them — and uniform in character as between A and B sections. Arias in the later operas are both fewer and longer. Internally, they have become more varied and less continuous in their flow. 'Motto' openings followed by a cadenza as well as terminal cadenzas are common in the vocal part. Whereas the B section was formerly contrasted texturally (being more thinly scored) rather than thematically with the A section, the reverse is now more general; differences of tempo between the sections are not uncommon. Once again, librettists must be held partly responsible, for these contrasts mirror the use of antithesis and paradox in verse of the Metastasian age.

Where Vivaldi discards the *da capo* layout, the reason is almost always to be found in the unitary construction of the text. Not surprisingly, old or old-style librettos like those of *L'incoronazione du Dario* and *Orlando* afforded him most scope for through-composed arias which, on account of their brevity, are accompanied by continuo alone. There is one outstanding aria, however, which respects the *da capo* of the text without reproducing it literally in the music: Clistene's 'Non so donde viene' (*L'Olimpiade*, III,6). There are no breaks between sections: the music set to the first quatrain modulates to the dominant; that of the second quatrain moves to the relative major; the reprise of the opening lines relates to the first section as a recapitulation to an exposition in sonata form. This partial dissociation between musical and poetic form in an aria from the 1730s is a remarkable foretaste of developments in the aria later in the century.

The number of duets and ensembles Vivaldi could include in his operas was limited by the parsimony of librettists, itself a response to actual conditions of performance. He left four particularly fine examples: the duet 'Ne' giorni tuoi felici' in *L'Olimpiade* (I, 10), the terzett 'S'egli è ver' in *La fida ninfa* (I, 12), the quartet 'Io crudel?' in *Farnace* (III, 7), later borrowed for *Bajazet*, and the quintet 'Anima mia, mio ben' (based on the quartet in *La Candace*) in *La verità in cimento*. When the participants have a common text, as in the terzett, the music may be set after the fashion of a chorus, either contrapuntally or homophonically. If the element of dialogue is present, or if the characters voice contrasted thoughts, a different treatment is needed. Vivaldi follows a common practice by introducing his characters separately, one after the other, so that they can establish a separate personality (and acquaint the audience with their words). The next stage is to overlap their phrases, producing sometimes quite intricate contrapuntal patterns. In preparation for the main cadences the voices unite homophonically. The *Farnace* quartet demonstrates in its 105 bars Vivaldi's superb control of pace, his gift of succinct characterization and his secure sense of form. It opens immediately with a tirade by Berenice against her hated son-in-law Farnace, now her captive. More tersely and less ferociously, Pompey (Pompeo) echoes her sentiments. Farnace's wife Tamiri now pleads hysterically with her mother for his life, the gasping, tonally unstable vocal line showing graphically her state of mind. Finally, Farnace enters, stoically accepting his fate. A few further exchanges lead to a ritornello in the mediant minor. During this first section (bars 1–40) there are only two bars (31–2) of ensemble writing, Berenice and Pompey singing in thirds. The second section (bars 41–83) goes through the text once more, as in a conventional aria, returning to the home key for a concluding ritornello. This time, however, frequent overlaps and one passage of ensemble writing (bars 63–5) increase the urgency and intensity. In the third section, equivalent to the B section of an aria, the voices are coupled, following the libretto, in pairs (Berenice–Pompey and Tamiri–Farnace), finally coming

189

together in a peroration. A reprise of the first two sections is not required, but Vivaldi rounds off the movement with a ritornello.

Choruses in the operas are as perfunctory as they are infrequent. The briefest binary form, with or without ritornellos, is preferred, and the texture is resolutely homophonic. Sometimes, indeed, the chorus part, to be sung in unison, is written on one stave. The borrowing or adaptation of an old chorus for a new work is often practised. One choral movement, written for performance in Rome, where elaborate choruses were part of local operatic tradition, does something to redeem this unimpressive showing. 'Dopo i nembi', which concludes *Giustino*, is a 62-bar-long chaconne of some contrapuntal merit. In the extract below, in which the voices (words omitted) are doubled by instruments, the delayed entry of the tenor in the first statement of the ostinato and the imitative interplay of soprano and alto in the second are particularly attractive.

Vivaldi's use in operas of instruments other than the orchestral quartet of strings and continuo reveals, as one would expect,

Ex. 28

his sure grasp of their technique and expressive potential. Few scores are without a pair of horns in F, which are summoned for arias, ensembles or choruses in hunting style. He notates for horns in three ways:

1. Parts ascending no further than the twelfth harmonic transpose down an octave. Walter Kolneder has argued, referring to the concerto RV 538/P.320, which features this transposition, that such parts, being written for a horn in 'high' F, sound at written pitch (one recalls a similar theory about the horn parts in the first 'Brandenburg' Concerto).[11] Were this so, however, the horn pedal-notes in *Farnace* ('Nell'intimo del petto', I,7) and *L'Olimpiade* ('Mentre dormi amor fomenti', I,8) would shriek out from the top of the texture.
2. Parts ascending to the 18th harmonic (g'') are written at sounding pitch.
3. A few parts ascending to the 13th harmonic employ the modern transposition for horn in F, sounding down a fifth.

If his use of the horns in a hunting vein is disappointingly conventional, Vivaldi's horn pedals are little short of sensational. The device was not entirely new, Vinci having exploited it as early as 1725, but Vivaldi introduces special, magical touches in both arias. In *L'Olimpiade* a single horn restricted to the sounding notes f-c'-f' is accompanied by muted strings

[11] *Antonio Vivaldi: His Life and Work*, p. 140.

expressive of sleep. In *Farnace* two horns in unison playing the notes c'-f'-g'-$b\flat'$ usher in the first stirrings of Gilade's love for Farnace's captive sister Selinda. Remarkably, the aria is in C minor. Vivaldi's use of the natural horn in a key foreign to its harmonic series is several decades ahead of its time. This aria was retained in the later version of *Farnace*, where Vivaldi, aware of the technical problems of sustaining long notes on a wind instrument (a g' is sustained *piano* from the 32nd to the 44th bar), wrote a characteristically precise instruction: 'This horn pedal must never cease sounding, so two horns have to play in unison softly throughout, taking turns to draw breath.'[12] The modern habit of 'bumping up', it seems, was familar to him.

Many operas introduce trumpets in C or D, sometimes accompanied by timpani (called 'tamburri', 'timballi' or 'timpani'), in martial or festive movements. In comparison with their imaginative use in the sacred music (for example in the *Gloria* RV 589 and the *Dixit Dominus* RV 594) their operatic appearances are unexciting.

Oboes and recorders, always in pairs, are used together with strings in an obbligato or semi-obbligato rôle to lend a bucolic touch. The appearance of both in 'Bel riposo de' mortali' (*Giustino*, I,4), a gentle pastorale, is typical. Sometimes, oboes are complemented by a bassoon. This instrument is used only once as a true obbligato instrument, to accompany the huffing and puffing of the comical old philosopher Niceno (*L'incoronazione di Dario*, I,19), ancestor to Doctor Bartolo.

Those instruments introduced as occasional novelties that have not been discussed in the previous chapter include the solo violin and cello, the psaltery (in *Giustino*), the *flauto grosso* (probably a tenor recorder: used in *Tito Manlio* and *La verità in cimento*, which also require the *flautino*), the flute and the solo

[12] 'Questo pedale del corno non deve mai mancare; per tanto devono suonare due corni unisoni e sempre piano affine uno lascia prendere fiato all'altro.'

Ex. 29

(Allegro)

Non lu - sin - ghi il co - re a - man - te, Im - por - tu - na la ven -

fag.

solo
vcl.

- det - ta, im - por - tu - na_ la ven - det - ta   Con lo

harpsichord. The solo violin is generally used in some special way: with solo cello in parallel tenths in 'Sentirò fra ramo e ramo' (*Dario*, III, 2) in imitation of bird-song; on stage in 'L'ombre, l'aure e ancora il rio' (*Ottone in Villa*, II, 3) to evoke the breezes; as an echo-effect in *Orlando finto pazzo*. The flute obbligato in 'Sol da te, mio dolce amore' (*Orlando*, I, 11), hauntingly lyrical in its more subdued moments, includes passages (some with 48 notes to the bar) of a technical difficulty surpassing that of his flute concertos. Vivaldi uses solo harpsichords (more than one instrument was employed for operatic performances) in 'Io son quel gelsomino' (*Arsilda*, I, 15) for purely colouristic effect; not for him the bold virtuosic display of 'Vo' far guerra' in Handel's *Rinaldo*.

Despite their many beautiful moments, Vivaldi's operas cannot lay claim to the historical importance of his concertos. Yet the vigour, complexity and variety of their instrumental writing, especially in the works of the first decade, set a fashion for his older contemporaries. Had he begun to write operas earlier, or had the rise of the Neapolitans occurred later, their orchestra-dominated style might have established itself more firmly. Though he continued after the critical period around

193

1725 to produce innovations, these never became consolidated in a 'late-period' style. A work like *Catone in Utica* betrays a self-consciousness foreign to the early operas for S. Angelo and S. Moisè: the malaise of a composer whose ambition has outlasted his capacity for self-renewal.

THE SACRED VOCAL MUSIC

No area of Vivaldi's creativity is so hard to survey as his sacred vocal music, because the factors most subject to variation— the nature of the texts set, the scale of the setting and the forces used — occur in so many combinations. A Vespers psalm, for example, may be set as one long movement (*Beatus vir* RV 598) or several movements (*Beatus vir* RV 597); its vocal complement may be solo voice (*Nisi Dominus* RV 608), choir alone (*Laudate Dominum* RV 606) or single or double choir with soloists (*Dixit Dominus* RV 594); the work may be *a cappella* (in eighteenth-century usage this means not that instruments are absent but that they double the voices strictly) as in the *Credidi* RV 605, include independent instrumental parts, as in *Lauda Jerusalem* RV 609, or treat the instruments in both fashions at different times.

The most important distinction to be drawn, however, is that between settings of liturgical and non-liturgical texts. The Ryom catalogue lists in the first category: one complete Mass, and separate settings of the *Kyrie, Gloria* (twice) and *Credo* (twice);[13] Vespers music comprising the response *Domine ad adiuvandum*, Psalms 69, 109 (twice), 110, 111 (twice), 112 (four times), 113, 115, 116, 121, 126 and 147 (all numberings according to the Vulgate), nine assorted hymns and antiphons, including three settings of the *Salve Regina*, and the *Magnificat* in four closely-related versions. The non-liturgical category

[13] The authenticity of the complete Mass and the *Credo* RV 592, both preserved in Warsaw, requires confirmation. All statistics given here refer to extant works, discounting minor variants.

embraces the oratorio *Juditha triumphans*, twelve solo motets, eight *introduzioni* and three independent movements, one of which (the *Aria de Sanctis* 'Eja voces plausum date' RV 647) is a *contrafactum* of the aria 'Benché nasconda la serpe in seno' in *Orlando* (II,2).[14]

It is convenient to begin with the works on non-liturgical texts, as they bear the closest resemblance to the cantatas and operas. Quantz supplies a good definition of the Italian motet of his day: 'In Italy one nowadays applies this term to a sacred solo cantata with Latin text consisting of two arias, two recitatives and a concluding 'Alleluia', commonly performed by one of the best singers during Mass, after the Credo.'[15] Mozart's *Exsultate, jubilate* K.165 is a late representative of the genre. As in most of his cantatas Vivaldi omits the introductory recitative, but because of the separate 'Alleluia' movement (through-composed with a hint of ritornello form), the second of the two arias, which with few exceptions are in a straightforward *da capo* form, can offer a contrast of key.

The *introduzioni* are very similar to the motets, though having no 'Alleluia'. As the name suggests, these are introductory movements, to the *Gloria*, to the *Dixit Dominus* or to the *Miserere*; exceptionally, *Jubilate, o amaeni*, RV 639/639a, leads into the *Gloria* RV 588 without a break.

Motets and *introduzioni* are scored alike for soprano or alto with strings and continuo. The instrumental accompaniment is more discreet than in most of Vivaldi's operatic arias before the 1720s, and the vocal writing correspondingly more florid; yet their style, and what little other evidence exists, suggests that most were written in his first flush of sacred vocal composition following Gasparini's departure from the Pietà. Though

---

[14] The same aria appears with new words in *L'Atenaide*. It was also borrowed (as 'So che nasconde in livore') for the pasticcio *Catone* (1732) arranged by Handel for the King's Theatre.

[15] *Versuch*, p. 288n.

unashamedly treble-dominated and not particularly subtle in their manner of expression, these 'concertos for voice' have considerable melodic appeal. The dog-Latin of their anonymous texts, in which Arcadian images such as the warbling nightingale (Filomena) incongruously appear, is less admirable.

The earliest known performance of an oratorio at the Pietà dates from 1684. From then until 1820 well over 50 oratorios of which librettos have been preserved were produced by successive *maestri di coro*, the most active being Gasparini (eight between 1701 and 1713), A. Bernasconi (five, 1744–51) and B. Furlanetto (31, 1768–1808).[16] As befitted an institution for the female sex, a large proportion celebrated biblical heroines such as Mary Magdalene, Athalia, Abigail and Susannah. Vivaldi's 'sacrum militare oratorium' *Juditha triumphans,* whose bellicosity, as we have seen, suited the times,[17] was the first on that subject for the Pietà; Cassetti's libretto was refurbished for a setting by G. Latilla (1757), and Furlanetto returned to the story in 1787.

In *Juditha* Vivaldi puts virtually the whole of the Pietà's arsenal of instruments on display. The score calls for two recorders, two oboes, soprano chalumeau, two clarinets, two trumpets with timpani, mandolin, four theorboes (playing in two parts), obbligato organ, five *viole all'inglese* and viola d'amore in addition to strings and continuo. In many cases the same player probably doubled on more than one instrument, since, for example, only one kind of woodwind instrument is heard at a time.

Juditha completely lacks duets and other ensembles; the only

---

[16] Statistics based on Maria Antonietta Zorzi, 'Saggio di bibliografia sugli oratorî sacri eseguiti a Venezia', *Accademie e biblioteche d'Italia,* vols. iv (1930–31), pp. 226–46, 394–403, 529–43, v (1931–32), pp. 79–96, 493–508, vi (1932–33), pp. 256–69, vii (1933–34), pp. 316–41.

[17] cf. p. 59f.

interaction of characters in the closed numbers is provided by one chorus ('O quam vaga, venusta') with a solo part for Vagaus, and an aria of Vagaus ('O servi, volate') with choral interjections. The choir, representing Assyrian warriors and Bethulian maidens in turn, has two further numbers in each of the two parts of the oratorio; these expand somewhat — but do not outgrow — the binary conception of the operatic chorus.

The ever-changing instrumentation of the arias serves in a rather rudimentary way the ends of dramatic characterization, although the prime aim is still to depict a situation as viewed by a character rather than a character as revealed by a situation. Judith has to herself the 'feminine' tones of viola d'amore, *viola all'inglese*, chalumeau and mandolin, while Vagaus, Holophernes's obsequious henchman, flatters him to the strains of oboes, recorders and theorboes. Of sterner stuff, Holophernes makes do with orchestral strings for all his arias save one ('Noli, o cara') when, in a rush of tenderness, he woos Judith with the aid of oboe and obbligato organ.

Excellent though most of the arias are in their own right, *Juditha* suffers from a dramatic diffuseness exceeding even that of the operas. Vivaldi neglects his opportunity to build up excitement in preparation for Holophernes's beheading, and the *accompagnato* during which Judith carries out her gruesome task is deplorably lame. A more dramatic moment arrives immediately after, when Vagaus, gingerly approaching and entering the love-tent, recoils in horror at the sight of his decapitated master and then launches into a vituperative 'revenge' aria, 'Armatae face'. No finer *scena* exists in the whole of Vivaldi's music. Over-all, however, the pace is too leisurely, the price paid for stringing together a long work from units whose length and structure are unusually uniform, even in the context of the time.

The works on liturgical texts offer a far greater variety of movement types. *Da capo* form is ruled out, since the words, while they sometimes permit a short refrain, cannot be coerced into the familiar tripartite arrangement. Shorter movements can be set in through-composed fashion, the stylization depending on the forces involved: arioso or *accompagnato* is appropriate in a work with solo voice (for example, 'Cujus animam/Quis non posset' in the *Stabat Mater*); chordal declamation in a choral work (for example, the 'Gratias agimus tibi' of the *Gloria* RV 589). Longer movements can be set fugally in traditional style (this holds good even in the solo voice medium), but the most common solution in works with obbligato instrumental parts is some kind of ritornello form. In movements for solo voice ritornello form (which, in its variety with two episodes, coincides with the plan of the A section in *da capo* form) can be taken over unaltered from the concerto. In movements with choir (e.g. the 'Credo in unum Deum' of RV 591) some adjustments have to be made so that the choir lends its weight to the ritornellos (the introduction excepted) as well as to the episodes. Where vocal soloists as well as a choir participate, the latter has overwhelmingly a 'ritornello' function.

The hymns follow their text in adopting a simple strophic pattern. An exception is the *Stabat Mater* RV 621. Whereas the other well-known settings from the period of Jacopone da Todi's poem, such as those by Astorga, Caldara, Pergolesi, A. and D. Scarlatti and Steffani, include all 20 stanzas (plus the 'Amen'), appropriate when the work is sung as a sequence at Mass, Vivaldi's setting uses only stanzas 1 to 10 as prescribed when the *Stabat Mater* is sung as a Vespers hymn at the two feasts of the Seven Dolours of the Blessed Virgin Mary (15th September and the Friday before Good Friday). The form is a compromise between strophic and 'cantata-style' setting. Movements 1 to 3 (on the text of stanzas 1 to 4) are repeated as movements 4 to 6 (on the text of stanzas 5 to 8). The remaining two stanzas and the 'Amen' are set individually. In this closely-knit work, whose sombre mood is dispelled only by a radiant *tierce de*

Picardie in the final chord, Vivaldi achieves a remarkable, almost oppressive degree of unity. Until the 'Amen', which has no original tempo marking, tempi range from *Adagissimo* to *Andante* (a foretaste of Haydn's *Seven Last Words from the Cross*). All the movements are either in F minor or C minor, and several are related in cyclic fashion.

Quite the most compelling feature of these works is the large (if not yet Bachian) scale on which many of the movements are built, and the careful planning that complements it. The *Beatus vir* RV 598 for two sopranos, alto and four-part choir, cast in a single, ritornello-form movement of 420 bars, exhibits a range of modulation and a thematic affinity between ritornello and episode unmatched by the instrumental models. In the second movements of the three great D major works — the two *Gloria* settings and the *Dixit Dominus* RV 594 — where, as a foil to the brilliant opening movements, Vivaldi moves to B minor and adopts a slow tempo, we find a deliberateness of tragic mien and epic proportion wholly foreign to the world of the concerto. He also shows unsuspected skill in combining motives originally heard separately. In the first 'Kyrie eleison' of the *Kyrie* in G minor, RV 587, the boldly modulating chords and striding arpeggio figures appearing successively in the orchestral introduction come together for the first time after the modulation to D minor. The 'In memoria aeterna' terzett of the *Beatus vir* RV 597 not only combines a vocal fugato with contrasted material from the introduction but also subsequently integrates the subject of this fugato with the two of another fugato heard later to the words 'ab auditione mala non timebit'.

In the multi-movement works there is a lurking danger that because of all the variety of key, scoring and style the work will dissolve, aesthetically speaking, into fragments. Vivaldi was not unconscious of the problem. In the *Beatus vir* RV 597 a repeated five-bar strain extracted from the opening movement comes back as a so-called 'antiphon' before five of the eight remaining movements. This rather artificial device soon becomes wearisome, particularly as the refrain is not intrinsically very attractive. More successful is the reprise of the opening movement near the end of a work. In psalm settings this generally occurs at the start of the Doxology ('Gloria Patris'), so that the following words, 'Sicut erat in principio', can have punning significance.[18] In the *Gloria* RV 589 Vivaldi is inspired to prepare for the reprise (on 'Quoniam tu solus sanctus') by introducing the five-note motive following its initial octaves (see Ex. 1, p.97) into the preceding aria, 'Qui sedes'.

From the Governors' commendation of Vivaldi in 1715 it is evident that the Pietà required him to compose an 'entire' Mass (i.e. the five sections of the Ordinary) and a similar 'Vespers' (minus, perhaps, some or all of the antiphons). Some of the works preserved separately must therefore have been composed for the same service, and to that extent belong together. In the knowledge that the Pietà's *Maestro di Coro* had to supply new Mass and Vespers settings for the two principal feasts of the year — Easter, and the Visitation of the Blessed Virgin Mary — Piero Damilano has sought to identify among the extant works two Vespers cycles, taking into account not merely liturgical requirements but also congruence of scoring and key.[19] The attempt is valiant, but misconceived. It fails to reckon with the hymns and antiphons, which fall outside these two liturgies; it does not consider the near-certainty that several works in which male voices are prominent (for example, the *Beatus vir* RV 597 and the *Dixit Dominus* RV 594) were not composed for the Pietà; it includes a few spurious works; most important, it ignores connexions established by the bibliography of the manuscripts. This last factor still awaits thorough investigation, but one may

---

[18] J. S. Bach, who in his *Magnificat* BWV 243 begins the reprise on the very words 'Sicut erat in principio', is a less subtle punner.

[19] 'Antonio Vivaldi compose due vespri?', *Nuova Rivista Musicale Italiana*, vol. iii (1969), pp. 652–63.

give as an example the autograph manuscripts of the *Introduzione* and *Gloria* RV 639/588, the *Credo* 591, the *Laudate pueri Dominum* RV 602 and the *Laetatus sum* RV 607 — two Mass sections and two Vespers psalms with Marian associations — which are the only works among the Turin manuscripts written on a certain kind of paper. It is safest to conclude that the Turin manuscripts contain fragments of more than two Vespers cycles, together with other works composed individually.

Misconceptions also surround Vivaldi's numerous works 'in due cori'. Rather romantically in view of the lack of evidence, some writers have taken them to have been written for St Mark's, forgetting that while the use of *cori spezzati* may have originated there in the sixteenth century, it spread rapidly to become a universal means of achieving an exceptionally grand and spacious musical effect. *Lauda Jerusalem*, at any rate, was written for the Pietà in the late 1730s, for two of its girls, Margarita and Giulietta, are assigned by name to the solo soprano part of the first *coro*, and two more, Fortunata and Chiaretta, to that of the second *coro*.[20] All four sang in *Il coro delle muse* (1740), Chiaretta also in the late version (RV 611) of the *Magnificat*. Since the contemporary manuscript poem referred to earlier describes Fortunata as 'young', Giulietta as 'an adolescent' (giovinetta) and Chiaretta as 'a girl', a date before 1735 is unlikely.

By the eighteenth century the *concertato* style, the very basis of polychoral writing, had become obsolete. Increasingly, one finds alternate phrases of an essentially 'monochoral' piece allotted to each ensemble until they eventually join forces in a peroration; or there are imitative dialogues between the two ensembles reminiscent of those between the two violin parts in an orchestral ritornello. In both cases, antiphony is preserved, however artificially. More ominously for the style, polychoral-

[20] It is best to avoid translating *coro* as 'choir', as the term can refer to an ensemble of voices, instruments or both combined.

ity may survive only in the layout of the score, the composer simply writing in as many parts as the *cori* between them can provide, without regard for the spatial aspect.

All these tendencies characterize Vivaldi's works. At one extreme, one finds a monochoral work, the *Magnificat* RV 610, turned into one for two *cori* by the addition of the cues 'P.C.' (primo coro) and '2.C.' (secondo coro); at the other, the ornate and contrapuntally complex 'Sicut erat in principio' finale of the *Dixit Dominus* RV 594, where the two choirs and orchestras interweave in as many as seven real parts. Though the artistic possibilities of antiphony remain largely unexploited, these works do not disappoint in other respects. The little-known setting of the response *Domine ad adiuvandum me*, cast like a concerto in three movements, demonstrates in compact form Vivaldi's ability to weld very differently constructed movements into a perfect whole. An opening ritornello-form movement captures the urgency of the plea 'ad adiuvandum me festina'. It is followed by a setting in the relative minor for solo soprano of the first part of the Doxology; the singer slowly threads her way through a tight dialogue between the two orchestras. The 'a cappella' movement with united *cori* which follows (Vivaldi achieves greater luminosity in time-honoured fashion by having the first violins double the altos an octave higher and allotting the soprano line to the second violins) is shaped as an introduction and fugue, well knit together by a running bass in quavers.

The traditional element in Vivaldi's settings of liturgical texts should not be underestimated. Their fugue subjects tend to follow textbook patterns, unlike those in the instrumental music, and (in William Hayes's words) are 'well maintained'. Vivaldi is fond of pedal-note themes which suggest plainsong, though, unlike several in the sacred music of Leo, Pergolesi and Handel, they do not actually quote from it. The 'Amen' motive from the *Credo* RV 591 is typical:

Ex.30

The chaconne bass of the *Giustino* finale, metamorphosized into ponderous semibreves, serves the *Dixit Dominus* finale as a fugue subject-cum-ostinato, lending it a truly monumental character.[21] Its entry on first violins, the choirs momentarily pausing, recalls the instrumental interludes in Handel's great choral fugues. Towards the end, Vivaldi subjects his motive to diminution and inversion with a nice sense of climax if few contrapuntal pretensions.

Nevertheless, he was less at home with the *stile osservato* than, say, Lotti or Marcello. Significantly, the two unacknowledged borrowings from other composers so far traced in his music (outside the special case of opera) occur in this context. One, the 'Credidi a 5 a capella del Vivaldi' RV 605, is a clumsy *contrafactum* of an uninspired, anonymous *Lauda Jerusalem*, RV Anh. 35, found among the Turin manuscripts. Haste, or perhaps uneasiness in this style, may explain (though hardly excuse) Vivaldi's opportunism. In the other instance he made two separate adaptations of the 'Cum sancto spiritu' fugue from a *Gloria* (dated 9th September 1708) by G. M. Ruggieri, also preserved in Turin. Ruggieri's work is laid out for two orchestras of five-part strings, one with trumpet and the other with a pair of oboes, and two four-part choirs. In one adaptation, probably the earlier (for the *Gloria* RV 588), Vivaldi introduces Ruggieri's movement with a short peroration on a D major chord. His alterations, other than those implied by the reduction of forces to the level of a single orchestra and choir (both in four parts) tend to concentrate the movement and reduce the importance of the

---

[21] Couperin uses the motive similarly in the last movement of the sonata opening *La françoise* (composed *c*1692, published 1726).

203

instruments. The other adaptation (for the *Glória* RV 589) eliminates the peroration and tends to increase the rôle of the instruments (some passages for the solo trumpet are newly invented.) Moreover, it departs more radically from Ruggieri in word-setting and certain thematic details, greatly improving the original. No apologies need be made for these creative transformations, though what prompted the use of borrowed material remains obscure.

Vivaldi makes such sparing use of exotic instruments in the works belonging to this group that it is unnecessary to enlarge on incidental references already made. His methods of combining the string orchestra with the choir are so original and forward-looking, however, that they deserve close examination. They would have occurred only to a composer conversant with the practices of the instrumental concerto.

The problem lies in reconciling independence and idiomacy of part-writing in both choir and orchestra with an avoidance of the confusion and turgidity that can so easily result. He solves it by composing on two different planes, which we can term for convenience foreground and background. If instruments occupy the foreground with motivically-significant material, the voices

Ex. 31

will supply a simple background whose contribution, almost like that of a keyboard continuo, is perceived more in terms of texture and rhythm than of melody, as in the above bars from *In exitu Israel,* RV 604.

The roles can easily be reversed, as in the 'Et in terra pax' from the *Gloria* RV 588.

Ex. 32

In both examples one is aware of the part-writing within each section — choir or orchestra — but the dissociation of the two planes makes the relationship of, say, the tenor and the viola of very secondary importance. Analogous developments in the relationshipo of the wind and string sections of the orchestra itself are a vital element in the symphonic art of the later eighteenth century. To give Vivaldi a large share of the credit for the introduction of a 'symphonic' style to church music may seem a bold act, but the evidence justifies it.

It is ironic both that 'the Red Priest' came to write sacred vocal music through an accident of circumstances, and that he then revealed an exceptional talent for it. Fervour, exaltation, and mysticism; these qualities break forth from the scores. A further irony: the dramatic element is very subdued. One will

205

find no touches comparable with the diminished seventh on 'superbos' in the Bach *Magnificat* or the hammer blows on 'Conquissabit capita' in the *Dixit Dominus* of Handel. It is as if Vivaldi sought in church music a dignity and serenity for which his life as virtuoso and entrepreneur, invalid and globe-trotter, left him too little time.

Appendix A Calendar

(Figures in brackets denote the age reached by the person mentioned during the year in question.)

YEAR	AGE	LIFE	CONTEMPORARY MUSICIANS
1678		Antonio Lucio Vivaldi born, 4 March, at Venice. Eldest child of the violinist G. B. Vivaldi and his wife Camilla Vivaldi, née Calicchio. Officially baptized, 6 May.	G. M. Bononcini (36) dies, 18 Nov. Albinoni aged 7; Biber 34; Biffi *c* 12; Blow 29; A. M. Bononcini 1; G. Bononcini 8; Bonporti 6; Buxtehude 41; Caldara *c*7; Corelli 25; Couperin 10; Dall'Abaco 3; Fux 18; Gasparini 10; Keiser 4; Kuhnau 18; Lalande 21; Legrenzi 52; Lotti 12; Lully 46; A. Marcello 9; Mascitti *c*4; Pachelbel 25; Pasquini 41; C. F. Pollarolo *c*25; G. A. Pollarolo 2; Purcell 19; A. Scarlatti 18; Steffani 24; Stradella 34; Torelli 20; G. B. Vitali 46; T. A. Vitali 15; J. J. Walther *c*28; M. A. Ziani *c*25.
1679	1		Zelenka born, 16 Oct.
1680	2		Astorga born, 20 March.
1681	3		Telemann born, 14 March.
1682	4		Stradella (37) dies, 25 Feb.
1683	5		Graupner born, 13 Jan.;

YEAR	AGE	LIFE	CONTEMPORARY MUSICIANS
			Heinichen born, 17 Apri
			Rameau born, 24 Sept.
1684	6		Durante born, 31 March
			Manfredini born, 22 June
			J. G. Walther born, 1 Sept.
1685	7	Father enters orchestra of St Mark's, 23 April	G. M. Alberti born, 2 Sept; J. S. Bach born, 2 March; Handel born, 2 Feb.; D. Scarlatti born, 2 Oct.
1686	8		B. Marcello born, 1 Aug Porpora born, 17 Aug.
1687	9		Geminiani born, 5 Dec Lully (54) dies, 22 March Pisendel born, 26 Dec.
1688	10		Fasch born, 15 April; Pre dieri born, 13 Sept.
1689	11		Boismortier born, 23 Dec
1690	12		Legrenzi (63) dies, 2 May; Veracini born, 1 Feb
1691	13		
1692	14		Ristori born; Tartini borr 8 April; G. B. Vitali (60 dies, 12 Oct.
1693	15	Begins training for the priesthood. Tonsure, 18 Sept.; Porter, 19 Sept.	
1694	16	Lector, 21 Sept.	Leo born, 5 Aug.; Mic born, 5 Sept.; Roma born, 26 Oct.
1695	17	Exorcist, 25 Dec.	Locatelli born, 3 Sept Purcell (36) dies, 21 Nov
1696	18	Acolyte, 21 Sept.	Vinci born (or ?1690).
1697	19		Leclair born, 10 May Quantz born, 30 Jan.
1698	20		

208

YEAR	AGE	LIFE	CONTEMPORARY MUSICIANS
699	21	Sub-Deacon, 4 April.	Hasse born, 23/24 March.
700	22	Deacon, 18 Sept.	G. B. Sammartini born (or ?1701).
701	23		
702	24		
703	25	Priest, 23 March. Appointed violin master at the Pietà, commencing Sept.	
704	26	Salary raised, 17 Aug., in recognition of his teaching of the *viola all'inglese*	Biber (59) dies, 3 May.
705	27	12 trio sonatas (op. 1) published.	
706	28		Pachelbel (52) dies, 9 March.
707	29		Buxtehude (c70) dies, 9 May.
708	30		Blow (59) dies, 1 Oct.
709	31	12 violin sonatas (op. 2) ded. Frederik IV of Denmark, published. Voted out of office by the Pietà's governors, 24 Feb.	F. Benda born, 29 Nov.; Torelli (50) dies, 8 Feb.
710	32		Paganelli born, 6 March; Pasquini (72) dies, 21 Nov. Pergolesi born 4 Jan.
711	33	Reappointed violin master at the Pietà, 27 Sept. *L'estro armonico* (op. 3), ded. Ferdinando III of Tuscany, published.	Holzbauer born, 17 Sept.
712	34		
713	35	Gasparini's departure from the Pietà on sick leave approved by the gover-	Corelli (59) dies, 8 Jan.

YEAR	AGE	LIFE	CONTEMPORARY MUSICIANS
		nors, 23 April. First opera, *Ottone in Villa,* performed at Vicenza, May.	
1714	36	Association as impresario and composer with the S. Angelo theatre begins. *La stravaganza* (op. 4) published (possibly earlier).	C. P. E. Bach born, March; Gluck born, July; Jommelli born, 1 Sept.
1715	37	Meets Uffenbach, March. Voted special emolument, 2 June, for his composition of vocal works for the Pietà's chapel.	Wagenseil born, 15 Jan M. A. Ziani (*c*62) dies, 2 Jan.
1716	38	Voted out of office at the Pietà, 29 March; reinstated as *Maestro de' Concerti,* 24 May. Meets and befriends Pisendel. 6 sonatas (op. 5) published; 6 concertos (op. 6) and 12 concertos (op. 7) soon follow. *Juditha triumphans* performed, November.	
1717	39	Leaves the Pietà.	Monn born, 9 Apri Stamic born, 19 June.
1718	40	In Mantua as *Maestro di Cappella da Camera* to Prince Philip of Hesse-Darmstadt.	
1719	41		
1720	42	Returns to Venice. *Il teatro alla moda* (B. Marcello), Dec.	
1721	43		
1722	44		J. Benda born, 30 June Kuhnau (62) dies, 5 June

YEAR	AGE	LIFE	CONTEMPORARY MUSICIANS
			Nardini born, 12 April.
723	45	Visits Rome at Carnival time; is sketched by Ghezzi. The Pietà's governors agree, 2 July, to ask Vivaldi to compose, rehearse and direct the performance of two new concertos every month.	C. F. Pollarolo (c70) dies; Gassmann born, 4 May.
724	46	Probably again in Rome for Carnival. Venetian début of Anna Girò, Autumn.	
725	47	*Il cimento dell'armonia e dell'inventione* (op. 8), ded. Count Morzin, published. Wedding of Louis XV, 5 Sept., celebrated in a serenata by Vivaldi.	A. Scarlatti (65) dies, 22 Oct.
726	48		A. M. Bononcini (49) dies, 8 July; Lalande (68) dies, 18 June.
727	49	Birth, 14 Aug., of twin daughters to Louis XV celebrated in *L'unione della pace e di Marte* and a *Te Deum* (sung 19 Sept.). *La cetra* (op. 9) published.	Gasparini (59) dies, 22 March; Traetta born, 30 March; J. J. Walther (c67) dies, 2 Nov.
728	50	Meets Emperor Charles VI, Sept. 6 flute concertos (op. 10) published.	Piccini born, 16 Jan. Steffani (73) dies, 12 Feb.
729	51	G. B. Vivaldi petitions, 30 Sept., for one year's leave of absence from St Mark's 'to accompany a son to Germany'. 12 concertos	Heinichen (46) dies, 16 July; Sarti born, 1 Dec.

211

Appendix A—Calendar

YEAR	AGE	LIFE	CONTEMPORARY MUSICIANS
		(opp. 10 and 11) published.	
1730	52	In Bohemia.	Vinci (c34) dies, 27/29 May.
1731	53		Cannabich bapt., 28 Dec.; Pugnani born, 27 Nov.
1732	54	*La fida ninfa* inaugurates Verona's Teatro Filarmonico, 6 Jan.	Biffi (c66) dies; J. Haydn born, 31 March.
1733	55	Meets Holdsworth, 13 Feb.	Couperin (64) dies, 12 Sept.
1734	56		
1735	57	Collaborates with Goldoni on *Griselda,* Spring. Re-engaged at the Pietà as *Maestro de' Concerti,* 5 Aug.	J. C. Bach born, 5 Sept.
1736	58		Caldara (66) dies, 27 Dec. Pergolesi (26) buried, 1' March.
1737	59	Dispute with management of Ferrara opera over choice of works and payment, Jan. In Verona for successful performance of *Catone in Utica,* March. Cardinal Ruffo forbids him entry into Ferrara to direct the opera, Nov. Bentivoglio, his patron, intercedes unsuccessfully.	M. Haydn born, 14 Sept. Mysliveček born, 9 March
1738	60	Leads the orchestra in a celebration, 7 Jan., of the centenary of the Schouwburg theatre, Amsterdam.	
1739	61	*Siroe* badly received at Ferrara, Jan. *Feraspe,* last	Dittersdorf born, 2 Nov. Keiser (65) dies, 12 Sept.

YEAR	AGE	LIFE	CONTEMPORARY MUSICIANS
		known opera, performed at Venice. *Il Mopso* performed at the Pietà before Ferdinand of Bavaria. De Brosses reports meetings with Vivaldi, 29 Aug.	B. Marcello (52) dies, 24/25 July; Vaňhal born, 12 May.
740	62	*Il coro delle muse* (sinfonia and concertos contributed by Vivaldi) performed, 21 March, before Frederick Christian of Saxony. The Pietà's governors note, 20 April, his impending departure from Venice.	Lotti (74) dies, 5 Jan.; Paisiello born, 9 May.
741	63	In Vienna, where he sells concertos to Count Collalto, 28 June. Dies there in poverty, 28 July, from an 'internal inflammation'. Buried the same day in the Hospital Cemetery.	Fux (81) dies, 14 Feb.; Grétry born, 11 Feb.; Naumann born, 17 April; G. M. Alberti aged 56; Albinoni 70; Astorga 61; C. P. E. Bach 27; J. C. Bach 6; J. S. Bach 56; F. Benda 32; J. Benda 19; Boismortier 52; G. Bononcini 71; Bonporti 69; Cannabich 10; Dall'Abaco 66; Dittersdorf 2; Durante 57; Fasch 53; Gassmann 18; Geminiani 54; Gluck 27; Graupner 58; Handel 56; Hasse 42; J. Haydn 9; M. Haydn 4; Holzbauer 40; Jommelli 27; Leclair 44; Leo 47; Locatelli 46; Manfredini 57; A. Marcello 72; Mascitti *c*77; Miča 47; Monn

YEAR	AGE	LIFE	CONTEMPORARY MUSICIANS

24; Mysliveček 4; Nardini 19; Paganelli 31; Piccini 13; Pisendel 54; G. A. Pollarolo *c*70; Porpora 55; Predieri 53; Quantz 44; Rameau 58; Ristori 49; Roman 47; G. B. Sammartini *c*40; Sarti 12; D. Scarlatti 56; Stamic 24; Tartini 49; Telemann 60; Traetta 14; Vanhal 2; Veracini 51; T. A. Vitali 78; Wagenseil 26; J. G. Walther 57; Zelenka 62.

Appendix B Catalogue of works

INTRODUCTORY NOTES

1. RV numbers are taken from P. Ryom, *Verzeichnis der Werke Antonio Vivaldis: kleine Ausgabe* (Leipzig, 1974), which contains concordance tables for Pincherle, Fanna, Rinaldi and Ricordi numbers.
2. Except where a contrary indication is given, the presence of a *basso* or *basso continuo* part is presumed.
3. The = sign refers the reader to a work identical with the one under consideration except for (a) the key of one or more movements or (b) the choice of instrument(s) for its solo part(s).
4. A number following a publisher's name (e.g. Witvogel 48) is that assigned to a particular work or collection by the publisher himself and quoted in his catalogues.
5. Places and dates given for opera performances refer to *first* performances; revivals are not mentioned unless they entailed a significant change of title or very considerable modification.
6. The spelling and punctuation of titles and text incipits, often inconsistent in the original sources, have been normalized.
7. Operas described as 'lost' often survive partially, in the shape of one or more separate numbers (generally, arias).

ABBREVIATIONS

A	alto	est	*estate* (Summer Season)
aut	Autumn Season		
bn	bassoon	fl	flute (transverse)
carn	*carnevale* (Carnival or Winter Season)	flaut	*flautino*
		hn	horn
chal	chalumeau	hpd	harpsichord
cl	clarinet		

Appendix B—Catalogue of works

inscr.	inscribed (or dedicated) to	rec	recorder (alto)
		tpt	trumpet
lib.	*libro* (volume)	trb	trombone
mand	mandolin	th	theorbo
ob	oboe	v	voice
org	organ	vn	violin
prim	*primavera* (Spring of Ascensiontide Season)	vla	viola
		vla d'am	viola d'amore
		vlc	violoncello
S	soprano	vne	violone

INSTRUMENTAL MUSIC

Sonatas for violin

RV No.	KEY	OBSERVATIONS
1	C	op. 2 no. 6
2	C	inscr. Pisendel
3	C	
4	C	incomplete
5	c	
6	c	inscr. Pisendel
7	c	incomplete
8	c	op. 2 no. 7
9	D	op. 2 no. 11
10	D	
11	D	incomplete
12	d	
13	d	
14	d	op. 2 no. 3
15	d	
16	e	
17	e	incomplete
17a	e	
18	F	op. 5 no. 1 (=13)
19	F	inscr. Pisendel
20	F	op. 2 no. 4
21	f	op. 2 no. 10

216

RV No.	KEY	OBSERVATIONS
22	G	
23	G	op. 2 no. 8
24	G	
25	G	inscr. Pisendel
26	g	
27	g	op. 2 no. 1
28	g	
29	g	inscr. Pisendel
30	A	op. 5 no. 2 (=14)
31	A	op. 2 no. 2
32	a	op. 2 no. 12
33	B♭	op. 5 no. 3 (=15)
34	B♭	
35	b	op. 5 no. 4 (=15)
36	b	op. 2 no. 5
37	b	incomplete
754	C	
755	D	
756	E♭	
757	g	
758	A	
759	B♭	
760	b	

Sonatas for cello

38	d	lost
39	E♭	
40	e	Le Cène edn. no. 5
41	F	Le Cène edn. no. 2
42	g	
43	a	Le Cène edn. no. 3
44	a	
45	B♭	Le Cène edn. no. 4
46	B♭	Le Cène edn. no. 6
47	B♭	Le Cène edn. no. 1

217

RV No.	KEY	OBSERVATIONS

Other sonatas for one instrument

48	C	fl
49	d	fl
50	e	fl
51	g	fl
52	F	rec
53	c	ob
54	C	op. '13' no. 1
55	C	op. '13' no. 5
56	C	op. '13' no. 2
57	G	op. '13' no. 3
58	g	op. '13' no. 6
59	A	op. '13' no. 4

musette/
vièle/rec/
ob/vn
spurious

Sonatas for two violins

60	C	? spurious
61	C	op. 1 no. 3
62	D	op. 1 no. 6
63	d	op. 1 no. 12 *Follia*
64	d	op. 1 no. 8
65	E♭	op. 1 no. 7
66	E	op. 1 no. 4
67	e	op. 1 no. 2
68	F	bass optional
69	F	op. 1 no. 5
70	F	bass optional
71	G	bass optional
72	g	op. 5 no. 6 (=18)
73	g	op. 1 no. 1
74	g	
75	A	op. 1 no. 9
76	B♭	op. 5 no. 5 (=17)
77	B♭	bass optional
78	B♭	op. 1 no. 10
79	b	op. 1 no. 11

RV No.	KEY	OBSERVATIONS

Other sonatas for two instruments

80	G	2 fl
81	g	2 ob
82	C	vn, lute *Trio* inscr. Count Wrtby
83	c	vn, vlc
84	D	fl, vn untitled
85	g	vn, lute *Trio* inscr. Count Wrtby
86	a	rec, bn

Sonatas for more than two instruments

—	C	vn, ob, org, chal chal optional
130	E♭	2 vn, vla *Sonata'al Santo Sepolcro*
169	b	2 vn, vla *Sinfonia al Santo Sepolcro*

Concertos without orchestra

87	C	rec, ob, 2 vn
88	C	fl, ob, vn, bn
89	D	fl, 2 vn
90	D	fl/rec/vn, ob/vn, vn, bn/vlc *Il gardellino*
91	D	fl, vn, bn
92	D	rec, vn, bn/vlc
93	D	lute, 2 vn inscr. Count Wrtby
94	D	rec, ob, vn, bn
95	D	rec/vn, ob/vn, vn, bn *La pastorella*
96	d	fl, vn, bn untitled
97	F	vla d'am, 2 hn, 2 ob, bn
98	F	fl, ob, vn, bn *Tempesta di mare*
99	F	fl, ob, vn, bn
100	F	fl, vn, bn
101	G	rec, ob, vn, bn
102	G	fl, 2 vn
103	g	rec, ob, bn
104	g	fl/vn, 2 vn, bn *La notte*
105	g	rec, ob, vn, bn
106	g	fl/vn, vn, bn/vlc
107	g	fl, ob, vn, bn
108	a	rec, 2 vn

Appendix B—Catalogue of works

RV No.	KEY	OBSERVATIONS

Concertos and sinfonias for string orchestra

RV No.	KEY	OBSERVATIONS
109	C	*Concerto*
110	C	*Concerto*
111	C	*Concerto*
111a	C	*Sinfonia*
112	C	*Sinfonia*
113	C	*Concerto*
114	C	*Concerto*
115	C	*Concerto ripieno*
116	C	*Sinfonia*
117	C	*Concerto*
118	c	*Concerto*
119	c	*Concerto*
120	c	*Concerto*
121	D	*Concerto*
122	D	*Sinfonia*
123	D	*Concerto*
124	D	*Concerto* op. 12 no. 3
125	D	*Sinfonia* incomplete
126	D	*Concerto*
127	d	*Concerto*
128	d	*Concerto*
129	d	*Concerto madrigalesco*
131	E	*Sinfonia*
132	E	*Sinfonia* ?spurious
133	e	*Concerto*
134	e	*Sinfonia/Concerto*
135	F	*Sinfonia*
136	F	*Concerto*
137	F	*Sinfonia*
138	F	*Concerto*
139	F	*Concerto*
140	F	*Concerto/Sinfonia*
141	F	*Concerto*
142	F	*Concerto*
143	f	*Concerto*

RV No.	KEY	OBSERVATIONS
144	G	*Introdutione* ?spurious
145	G	*Concerto*
146	G	*Concerto/Sinfonia*
147	G	*Sinfonia*
149	G	*Sinfonia*
150	G	*Concerto*
151	G	*Concerto alla rustica*
152	g	*Concerto ripieno*
153	g	*Concerto*
154	g	*Concerto*
155	g	*Concerto*
156	g	*Concerto*
157	g	*Concerto*
158	A	*Concerto ripieno*
159	A	*Concerto*
160	A	*Concerto*
161	a	*Concerto*
162	B♭	*Sinfonia*
163	B♭	*'Conca'*
164	B♭	*Concerto*
165	B♭	*Concerto*
166	B♭	*Concerto*
167	B♭	*Concerto*
168	b	*Sinfonia*

Concertos for violin and string orchestra

170	C	
171	C	inscr. 'Sua Maestà Cesarea e Cattolica'
172	C	inscr. Pisendel
172a	C	incomplete
173	C	op. 12 no. 4
174	C	lost
175	C	Witvogel 48 no. 3
176	C	
177	C	
178	C	op. 8 no. 12 =RV 449

Appendix B—Catalogue of works

RV No.	KEY	OBSERVATIONS
179	C	
180	C	op. 8 no. 6 *Il piacere*
181	C	
181a	C	op. 9 no. 1
182	C	
183	C	
184	C	
185	C	op. 4 no. 7
186	C	
187	C	
188	C	op. 7 no. 2
189	C	Witvogel 35 no. 1
190	C	
191	C	
192	C	*Sinfonia*
193	C	lost
194	C	
195	C	J. Roger 417 no. 6
196	c	op. 4 no. 10
197	c	
198	c	
198a	c	op. 9 no. 11
199	c	*Il sospetto*
200	c	lost
201	c	
202	c	op. 11 no. 5
761	c	*Amato bene*
203	D	incomplete
204	D	op. 4 no. 11
205	D	inscr. Pisendel
206	D	
207	D	op. 11 no. 1
208	D	*Grosso Mogul*
208a	D	op. 7 no. 11 (=lib. 2 no. 5)
209	D	
210	D	op. 8 no. 11

RV No.	KEY	OBSERVATIONS
211	D	
212	D	*Concerto fatto per la solennità della S. Lingua di S. Antonio in Padova 1712*
212a	D	
213	D	
214	D	op. 7 no. 12 (=lib. 2 no. 6)
215	D	
216	D	op. 6 no. 4
217	D	
218	D	
219	D	
220	D	J. Roger 432 no. 6
221	D	'violino in tromba'
222	D	
223	D	=RV 762
224	D	
224a	D	
225	D	
226	D	
227	D	
228	D	
229	D	
230	D	op. 3 no. 9
231	D	
232	D	
233	D	
234	D	*L'inquietudine*
752	D	lost
235	d	
236	d	op. 8 no. 9 =RV 454
237	d	inscr. Pisendel
238	d	op. 9 no. 8
239	d	op. 6 no. 6
240	d	
241	d	
242	d	op. 8 no. 7 inscr. Pisendel

Appendix B—Catalogue of works

RV No.	KEY	OBSERVATIONS
243	d	'violino senza cantin'
244	d	op. 12 no. 2
245	d	
246	d	
247	d	
248	d	
249	d	op. 4 no. 8
250	E♭	
251	E♭	
252	E♭	
253	E♭	op. 8 no. 5 *La tempesta di mare*
254	E♭	
255	E♭	lost
256	E♭	*Il ritiro*
257	E♭	
258	E♭	
259	E♭	op. 6 no. 2
260	E♭	
261	E♭	
262	E♭	
263	E	
263a	E	op. 9 no. 4
264	E	
265	E	op. 3 no. 12
266	E	
267	E	
268	E	
269	E	op. 8 no. 1 *La primavera*
270	E	*Il riposo/Concerto per il santissimo natale*
271	E	*L'amoroso*
762	E	=RV 223
273	e	
274	e	
275	e	J. Roger 433 no. 12
275a	e	=RV 430
276	e	

224

RV No.	KEY	OBSERVATIONS
277	e	op. 11 no. 2 *Il favorito*
278	e	
279	e	op. 4 no. 2
280	e	op. 6 no. 5
281	e	
282	F	
283	F	
284	F	op. 4 no. 9
285	F	
285a	F	op. 7 no. 5
286	F	*Concerto per la solennità di S. Lorenzo*/inscr. Anna Maria
287	F	
288	F	
289	F	
290	F	lost
291	F	no. 6 in Walsh edn. of op. 4
292	F	
293	F	op. 8 no. 3 *L'autunno*
294	F	*Il ritiro*
294a	F	op. 7 no. 10 (=lib. 2 no. 4) *Il ritiro*
295	F	
296	F	
297	f	op. 8 no. 4 *L'inverno*
298	G	op. 4 no. 12
299	G	op. 7 no. 8 (=lib. 2 no. 2)
300	G	op. 9 no. 10
301	G	op. 4 no. 3
302	G	
303	G	
304	G	lost
305	G	lost
306	G	
307	G	
308	G	op. 11 no. 4
309	G	*Il mare tempestoso* lost

RV No.	KEY	OBSERVATIONS
310	G	op. 3 no. 3
311	G	'violino in tromba'
312	G	
313	G	'violino in tromba'
314	G	inscr. Pisendel
314a	G	
315	g	op. 8 no. 2 *L'estate*
316	g	lost
316a	g	op. 4 no. 6
317	g	op. 12 no. 1
318	g	op. 6 no. 3
319	g	
320	g	incomplete
321	g	
322	g	incomplete
323	g	
324	g	op. 6 no. 1
325	g	
326	g	op. 7 no. 3
327	g	
328	g	
329	g	
330	g	
331	g	
332	g	op. 8 no. 8
333	g	
334	g	op. 9 no. 3
335	A	*The Cuckow*
336	A	op. 11 no. 3
337	A	lost
339	A	
340	A	inscr. Pisendel
341	A	Witvogel 35 no. 4
342	A	
343	A	
344	A	

RV No.	KEY	OBSERVATIONS
345	A	op. 9 no. 2
346	A	
347	A	op. 4 no. 5
348	A	op. 9 no. 6
349	A	
350	A	
351	A	lost
352	A	
353	A	
763	A	*L'ottavina*
768	A	
354	a	op. 7 no. 4
355	a	
356	a	op. 3 no. 6
357	a	op. 4 no. 4
358	a	op. 9 no. 5
359	B♭	op. 9 no. 7
360	B♭	incomplete
361	B♭	op. 12 no. 6
362	B♭	op. 8 no. 10 *La caccia*
363	B♭	*Il corneto da posta*
364	B♭	J. Roger 433 no. 8
364a	B♭	*L'élite des concerto italiens*
365	B♭	
366	B♭	
367	B♭	
368	B♭	
369	B♭	
370	B♭	
371	B♭	
372	B♭	
373	B♭	op. 7 no. 9 (=lib. 2 no. 3) ?spurious
374	B♭	op. 7 no. 6
375	B♭	
376	B♭	
377	B♭	

RV No.	KEY	OBSERVATIONS
378	B♭	
379	B♭	op. 12 no. 5
380	B♭	
381	B♭	
382	B♭	
383	B♭	
383a	B♭	op 4 no. 1
384	b	
385	b	
386	b	
387	b	
388	b	
389	b	
390	b	
391	b	op. 9 no. 12

Concertos for viola d'amore and string orchestra

392	D
393	d
394	d
395	d
395a	d
396	A
397	a

Concertos for cello and string orchestra

398	C
399	C
400	C
401	c
402	c
403	D
404	D
405	d
406	d
407	d
408	E♭

RV No.	KEY	OBSERVATIONS
409	e	
410	F	
411	F	
412	F	
413	G	
414	G	
415	G	
416	g	
417	g	
418	a	
419	a	
420	a	
421	a	
422	a	
423	B♭	
424	b	

Concerto for mandolin and string orchestra

425	C	

Concertos for flute and string orchestra

426	D	
427	D	
428	D	op. 10 no. 3 *Il gardellino*
429	D	
430	e	=RV 275a
431	e	incomplete
432	e	incomplete
433	F	op. 10 no. 1 *La tempesta di mare*
434	F	op. 10 no. 5 =RV 442
435	G	op. 10 no. 4
436	G	
437	G	op. 10 no. 6
438	G	
439	g	op. 10 no. 2 *La notte*
440	a	

Appendix B—Catalogue of works

Concertos for recorder and string orchestra

RV No.	KEY	OBSERVATIONS
441	c	
442	F	=RV 434

Concertos for 'flautino' and string orchestra

443	C	
444	C	
445	a	

Concertos for oboe and string orchestra

446	C	
447	C	
448	C	
449	C	op. 8 no. 12 =RV 178
450	C	
451	C	
452	C	
453	D	
454	d	op. 8 no. 9 =RV 236
455	F	inscr. 'Sassonia'
456	F	*Harmonia mundi* no. 5
457	F	
458	F	
459	g	
460	g	op. 11 no. 6
461	a	
462	a	
463	a	
464	B♭	op. 7 no. 7 (=lib. 2 no. 1) ?spurious
465	B♭	op. 7 no. 1 ?spurious

Concertos for bassoon and string orchestra

466	C	
467	C	
468	C	
469	C	
470	C	

RV No.	KEY	OBSERVATIONS
471	C	
472	C	
473	C	
474	C	
475	C	
476	C	
477	C	
478	C	
479	C	
480	c	
481	d	
482	d	
483	E♭	
484	e	
485	F	
486	F	
487	F	
488	F	
489	F	
490	F	
491	F	
492	G	
493	G	
494	G	
495	g	
496	g	inscr. 'Ma: de Morzin'
497	a	
498	a	
499	a	
500	a	
501	B♭	
502	B♭	inscr. Gioseppino Biancardi
503	B♭	
504	B♭	

Concertos for two violins and string orchestra

505	C	

RV No.	KEY	OBSERVATIONS
506	C	
507	C	
508	C	
509	c	
510	c	
511	D	
512	D	
513	D	Witvogel 48 no. 6
514	d	
515	E♭	
516	G	
517	g	
518	A	
519	A	op. 3 no. 5
520	A	incomplete
521	A	
522	a	op. 3 no. 8
523	a	
524	B♭	
525	B♭	
526	B♭	incomplete
527	B♭	
528	B♭	
529	B♭	
530	B♭	op. 9 no. 9
764	B♭	=RV 548

Other concertos for two instruments and string orchestra

531	g	2 vlc
532	G	2 mand
533	C	2 fl
534	C	2 ob
535	d	2 ob
536	a	2 ob
537	C	2 tpt
538	F	2 hn

RV No.	KEY	OBSERVATIONS
539	F	2 hn
766	c	vn, org
540	d	vla d'am, lute
541	d	vn, org
542	F	vn, org
543	F	vn, ob (unison)
544	F	vn, vlc *Il proteo ossia il mondo al rovescio*
767	F	vn, org
545	G	ob, bn
546	A	vn, vlc/ vn, vlc *all'inglese*
547	B♭	vn, vlc
548	B♭	vn, ob =RV 764

Concertos for several violins and string orchestra

549	D	4 vn (vlc in 3rd movement) op. 3 no. 1
550	e	4 vn op. 3 no. 4
551	F	3 vn
552	A	*Concerto con violino principale et altro* [=3!] *violino per eco in lontano*
553	B♭	4 vn

Other concertos for several instruments and string orchestra

554	C	vn, org/vn, ob
554a	C	vn, org/vn, vlc
555	C	3 vn, ob, 2 rec, 2 vla *all'inglese,* chal, 2 vlc, 2 hpd (2 tpt, 2 vne in 3rd movement)
556	C	2 ob, 2 cl, 2 rec, 2 vn, bn (lute in 2nd movement) *Concerto per la solennità di S. Lorenzo*
557	C	2 vn, 2 ob, ?bn (2 rec, bn in 2nd movement)
558	C	2 vn 'in tromba marina', 2 rec, 2 tpt, 2 mand, 2 chal, 2 th, vlc
559	C	2 cl, 2 ob
560	C	2 cl, 2 ob
561	C	vn, 2 vlc
562	D	vn, 2 ob, 2 hn *Concerto per la solennità di S. Lorenzo*
562a	D	vn, 2 ob, 2 hn, timp
563	D	vn, 2 ob

233

Appendix B—Catalogue of works

RV No.	KEY	OBSERVATIONS
564	D	2 vn, 2 vlc
564a	D	2 vn, 2 ob, bn
565	d	2 vn, vlc op. 3 no. 11
566	d	2 vn, 2 rec, 2 ob, bn
567	F	4 vn, vlc op. 3 no. 7
568	F	vn, 2 ob, 2 hn, bn
569	F	vn, 2 ob, 2 hn, bn (vlc in 3rd movement)
570	F	fl, ob, bn (vn in 1st movement) *Tempesta di mare*
571	F	vn, 2 ob, 2 hn, vlc, bn
572	F	2 fl, 2 ob, vn, vlc *Il proteo ossia il mondo al rovescio*
573	F	lost
574	F	vn, 2 trbn da caccia, 2 ob, bn inscr. 'S.A.S.I.S.P.G. M.D.G.S.M.B.'
575	G	2 vn, 2 vlc
576	g	vn, 2 rec, 2 ob, bn inscr. 'Sua Altezza Reale [di] Sassonia'
577	g	vn, 2 ob, 2 rec, 3 ob, bn inscr. 'L'orchestra di Dresda'
578	g	2 vn, vlc op. 3 no. 2
579	B♭	vn, ob, chal, 3 vla *all'inglese* *Concerto funebre*
580	b	4 vn, vlc op. 3 no. 10

Concertos for violin and two string orchestras

581	C	*Concerto per la Santissima Assontione di Maria Vergine*
582	D	*Concerto per la Santissima Assontione di Maria Vergine*
583	B♭	

Concertos for several instruments and two orchestras

584	F	*Coro 1* vn, org; *Coro 2* vn, org unfinished
585	A	*Coro 1* 2 vn, 2 rec (th/org in 2nd movement, vlc in 3rd movement); *Coro 2* 2 vn, 2 rec, org (vlc in 4rd movement)

VOCAL MUSIC

Masses and Mass sections

RV No.	KEY	TITLE OR DESCRIPTION
586	C	*Sacrum* (complete Mass)
587	g	*Kyrie* (2 *cori*)
588	D	*Gloria* (introduced by RV 639/639a)
589	D	*Gloria*
590	?	*Gloria* (lost)
591	e	*Credo*
592	G	*Credo*

Psalms, etc.

593	G	*Domine ad adiuvandum me* (response, 2 *cori*)
594	D	*Dixit Dominum* (Ps. 109, 2 *cori*)
595	D	*Dixit Dominus* (Ps. 109)
596	C	*Confitebor tibi Domine* (Ps. 110)
597	C	*Beatus vir* (Ps. 111, 2 *cori*)
598	B♭	*Beatus vir* (Ps. 111)
599	B♭	*Beatus vir* (Ps. 111, lost)
600	c	*Laudate pueri* (Ps. 112, 2 *cori*)
601	G	*Laudate pueri* (Ps. 112)
602	A	*Laudate pueri* (Ps. 112, 2 *cori*)
602a	A	modification of RV 602
603	A	*Laudate pueri* (Ps. 112, 2 *cori*, modification of RV 602)
604	C	*In exitu Israel* (Ps. 113)
605	C	*Credidi* (Ps. 115, *contrafactum* of anonymous *Lauda Jerusalem*, RV Anh. 35)
606	d	*Laudate Dominum* (Ps. 116)
607	F	*Laetatus sum* (Ps. 121)
608	g	*Nisi Dominus* (Ps. 126)
609	e	*Lauda Jerusalem* (Ps. 147, 2 *cori*)
610	g	*Magnificat*
610a	g	version of RV 610 for 2 *cori*
610b	g	modification of RV 610
611	g	*Magnificat* (later modification of RV 610)

Hymns, antiphons, etc.

612	C	*Deus tuorum militum* (hymn)
613	B♭	*Gaude Mater* (hymn)
614	F	*Laudate Dominum omnes gentes* ('offertory')

Appendix B—Catalogue of works

---

[1] Without additional accompanying strings.
[2] RV 646–648 are *contrafacta* of arias in RV 700 (RV 646, 648) and RV 728 (RV 647).

RV No.	TITLE OR DESCRIPTION
647	*Eja voces plausum date* ('Aria de Sanctis')
648	*Ihr Himmel nun* ('Concertus Italicus')

Solo cantatas for soprano

649	*All'ombra d'un bel faggio*
650	*All'or che lo sguardo*
651	*Amor, hai vinto*
652	*Aure, voi più non siete*
653	*Del suo natio rigore*
654	*Elvira, Elvira, anima mia*
655	*Era la notte*
656	*Fonti di pianto, piangete*
657	*Geme l'onda che parte*
658	*Il povero mio cor*
659	*Indarno cerca la tortorella*
660	*La farfalletta s'aggira*
661	*Nel partir da te, mio caro*
662	*Par che tardo*
663	*Scherza di fronda*
664	*Seben vivono senz'alma*
665	*Sì levi dal pensier*
666	*Sì, sì, luci adorate*
667	*Sorge vermiglia in ciel*
668	*T'intendo, sì, mio cor*
669	*Tra l'erbe i zeffiri*
753	*Prendea con mandi latte*

Solo cantatas for alto

670	*Alla caccia, alla caccia*
671	*Care selve, amici prati*
672	*Filli di gioia*
673	*Ingrata Lidia, hai vinto*
674	*Perfidissimo cor*
675	*Piango, gemo, sospiro*
676	*Pianti, sospiri*
677	*Qual per ignoto*

Cantatas for soprano with instrumental accompaniment

678	*All'ombra di sospetto* (fl)
679	*Che giova il sospirar* (2 vn, vla)
680	*Lungi dal vago* (vn)

Appendix B—Catalogue of works

[3] 'In praise of Monsignor da Bagni, Bishop of Mantua'.
[4] 'In praise of His Highness Prince Philip of Hesse-Darmstadt, Governor of Mantua'.

RV No.	TITLE	LIBRETTIST	PLACE, DATE
Oratorios			
643	Moyses Deus Pharaonis (lost)	unknown	Venice, 1714
644	Juditha triumphans	G. Cassetti	Venice, 1716 Nov.
645	L'adorazione delli tre rè magi al bambino Gesù	unknown	Milan, 1722
Serenatas, etc			
687	'Dall'eccelsa mia reggia' (2 v, Gloria, Imeneo)	unknown	?Venice, 1725 aut
688	Le gare del dovere (3 v, lost)[5]	unknown	Venice, 1719
689	Le gare della giustitia e della pace (lost)	G. B. Catena	?Venice
690	'Mio cor, povero cor' (3 v)	unknown	unknown
691	Il Mopso ('Egloga Pescatoria', 5 v, lost)	E. Nonnanuci[6]	Venice, 1739
692	'Questa Eurilla gentil' (4 v)[7]	unknown	Mantua, 1726, 31 July
693	La Sena festeggiante (3 v)	D. Lalli	unknown
694	L'unione della pace e di Marte (3 v, lost)[8]	A. Grossatesta	Venice, 1727 aut

[5] 'A tribute in praise of the singular merit of Francesco Querini'.

[6] Pseudonym of G. Cendoni.

[7] 'In celebration of the birthday of Philip, Landgrave of Hesse-Darmstadt'.

[8] 'In celebration of the birth of the two royal twin princesses, Mme de France and Mme de Navarre'.

RV No.	TITLE	LIBRETTIST	PLACE, DATE
Operas			
695	*L'Adelaide* (lost)	A. Salvi	Verona, 1735
696	*Alvilda, regina de' Goti* (lost)[9]	A. Zeno	Prague, 1731 prim
697	*Argippo* (lost)	D. Lalli	Prague, 1730 aut
698	*Aristide* (lost)	C. Goldoni	Venice, 1735 aut
699	*Armida al campo d'Egitto* (Act II lost)	G. Palazzi	Venice, 1718 carn
700	*Arsilda, regina di Ponto*	D. Lalli	Venice, 1716 aut
701	*Artabano, rè de' Parti* (modification of RV 706, lost)	A. Marchi	Venice, 1718 carn
702	*L'Atenaide*	A. Zeno	Florence, 1729 carn
703	*Bajazet* (*Tamerlano*) (pasticcio)	A. Piovene	Verona, 1735 carn
704	*La Candace o siano li veri amici* (lost)	F. Silvani — D. Lalli	Mantua, 1720 carn
705	*Catone in Utica* (Act I lost)	P. Metastasio	Verona, 1737, March
706	*La costanza trionfante degl'amori e de gl'odii* (lost)	A. Marchi	Venice, 1716 carn
707	*Cunegonda* (lost)	A. Piovene	Venice, 1726 carn
708	*Doriclea* (modification of RV 706, lost)	A. Marchi	Prague, 1732 carn
709	*Dorilla in Tempe*	A. M. Lucchini	Venice, 1726 aut
710	*Ercole sul Termodonte* (lost)	G. F. Bussani	Rome, 1723 carn
711	*Farnace*[10]	A. M. Lucchini	Venice, 1727 carn
712	*La fede tradita e vendicata* (lost)	F. Silvani	Venice, 1726 carn

[9] Recitatives and comic arias ('arie bernesche') not by Vivaldi.

[10] Acts I and II of a new version for Ferrara (1739 carn) survive.

RV No.	TITLE	LIBRETTIST	PLACE, DATE
713	*Feraspe* (lost)	?F. Silvani	Venice, 1739 aut
714	*La fida ninfa*	S. Maffei	Verona, 1732, Jan.
715	*Filippo, rè di Macedonia* (lost)[11]	D. Lalli	Venice, 1721 carn
716	*Ginevra, principesa di Scozia* (lost)	A. Salvi	Florence, 1736 carn
717	*Giustino*	N. Beregan —	
		P. Pariati	Rome, 1724 carn
718	*Griselda*	A. Zeno —	
		C. Goldoni	Venice, 1725 prim
719	*L'incoronazione di Dario*	A. Morselli	Venice, 1717 carn
720	*Gli inganni per vendetta* (modification of RV 699, lost)	G. Palazzi	Vicenza, 1720
721	*L'inganno trionfante in amore* (lost)	M. Noris —	
		G. M. Ruggieri	Venice, 1725 aut
722	*Ipermestra* (lost)	A. Salvi	Florence, 1727 carn
723	*Motezuma* (lost)	G. Giusti	Venice, 1733 aut
724	*Nerone fatto Cesare* (pasticcio, lost)	M. Noris	Venice, 1715 carn
725	*L'Olimpiade*	P. Metastasio	Venice, 1734 carn
726	*L'oracolo in Messenia* (lost)	A. Zeno	Venice, 1738 carn
727	*Orlando finto pazzo*	G. Braccioli	Venice, 1714 aut
728	*Orlando (furioso)*	G. Braccioli	Venice, 1727 aut
729	*Ottone in Villa*	D. Lalli	Vicenza, 1713, May
730	*Rosilena ed Oronta* (lost)	G. Palazzi	Venice, 1728 carn

[11] Acts I and II by G. Boniventi, Act III by Vivaldi.

RV No.	TITLE	LIBRETTIST	PLACE, DATE
731	*Rosmira* (pasticcio)	S. Stampiglia	Venice, 1738 carn
732	*Scanderbeg* (lost)	A. Salvi	Florence, 1718 est
733	*Semiramide* (lost)	F. Silvani	Mantua, 1732 carn
734	*La Silvia* (lost)	P. P. Bissarri	Milan, 1721, Aug
735	*Siroe, rè di Persia* (lost)	P. Metastasio	Reggio, 1727 prim
736	*Teuzzone*	A. Zeno	Mantua, 1719 carn
737	*Tieteberga* (lost)	A. M. Lucchini	Venice, 1717 aut
738	*Tito Manlio*	M. Noris	Mantua, 1719 carn
Anh. 56	*Tito Manlio* (lost)[12]		Rome, 1720 carn
739	*La verità in cimento*	G. Palazzi and D. Lalli	Venice, 1720 aut
740	*La virtù trionfante dell'amore e dell'odio ovvero il Tigrane*[13]	F. Silvani	Rome, 1724 carn

[12] Act I by G. Boni, Act II by G. Giorgio. Act III by Vivaldi.
[13] Act I by B. Micheli, Act III by N. Romaldi. Only Act II (Vivaldi) survives.

RV 741–750 are works preserved in too fragmentary a state or cited too imprecisely to be included in the main series RV 1–740 or its supplement RV 751–768. The Ryom catalogue has in addition an appendix (*Anhang*) containing 68 works incorrectly attributed elsewhere to Vivaldi or of uncertain authorship. The same author's *Les manuscrits de Vivaldi* refers to works identified by the RV numbers 770, 772, 779 and 780, from which it is clear that in the revised edition of the *Verzeichnis der Werke Antonio Vivaldis*, currently in preparation, and his larger catalogue, *Répertoire des œuvres d'Antonio Vivaldi*, which is due to appear shortly, the series has been extended by at least 11 numbers. RV 770 is the former RV 395a, the change of number resulting from Ryom's identification of the violin rather than the viola d'amore as the solo instrument in the variant of RV 395. RV 772 is a violin concerto newly discovered in Venice. RV 779 is the Dresden quartet sonata. RV 780 is the concerto for violin and cello (also, two *viole all'inglese*) RV 546 in a version Ryom supposes— in the present author's view erroneously — to be for solo harpsichord.

Appendix C Personalia

Alberti, Giuseppe Matteo (1685–1751), Italian composer, born Bologna. His light and tuneful works, mostly concertos and sinfonias for strings with or without solo violin, were very popular in northern Europe in the first half of the eighteenth century. No relation of the harpsichordist and singer Domenico Alberti (1710–46).

Albinoni, Tomaso (1671–1751), Italian composer. Born into a wealthy Venetian family of paper-manufacturers, he began his musical career as a *dilettante*. His compositions include numerous operas, serenatas, cantatas, sonatas and concertos. His solo concertos and the intermezzos *Vespetta e Pimpinone* were widely performed.

Bach, Carl Philipp Emanuel (1714–88), German composer and theorist, born Weimar. Second son of Johann Sebastian Bach. From 1740 to 1767 he served Frederick of Prussia as first harpsichordist, subsequently moving to Hamburg. Of his theoretical writings the *Versuch über die wahre Art das Clavier zu spielen* (1753–62) is the most important, illuminating many aspects of mid-century performance practice in Germany.

Bentivoglio d'Aragona, Guido (1705–59), Italian nobleman (*Marchese*), born Venice. His promising ecclesiastical career was cut short by the death of an elder brother, following which he settled in Ferrara, in whose administration he participated.

Boniventi, Giuseppe (fl. 1690–1727), Italian composer, born Venice. *c*1707 he was *Maestro di Cappella* to Duke Ferdinando Carlo of Mantua. From 1712 to 1718 he was *Kapellmeister* to the Margrave of Baden-Durlach. His output consists largely of operas.

Boni, Pietro Giuseppe Gaetano (fl. 1700–41), Italian composer, born

244

Bologna. He lived in Rome from 1711 to at least 1720. His small output is most notable for its instrumental works.

Brosses, Charles de (1709–77), first president of the *Parlement* of Dijon, classical scholar and historian. He undertook a tour of Italy in 1739–40. His *Lettres historiques et critiques sur l'Italie* (also known as *Lettres familières*) are largely based on letters written to various friends during the tour and contain many illuminating observations on music.

Charles VI (1685–1740), last emperor of the direct Habsburg line, succeeding his brother Joseph I in 1711. He had wide cultural interests and possessed some ability as a composer and accompanist. During his reign the court opera at Vienna flourished.

Corelli, Arcangelo (1653–1713), Italian composer, born Fusignano near Ravenna. His early years were spent in Bologna (hence his nickname 'Il Bolognese') but in 1675 at latest he came to Rome, where he directed orchestras and enjoyed the patronage of Queen Christina of Sweden and the cardinals Pamphili and Ottoboni. His published collections of trio sonatas (opp. 1–4), solo sonatas (op. 5) and concertos (op. 6) were classic works in their period.

Denzio, Antonio (*fl.* early eighteenth century), Venetian impresario and singer. During a long period of activity (1724–34) at the Sporck theatre in Prague Denzio was responsible for nearly 60 productions. His repertoire embraced works by Albinoni, Boniventi, Gasparini, Lotti, Orlandini, Porta and Vivaldi.

Francis I (1708–65), Duke of Lorraine from 1729 to 1737, Grand Duke of Tuscany from 1737 to 1765 and (by virtue of his marriage in 1736 to the Habsburg princess Maria Theresa) Austrian Emperor from 1745 to 1765 in succession to Charles VII.

Frederick IV (1671–1730), King of Denmark and Norway from 1699. He visited Venice in 1693 and 1708–9.

Frederick Augustus II (1696–1763), Elector of Saxony from 1733 and (as Augustus III) King of Poland from 1736. Noted for his patronage of the arts. Before his accession he visited Venice on three occasions: 1712, 1713 and 1716–17.

Frederick Christian (1722-63), Crown Prince of Saxony. As he outlived his father Frederick Augustus II (q.v.) by only two months his reign as Elector was very brief.

Gambara, Annibale (1682–1709), Venetian nobleman (*Conte*) of Brescian extraction.

Gasparini, Francesco (1668–1727), Italian composer, born Camajore near Lucca. A pupil of Pasquini and Corelli in Rome and Lotti in Venice. *Maestro di Coro* at the Pietà from 1700 to 1713, when he moved to Rome. Composer of over 60 operas and the manual for accompanists *L'armonico pratico al cimbalo* (1708).

Gasparini, Michel Angelo (died *c* 1732), Italian singer, singing teacher and composer, probably a brother of Francesco Gasparini.

Gentili, Giorgio (*c* 1669–1731 or later), Italian composer, born Venice. He was principal violinist of the St Mark's orchestra and from *c* 1702 to *c* 1717 *Maestro di Istrumenti* at the Mendicanti. Six collections of his instrumental music, including two of concertos (opp. 5 and 6) were published between 1701 and 1716.

Ghezzi, Pier Leone (1674–1755), Italian painter, born Rome. Famous for his caricatures and sketches of Roman life, which have earned him the nickname 'the Roman Hogarth'.

Giacomelli (or *Jacomelli*), *Geminiano* (*c* 1692–1740), Italian composer, born Piacenza. Appointed *Maestro di Cappella* to the Duke of Parma in 1724. In 1738 made *Maestro di Cappella* of the Holy House of Loreto. His compositions include operas and church music.

Goldoni, Carlo (1707–93), Italian dramatist, born Venice. Famed above all for his sparkling comedies, he also wrote several librettos for comic operas and intermezzos. His Memoirs came out in Paris in 1787.

Grua, Carlo Pietro (*c* 1665–1726), Italian composer, born Florence. Most of his working life was spent at German courts. From 1719 he was *Maestro di Coro* at the Pietà. Often confused with a homonymous son, also a composer.

Hasse, Johann Adolf (1699–1783), German composer, born Bergedorf near Hamburg. The most successful opera composer of his generation, equally esteemed in Italy, where he spent many years and was nicknamed 'Il Sassone', and Germany. *Kapellmeister* to the Saxon court from 1731 to 1763. Besides operas his output includes much church music and some instrumental music.

Heinichen, Johann David (1683–1729), German composer, born Krössuln. He lived in Italy from 1710 to 1716, mostly in Venice. *Kapellmeister* to the Saxon court from 1716.

Holdsworth, Edward (1684–1746), English classical scholar and poet (in Latin). Employed as a cicerone to young gentlemen on the Grand Tour, he visited Italy several times, where he fulfilled 'commissions' for his friend and correspondent Charles Jennens (q.v.).

Jennens, Charles (1700–73), English landowner, man of letters and connoisseur of music. Friend and patron of Handel, for whom he provided several oratorio librettos, including *Saul, Messiah* and *Belshazzar*. His large musical library inherited by the Earls of Aylesford, was sold by auction in 1873 and 1918, a portion passing via Newman Flower to Manchester Public Libraries.

Le Cène, Michel-Charles (1683/4–1743), music publisher, born Honfleur. Son of a Huguenot émigré, he became associated with the publishing house of Estienne Roger through his marriage to Roger's elder daughter Françoise. In 1722 he succeeded Jeanne Roger, the younger daughter, as head of the firm.

Locatelli, Pietro (1695–1764), Italian composer and violinist, born Bergamo. The 'Paganini of the 18th century', he was also an inventive, sometimes profound, composer of instrumental works, of which nine *opera,* including the twelve solo concertos, op. 3, entitled *L'arte del violino* (1733), came out between 1721 and 1762. Much travelled, he settled permanently in Amsterdam in 1729.

Lotti, Antonio (1666–1740), Italian composer, born Venice. For most of his life he was associated with St Mark's, where he was appointed *Primo Maestro* in 1736. Director of the Dresden court opera from 1717 to 1719. His works include operas, cantatas and church music. Among his pupils were D. Alberti, F. and M. A. Gasparini, Galuppi and B. Marcello.

Marcello, Alessandro (1669–1747), Italian amateur composer, born Venice. In addition to writing a small number of cantatas and instrumental works, he fostered music through weekly 'academies' at his house attended, among others, by Gasparini, Lotti and Tartini.

Marcello, Benedetto (1686–1739), Italian amateur composer and writer, born Venice. Brother of A. Marcello. He held several important official posts in Venice and the provinces, but found time to compose an impressive quantity of works, of which his *Estro poetico-armonico* (1724–6), a setting of 50 psalms in Italian paraphrase, and his solo cantatas were the most celebrated. His best-known literary work is the satire *Il teatro alla moda* (1720).

Mattheson, Johann (1681–1764), German critic and composer, born Hamburg. Friend of Handel. Cantor of Hamburg Cathedral from 1715 to 1728 and for many years Secretary to the English Resident. His often strongly polemical writings mark the birth of music criticism in the modern sense.

Metastasio, Pietro (1698–1782), Italian dramatist and poet (real name P. Trapassi), born Rome. Appointed 'Caesarean Poet' to the Viennese court, succeeding Zeno and Pariati, in 1729. The most popular and influential librettist of his century, famed for the limpid elegance of his verse and the cogent structure of his plots.

Pergolesi, Giovanni Battista (1710–36), Italian composer, born Jesi. His meteoric career provided Europe with a romantic legend. Though his most famous works deservedly remain the intermezzos *La serva padrona* (1733) and the *Stabat Mater* (1736), he produced many other masterpieces of opera and church music.

Philip of Hesse-Darmstadt (1671–1736), Prince. Son of Landgrave Ludwig VI and younger brother of his successor Ernst Ludwig, he was nevertheless often styled 'Landgrave' in Italy, where he served as Governor of Mantua on behalf of the Austrians from 1714 to 1735.

Porta, Giovanni (*c* 1690–1755), Italian composer, born Venice. From

1706 to 1716 he worked in Rome. *Maestro di Coro* at the Pietà from 1726 until 1737, when he became *Kapellmeister* to the Elector of Bavaria. His output consists principally of operas and church music.

Predieri, Luca Antonio (1688–1767), Italian composer, born Bologna. His early years were spent in Italy, but in 1737 he was invited to the Viennese court, where he remained. He composed mainly operas.

Quantz, Johann Joachim (1697–1773), German composer, flautist and theorist, born Oberscheden near Hanover. In the service of the Elector of Saxony from 1716 to 1741 and the King of Prussia thereafter. His compositions are dominated by flute concertos written for Frederick the Great. His flute tutor, *Versuch einer Anweisung die Flöte traversiere zu spielen* (1752), and his Autobiography (1755) are important documents in their respective areas.

Ristori, Giovanni Alberto (1692–1753), Italian composer, born Bologna. Having enjoyed success with his operas in Venice, he moved in 1715 to Dresden, where his father directed a troupe of comedians. He secured court appointments first as composer, later as organist and finally as deputy to J. A. Hasse.

Scarlatti, Alessandro (1660–1725), Italian composer, born Palermo. Resident at various times in Rome, Florence and Naples. A prolific and much-admired composer of operas, cantatas and church music. He is credited with the popularization of the *da capo* aria form. Father of the composer Domenico Scarlatti.

Stölzel, Gottfried Heinrich (1690–1749), German composer, born Crunstädtel near Schwarzenberg. From 1719 *Kapellmeister* to the court of Gotha.

Tartini, Giuseppe (1692–1770), Italian composer, violinist, violin teacher and theorist, born Pirano (Istria). From 1721 he was principal violinist in the orchestra of the Basilica del Santo in Padua, where he founded an internationally renowned school of violin playing in 1728. His instrumental compositions are distinguished by a cantabile style that looks forward to the classical period.

Telemann, Georg Philipp (1681–1767), German composer, born Magdeburg. Virtually self-taught, he became one of the most prolific, versatile and admired composers of his age. From 1721 he was City Cantor at Hamburg. His music is notable for the cosmopolitanism of its style.

Torelli, Giuseppe (1658–1709), Italian composer, born Verona. Except for a period of service (1697–1700) at Ansbach he was from 1686 a member of the orchestra of the Basilica of S. Petronio in Bologna. His concertos published as opp. 6 (1698) and 8 (1709) are significant landmarks in the history of the *genre*.

Treu, Daniel Gottlob (1695–1749), German composer, born Stuttgart. He served many minor princely houses as *Kapellmeister* and between 1725 and 1727 directed opera in Breslau, where he also spent his last years. He often italianized his name to Daniele Teofilo Fedele.

Uffenbach, Johann Friedrich Armand von (1687–1769), engineer, architect and dignitary (Burgomaster in 1762) in his native Frankfurt am Main. His enthusiasm for music brought him into contact with many leading musicians of his time.

Vandini, Antonio (c 1690–1770 or later), Italian cellist and composer, born Bologna. Cello master at the Pietà from 1720 until 1721, when he joined the orchestra of the Basilica del Santo in Padua. A friend of Tartini, with whom he travelled to Prague in 1723.

Vinciguerra VI di Collalto (1710–69), Austrian nobleman (*Graf*) of Italian extraction, born Vienna. His castle at Brtnice (Pirnitz) in Moravia was an important centre of instrumental music.

Walther, Johann Gottfried (1684–1748), German composer and lexicographer, born Erfurt. He met J. S. Bach at Weimar, where for many years he was town organist. His *Musicalisches Lexicon* (1732) is the father of all dictionaries of music, combining biography with the explanation of musical terms.

Zelenka, Jan Dismas (1679–1745), Bohemian composer, born Louňovice (Launowitz). In 1710 he was appointed a double-bass player to the Dresden court orchestra, remaining in this lowly post until 1735, when he received belated official recognition as a composer of church music. His often dark-hued compositions show strength and originality, as well as a fondness for contrapuntal complexity, large dimensions and elements of Czech folk music.

Zeno, Apostolo (1668–1750), Italian dramatist, poet and historian, born Venice. A founding member in 1691 of the Accademia degli Animosi (later affiliated to the Arcadian Academy). A founder of the Giornale de' letterati d'Italia. Court poet and historian at Vienna from 1718 to 1729. He sought to elevate *opera seria* by purging it of comic, unhistorical and dramatically irrelevant elements, a process continued by Metastasio (q.v.).

Appendix D Bibliography

As the following list is intended as a general guide to further reading on Vivaldi's life and works, the titles it contains coincide only in part with those to which reference has been made in the course of the present book. All titles, dates and places of publication quoted are, unless stated otherwise, those of the earliest editions.

I PRE-1850 WRITINGS

Avison, Charles, *An Essay on Musical Expression* (London, 1752).

Bach, Carl Philipp Emanuel, *Versuch über die wahre Art das Clavier zu spielen,* 2 vols. (Berlin, 1753–62).

Brosses, Charles de, *Letters historiques et critiques sur l'Italie,* 3 vols. (Paris, 1799).

Burney, Charles, *A General History of Music,* 4 vols. (London, 1776–89).

Conti, Abbé, *Lettres de M. l'Abbé Conti, noble vénitien, à Mme de Caylus.* MS. in Venice, Biblioteca Nazionale Marciana, Ms. fr. append. 58 (=10102).

Forkel, Johann Nikolaus, *Ueber Johann Sebastian Bachs Leben, Kunst und Kunstwerke* (Leipzig, 1802).

Gerber, Ernst Ludwig, *Historisch-biographisches Lexicon der Tonkünstler,* 2 vols. (Leipzig, 1790–2).

—— *Neues historisch-biographisches Lexicon der Tonkünstler,* 4 vols. (Leipzig, 1812–14).

Goldoni, Carlo, *Commedie,* vol. 13 (Venice, 1761).

—— *Mémoires de M. Goldoni pour servir à l'histoire de sa vie et à celle de son théâtre,* 3 vols. (Paris, 1787).

Hawkins, Sir John, *A General History of the Science and Practice of Music,* 4 vols. (London, 1776).

[Hayes, William], *Remarks on Mr. Avison's Essay on Musical Expression* (London, 1753).

Hiller, Johann Adam, *Lebensbeschreibungen berühmter Musikgelehrten und Tonkünstler neuerer Zeit* (Leipzig, 1784).

—— *Wöchentliche Nachrichten und Anmerkungen die Musik betreffend* (Leipzig, 10th March 1767).

[Marcello, Benedetto], *Il teatro alla moda* (Venice, [1720]).

Mattheson, Johann, *Das neu-eröffnete Orchestre* (Hamburg, 1713).

—— *Der vollkommene Capellmeister* (Hamburg, 1739).

Orloff, Grégoire, *Essai sur l'histoire de la musique en Italie*, 2 vols. (Paris, 1822).

Quadrio, Francesco Saverio, *Della storia e della ragione d'ogni poesia*, 5 vols. (Bologna-Milan, 1739–52).

Quantz, Johann Joachim, 'Herrn Johann Joachim Quantzens Lebenslauf, von ihm selbst entworfen', in Friedrich Wilhelm Marpurg, *Historisch-Kritische Beyträge zur Aufnahme der Musik,* vol. i (Berlin, 1754–5).

—— *Versuch einer Anweisung die Flöte traversiere zu spielen* (Berlin, 1752).

Wright, Edward, *Some observations made in travelling through France, Italy . . . in the years 1720, 1721 and 1722*, 2 vols. (London, 1730).

II   POST-1850 WRITINGS

(a) Books and Dissertations

Abbado, Michelangelo, *Antonio Vivaldi* (Turin, 1942).

Caffi, Francesco, *Storia della musica sacra nella già Cappella Ducale di San Marco in Venezia*, 2 vols. (Venice, 1854–5).

—— *Storia della musica teatrale in Venezia*, MS. notes in Venice, Biblioteca Nazionale Marciana, Cod. It. IV–747 (=10462–10465).

Candé, Roland de, *Vivaldi* (Paris, 1967).

Dunham, Mary Meneve, *The Secular Cantatas of Antonio Vivaldi in the Foà Collection* (diss., University of Michigan, 1969).

Eller, Rudolf, *Vivaldis Konzertform* (diss., University of Leipzig, 1956).

Giazotto, Remo, *Antonio Vivaldi* (Turin, 1973).

Hilgenfeldt, Carl Ludwig, *Johann Sebastian Bach's Leben, Wirken und Werke* (Leipzig, 1850).

Hutchings, Arthur, *The Baroque Concerto* (London, 1961).

Klein, Hans-Günther, *Der Einfluss der Vivaldischen Konzertform im Instrumentalwerk Johann Sebastian Bachs* (Baden-Baden, 1970).

Kolneder, Walter, *Antonio Vivaldi: Leben und Werk* (Wiesbaden, 1965). English translation as *Antonio Vivaldi: his life and work*, translated Bill Hopkins (London, 1970).

—— *Aufführungspraxis bei Vivaldi* (Leipzig, 1955).

—— *Die Solokonzertform bei Vivaldi* (Strasbourg/Baden-Baden, 1961).

—— *Melodietypen bei Vivaldi* (Berg am Irchel/Zürich, 1973).

Newman, William S., *The Sonata in the Baroque Era* (Chapel Hill, 1959).

Pincherle, Marc, *Antonio Vivaldi et la musique instrumentale*, 2 vols. (Paris, 1948).

—— *Vivaldi* (Paris, 1955). English translation as *Vivaldi: Genius of the Baroque*, translated Christopher Hatch (New York, 1957).

Preussner, Eberhard:, *Die musikalischen Reisen des Herrn von Uffenbach* (Kassel/Basel, 1949).

Rinaldi, Mario, *Antonio Vivaldi* (Milan, 1943).

Rarig, Howard R., *The Instrumental Sonatas of Antonio Vivaldi* (diss., University of Michigan, 1958).

Rowell, Lewis E., *Four Operas of Antonio Vivaldi* (diss., University of Rochester, 1959).

Ryom, Peter, *Les manuscrits de Vivaldi* (Copenhagen, 1977).

Schering, Arnold, *Geschichte des instrumentalkonzerts* (Leipzig, 1905).

Selfridge-Field, Eleanor, *Venetian Instrumental Music from Gabrieli to Vivaldi* (Oxford, 1975).

Stefani, Federigo, Sei lettere di *Antonio Vivaldi veneziano* (Venice, 1871).

Strohm, Reinhard, *Italienische Opernarien des frühen Settecento (1720–1730)*, 2 vols. (Cologne, 1976).

Talbot, Michael, *Vivaldi* (London, BBC Publications, forthcoming).

Wasiliewski, Wilhelm Joseph von, *Die Violine und ihre Meister* (Leipzig, 1868).

Zobeley, Fritz, *Rudolf Franz Erwein Graf von Schönborn (1677–1754)*

254

und seine Musikpflege (Würzburg, 1949).

(b) *Articles*

Arnold, Denis, 'Instruments and Instrumental Teaching in the Early Italian Conservatoires', *Galpin Society Journal,* vol. xviii (1965), pp. 72–81.

—— 'Orchestras in Eighteenth-Century Venice', *Galpin Society Journal,* vol. xix (1966), pp. 3–19.

—— 'Vivaldi's church music: an introduction', *Early Music,* vol. i (1973), pp. 66–74.

Cavicchi, Adriano, 'Inediti nell'epistolario Vivaldi-Bentivoglio' *Nuova Rivista Musicale Italiana,* vol. i (1967), pp. 45–79.

Damilano, Piero, 'Antonio Vivaldi compose due vespri?', *Nuova Rivista Musicale Italiana,* vol. iii (1969) pp. 652–63.

Gallo, Rodolfo, 'Antonio Vivaldi, il Prete Rosso: la famiglia, la morte', *Ateneo Veneto,* fasc. xii (Dec., 1938).

—— 'L'atto di morte di Antonio Vivaldi', *La scuola veneziana* (Siena, 1941), pp. 58–9.

Gentili, Alberto, 'La raccolta di antiche musiche "Renzo Giordano" alla Biblioteca Nazionale di Torino', *Accademie e Biblioteche d'Italia,* vol. iv (1930–1), pp. 117–25.

—— 'La raccolta di rarità musicali "Mauro Foà" alla Biblioteca Nazionale di Torino', *Accademie e Biblioteche d'Italia,* vol. i (1927–8), pp. 36–50.

—— 'Vivaldi and Stradella: a recent discovery', *The Musical Times,* vol. lxviii (1927), pp. 507–8.

Heller, Karl, 'Die Bedeutung J. G. Pisendels für die deutsche Vivaldi-Rezeption', *Bericht über den Internationalen Musikwissenschaftlichen Kongress Leipzig 1966* (Leipzig/Kassel, 1970), pp. 247–51.

Igoe, James T., 'Bachs Bearbeitungen für Cembalo solo. Eine Zusammenfassung', *Bach-Jahrbuch,* vol. lvii (1971), pp. 91–7.

Jung, Hans Rudolf, 'Die Dresdner Vivaldi-Manuskripte', *Archiv für Musikwissenschaft,* vol. xii (1955), pp. 314–18.

Kneidl, Pravoslav, 'Libreta italské opery v Praze v 18. století, *Strahovská Knihovna* (Prague, 1966), pp. 97–131.

Kolneder, Walter, 'Das Frühschaffen Antonio Vivaldis', *Kongress-*

Appendix D—Bibliography

Bericht Internationale Gesellschaft für Musikwissenschaft Utrecht 1952 (Amsterdam, 1953), pp. 254–62.

—— 'Die Klarinette als Concertino-Instrument bei Vivaldi', Die Musikforschung, vol. iv (1951), pp. 185–91.

—— 'Die Vivaldi Forschung; Geschichte, Probleme, Aufgaben', Österreichische Musikzeitschrift, vol. xx (1967), pp. 313–19.

—— 'Il concerto per due trombe di Antonio Vivaldi', Rivista Musicale Italiana, vol. lv (1953), pp. 54–63.

—— 'Noch einmal: Vivaldi und die Klarinette', Die Musikforschung, vol. viii (1955), pp. 209–11.

—— 'Vivaldis Aria-Concerto', Deutsches Jahrbuch der Musikwissenschaft, vol. ix (1964), pp. 17–27.

Lasocki, David, 'Vivaldi and the Recorder', Recorder and Music Magazine, vol. iii (1969), pp. 22–7.

Lebermann, Walter, 'Zur Besetzungsfrage der Concerti grossi von A. Vivaldi', Die Musikforschung, vol. vii (1954), pp. 337–9.

Newman, William S., 'The Sonatas of Albinoni and Vivaldi', Journal of the American Musicological Society, vol. v (1952), pp. 99–113.

Ohmura, Noriko, 'Vivaldi no orchestra o tomonawanai concerto (Vivaldi's Concertos without Orchestra)', Ongaku gaku, vol. xvii (1971), pp. 103–30. In Japanese, summary in English.

Pabisch, Hedy, 'Neue Dokumente zu Vivaldis Sterbetag', Österreichische Musikzeitschrift, vol. xxvii (1972), pp. 82–3.

Pincherle, Marc, 'Vivaldi and the Ospitali of Venice', Musical Quarterly, vol. xxiv (1938), pp. 300–12.

Rüegge, Raimund, 'Die Kirchenmusik von Antonio Vivaldi', Schweizerische Musikzeitung, vol. cxi (1971), pp. 135–9.

Rühlmann, Julius, 'Antonio Vivaldi und sein Einfluss auf Johann Sebastian Bach', Neue Zeitschrift für Musik, vol. lxiii (1867), pp. 393–7, 401–5, 413–16.

Ryom, Peter, 'La comparaison entre les versions différentes d'un concerto d'Antonio Vivaldi transcrit par J. S. Bach', Dansk Aarbog for Musikforskning 1966–7, pp. 91–111.

—— 'Le premier catalogue thématique des œuvres d'Antonio Vivaldi', Festskrift Jens Peter Larsen (Copenhagen, 1972), pp. 127–40.

—— 'Le premier catalogue thématique des œuvres d'Antonio

for Musikforskning 1972, pp. 81–100.

Salvatori, Arcangelo, 'Antonio Vivaldi (il Prete Rosso)', *Rivista della città di Venezia,* vol. vi (1928), pp. 325–46.

Scazzoso, Piero, 'La posizione storica di Antonio Vivaldi', *Rivista Musicale Italiana,* vol. xlix (1947), pp. 143–67.

Selfridge-Field, Eleanor, 'Annotated Membership Lists of the Venetian Instrumentalists' Guild 1672–1727', *R. M. A. Research Chronicle,* no. 9 (1971), pp. 1–52.

Talbot, Michael, 'The Concerto Allegro in the Early Eighteenth Century', *Music and Letters,* vol. lii (1971), pp. 8–18, 159–72.

Volek, Tomislav and Skalická, Marie, 'Vivaldis Beziehungen zu den böhmischen Ländern', *Acta Musicologica,* vol. xxxix (1967), pp. 64–72.

Waldersee, Paul Hermann Otto von, 'Antonio Vivaldis Violinconcerte unter besonderer Berücksichtigung der von Johann Sebastian Bach bearbeiteten', *Vierteljahrschrift für Musikwissenschaft,* vol. i (1885), pp. 356–80.

Wolff, Hellmut Christian, 'Vivaldi und der Stil der italienischen Oper', *Acta Musicologica,* vol. xl (1968), pp. 179–86.

(c) *Journals and Compilations*

Vivaldi, Antonio. Note e documenti sulla vita e sulle opere (Rome, Accademia Musicale Chigiana, 1939).

Vivaldi Informations, 2 vols. to date (Copenhagen, Société Internationale Antonio Vivaldi, 1971–3).

Vivaldiana I (Brussels, Centre International de Documentation Antonio Vivaldi, 1969).

(d) *Catalogues*

Altmann, Wilhelm, 'Thematischer Katalog der gedruckten Werke Antonio Vivaldis', *Archiv für Musikwissenschaft,* vol. iv (1922), pp. 262–79.

Damilano, Piero, 'Inventario delle composizioni musicali manoscritte di Antonio Vivaldi esistenti presso la Biblioteca Nazionale di Torino', *Rivista Italiana di Musicologia,* vol. iii (1968), pp. 109–79.

Fanna, Antonio, *Antonio Vivaldi: Catalogo numerico-tematico delle opere strumentali* (Milan, 1968).

257

Appendix D—Bibliography

Heller, Karl, *Die deutsche Überlieferung der Instrumentalwerke Vivaldis* (Leipzig, 1971).

Martin, Arlan Stone, *Vivaldi Violin Concertos. A Handbook* (Metuchen, N. J., 1972).

Ohmura, Noriko, *A reference concordance table of Vivaldi's instrumental works* (Tokyo, 1972).

Pincherle, Marc, *Inventaire-Thématique* (= vol. ii of *Antonio Vivaldi et la musique instrumentale*) (Paris, 1948).

Rinaldi, Mario, *Catalogo numerico tematico delle composizioni di A. Vivaldi* (Rome, 1945).

Ryom, Peter, Antonio Vivaldi: *Table de concordances des œuvres (RV)* (Copenhagen, 1973).

—— 'Inventaire de la documentation manuscrite des œuvres de Vivaldi, I. Biblioteca Nazionale di Torino, Première Partie: le fonds Foà', *Vivaldi Informations,* vol. ii (1973), pp. 61–112.

—— *Verzeichnis der Werke Antonio Vivaldis: kleine Ausgabe* (Leipzig, 1974).

Strohm, Reinhard, *Italienische Opernarien des frühen Settecento (1720–1730)* (Cologne, 1976). Vol ii contains a list of Vivaldi's operas and fragments thereof.

Appendix E

Index to individual works and published collections by Vivaldi mentioned in the text

INDIVIDUAL WORKS
(The work to which an 'RV' number refers can be identified from Appendix B.)

259

Appendix E—Index to individual works

260

Appendix E—Index to individual works

Appendix E—Index to individual works

Appendix E—Index to individual works

Appendix F

CONCORDANCE TABLE OF PINCHERLE (P.) AND RYOM (RV) NUMBERS

Sinfonias

P.	RV	P.	RV	P.	RV
1	Anh. 4	*Concertos*		22	184
2	116	P.	RV	23	507
3	149	1	356	24	422
4	140	2	522	25	741
5	135	3	357	26	176
6	147	4	185	27	114
7	122	5	188	28	523
8	146	6	354	29	189
9	719	7	180	30	400
10	700/736	8	178/449	31	398
11	162	9	181(a)	32	419
12	Anh. 68	10	358	33	399
13	132	11	173	34	421
14	125	12	195	35	418
15	111a	13	Anh. 15	36	554(a)
16	739	14	179/581	37	397
17	137	15	526	38	183
18	699/710	16	558	39	191
19	131	17	508	40	194
20	192	18	506	41	447
21	169	19	172(a)	42	461
22	168	20	170	43	448/470
23	112	21	177	44	451

P.	RV	P.	RV	P.	RV
45	472	81	87	117	311
46	477	82	88	118	414/438
47	499	83	445	119	409
48	467	84	556	120	413
49	469	85	534	121	303
50	450/471	86	129	122	312
51	466	87	555	123	145
52	479	88	186	124	307
53	536	89	463/500	125	273
54	557	90	473	126	281
55	468	91	452	127	134
56	475	92	355	128	492
57	476	93	175	129	545
58	561	94	113	130	494
59	190	95	111	131	493
60	161	96	310	132	516
61	110	97	550	133	532
62	187	98	279	134	425
63	115	99	301	135	575
64	117	100	298	136	306
65	505	101	280	137	484
66	171	102	299	138	313
67	109	103	300	139	431
68	182	104	435	140	436
69	474	105	101/437	141	438
70	498	106	277	142	432
71	478	107	308	143	151
72	497	108	276	144	278
73	560	109	275(a)/430	145	144
74	559	110	Anh. 64(a)	146	549
75	537	111	314(a)	147	230
76	533	112	302	148	580
77	108	113	133	149	204
78	444	114	150	150	216
79	443	115	Anh. 12	151	208(a)
80	440	116	Anh. 11	152	214

P.	RV	P.	RV	P.	RV
153	210	189	512	225	349
154	391	190	511	226	585
155	90/428	191	123	227	341
156	207	192	222	228	340
157	124	193	209	229	343
158	220	194	215	230	160
159	513	195	233	231	159
160	203	196	218	232	339
161	224(a)	197	126	233	396
162	228	198	92	234	350
163	213	199	231	235	158
164	582	200	232	236	352
165	212(a)	201	217	237	346
166	392	202	387	238	546
167	219	203	427	239	353
168	384	204	95	240	265
169	562	205	429	241	269
170	226	206	91	242	263(a)
171	229	207	94	243	267
172	388	208	234	244	268
173	205	209	93	245	264
174	223	210	563	246	271
175	121	211	227	247	266
176	404	212	519	248	270
177	206	213	347	249	567
178	385	214	345	250	565
179	221	215	348	251	284
180	424	216	336	252	291
181	403	217	Anh. 65	253	249
182	211	218	Anh. 14	254	239
183	386	219	335/518	255	285a
184	389	220	520	256	294(a)
185	390	221	342	257	293
186	225	222	552	258	242
187	453	223	344	259	236/454
188	564	224	521	260	238

P.	RV	P.	RV	P.	RV
261	98/433/	296	289	331	465
	570	297	566	332	326
262	434/442	298	487	333	374
263	244	299	488	334	464
264	456	300	491	335	373
265	573	301	139/543	336	315
266	540	302	535	337	332
267	568	303	482	338	362
268	571	304	486	339	334/460
269	240	305	489	340	359
270	241	306	455	341	530
271	292	307	490	342	104/439
272	246	308	544/572	343	317
273	569	309	584	344	379
274	542	310	243	345	361
275	285	311	541	346	364(a)
276	245	312	247	347	360
277	237	313	138	348	322
278	551	314	283	349	370
279	136	315	295	350	363
280	127	316	248	351	319
281	514	317	287	352	323
282	406/481	318	457/485	353	383
283	412	319	574	354	329
284	411	320	538	355	259
285	410	321	539	356	369
286	97	322	100	357	328
287	395(a)	323	99	358	366
288	394	324	288	359	576
289	393	325	282	360	107
290	286	326	578	361	157
291	141	327	383a	362	154
292	142		381/528	363	164
293	235	328	316(a)	364	377
294	128	329	324	365	527
295	296	330	318	366	517

P.	RV	P.	RV	P.	RV
367	553	394	153	421	260
368	583	395	321	422	119
369	417	396	368	423	515
370	372	397	745	424	408
371	152	398	166	425	250
372	325	399	320	426	201
373	375	400	167	427	120
374	327	401	501	428	251
375	371	402	103	429	254
376	365	403	105	430	258
377	376	404	106	431	197
378	165	405	367	432	480
379	333	406	548/764	433	483
380	378	407	155	434	401
381	496	408	330	435	510/766
382	502	409	380	436	509
383	577	410	163	437	261
384	495	411	531	438	118
385	579	412	382	439	257
386	504	413	196	440	441
387	503	414	259	441	130
388	547	415	253	442	297
389	525	416	198(a)	443	143
390	524	417	202	444	562a
391	529	418	252	445	Anh. 3
392	156	419	199	446	Anh. 3
393	331	420	262	447	Anh. 5

Index

Index

Index

Index